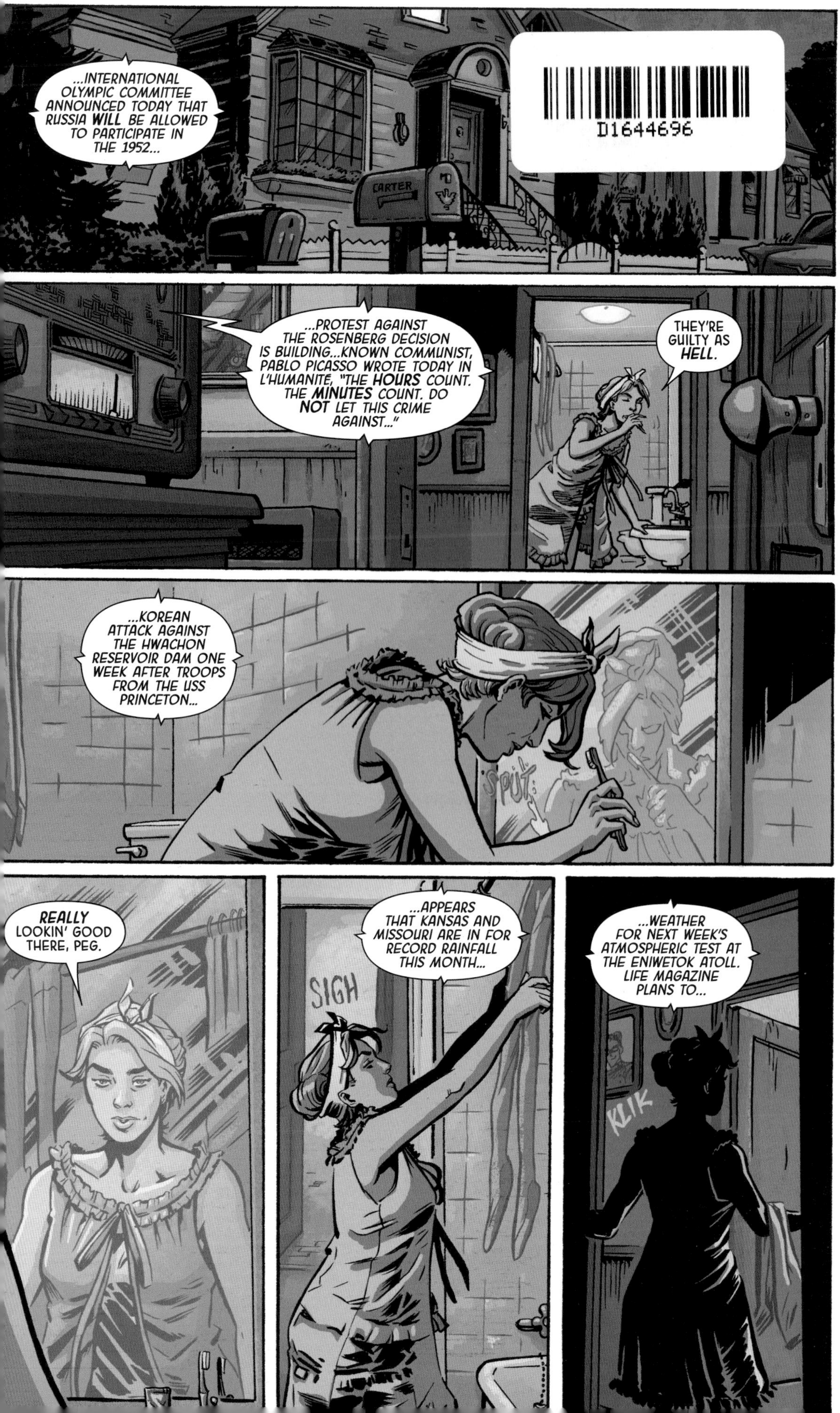
...INTERNATIONAL OLYMPIC COMMITTEE ANNOUNCED TODAY THAT RUSSIA WILL BE ALLOWED TO PARTICIPATE IN THE 1952...
CARTER
...PROTEST AGAINST THE ROSENBERG DECISION IS BUILDING...KNOWN COMMUNIST, PABLO PICASSO WROTE TODAY IN L'HUMANITE, "THE HOURS COUNT. THE MINUTES COUNT. DO NOT LET THIS CRIME AGAINST..."
THEY'RE GUILTY AS HELL.
...KOREAN ATTACK AGAINST THE HWACHON RESERVOIR DAM ONE WEEK AFTER TROOPS FROM THE USS PRINCETON...
SPUT
REALLY LOOKIN' GOOD THERE, PEG.
...APPEARS THAT KANSAS AND MISSOURI ARE IN FOR RECORD RAINFALL THIS MONTH...
SIGH
...WEATHER FOR NEXT WEEK'S ATMOSPHERIC TEST AT THE ENIWETOK ATOLL. LIFE MAGAZINE PLANS TO...
KLIK

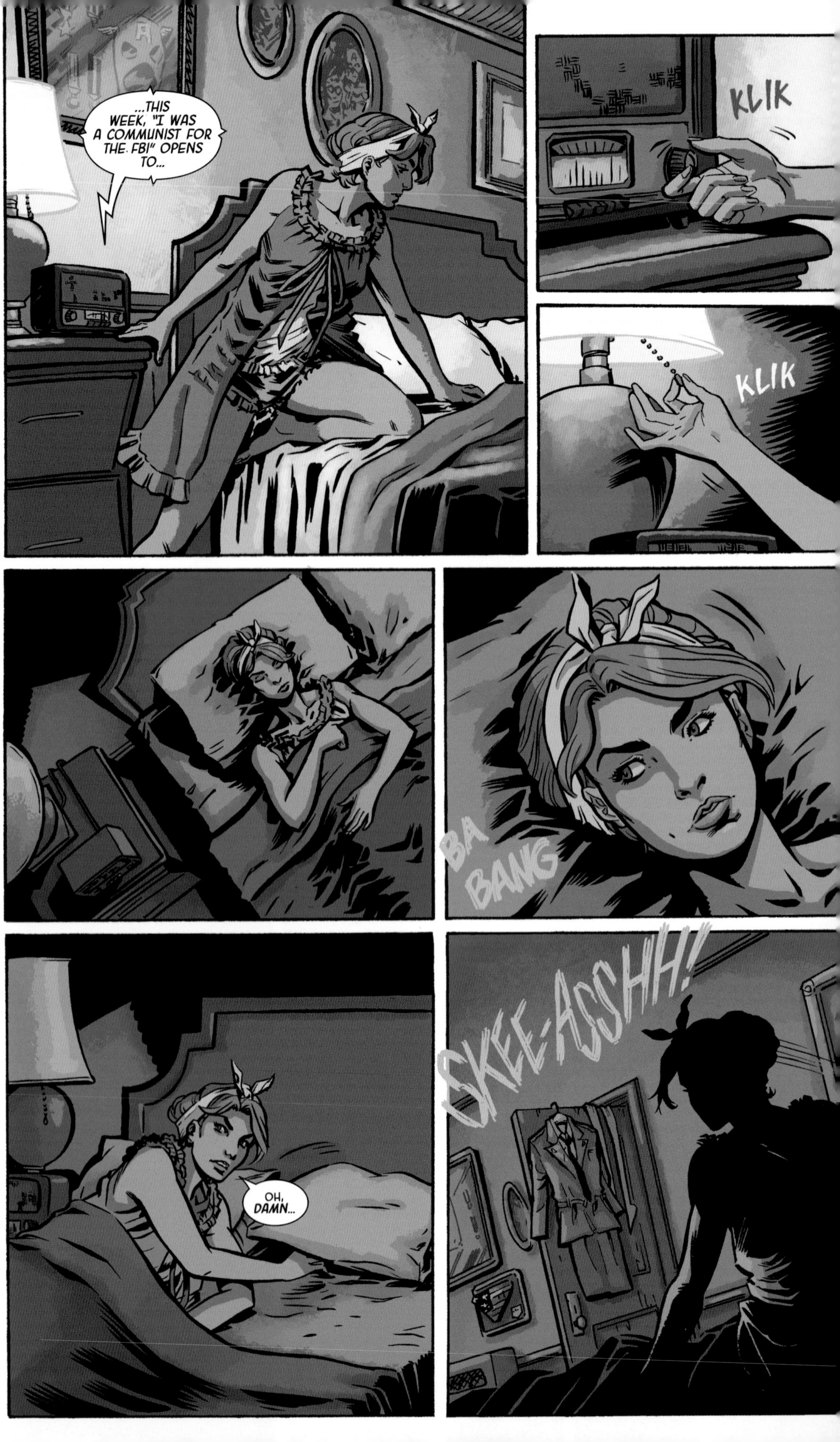
...THIS WEEK, "I WAS A COMMUNIST FOR THE FBI" OPENS TO...
KLIK
KLIK
BA BANG
OH, DAMN...
SKEE-ASSHH!

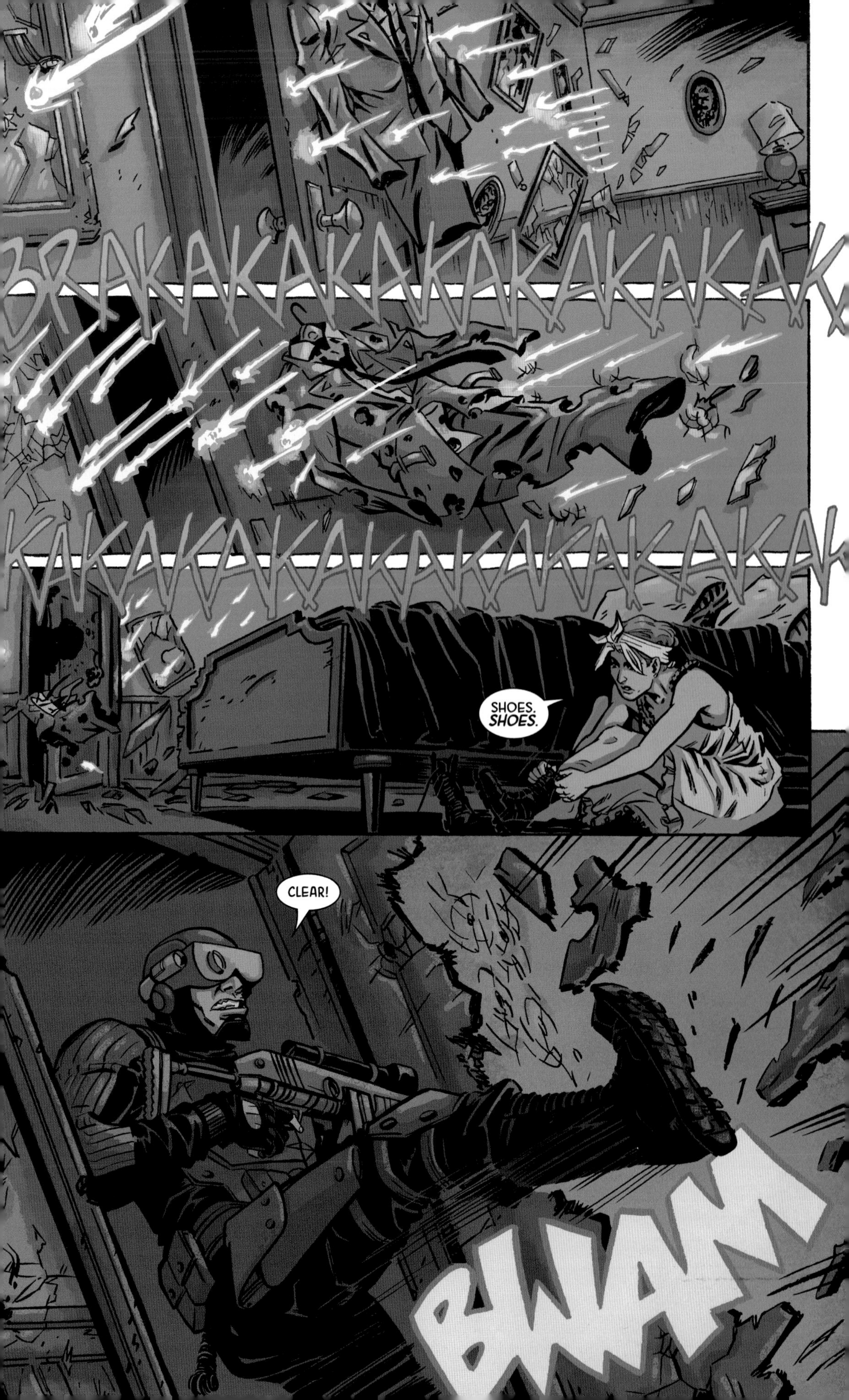
BRAKAKAKAKAKAKAKAKAK
KAKAKAKAKAKAKAKAKAKAK
SHOES. SHOES.
CLEAR!
BWAM

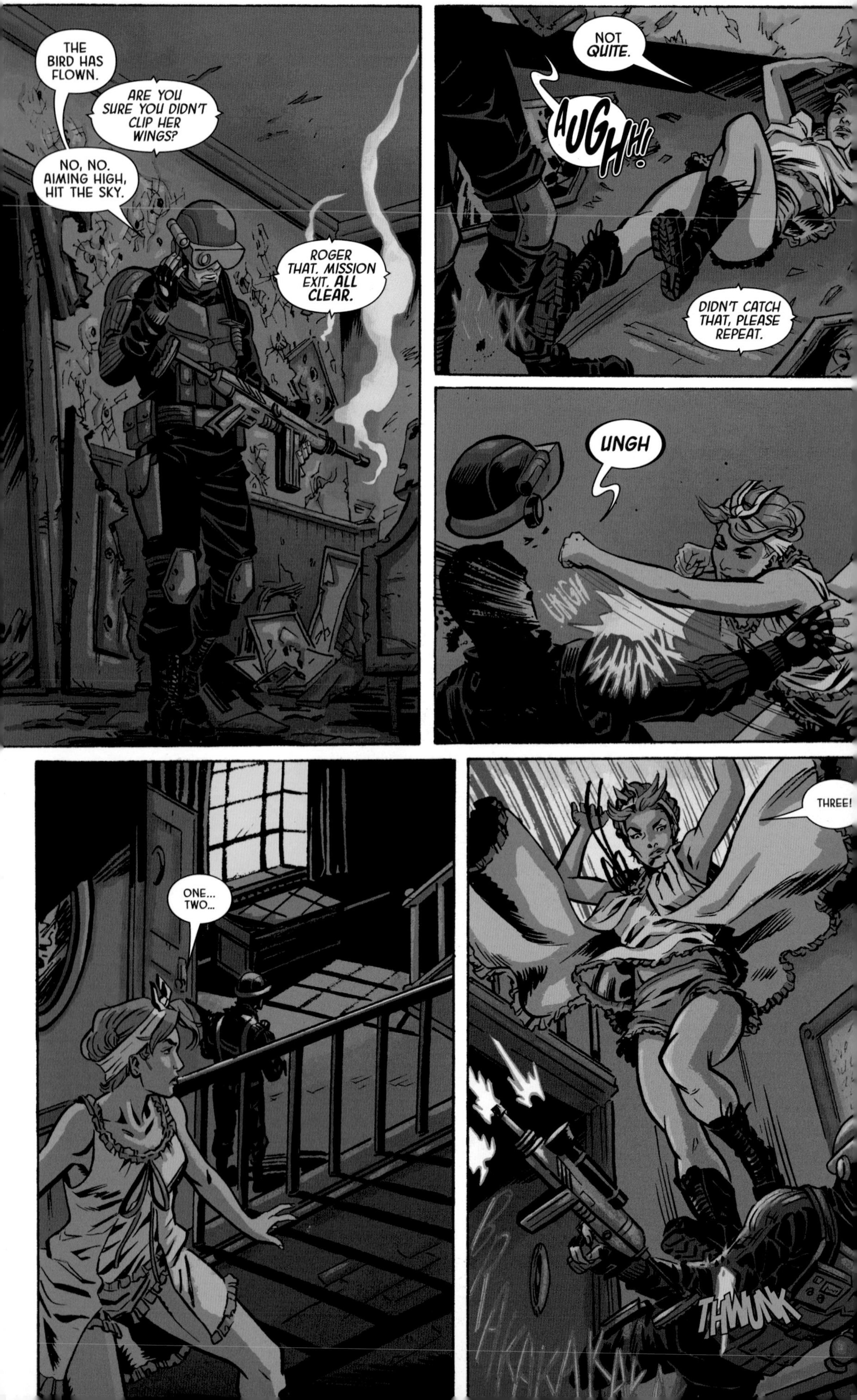
THE BIRD HAS FLOWN.
ARE YOU SURE YOU DIDN'T CLIP HER WINGS?
NO, NO. AIMING HIGH, HIT THE SKY.
ROGER THAT. MISSION EXIT. ALL CLEAR.
NOT QUITE.
AUGHH!
DIDN'T CATCH THAT, PLEASE REPEAT.
UNGH
ONE... TWO...
THREE!
THWUNK

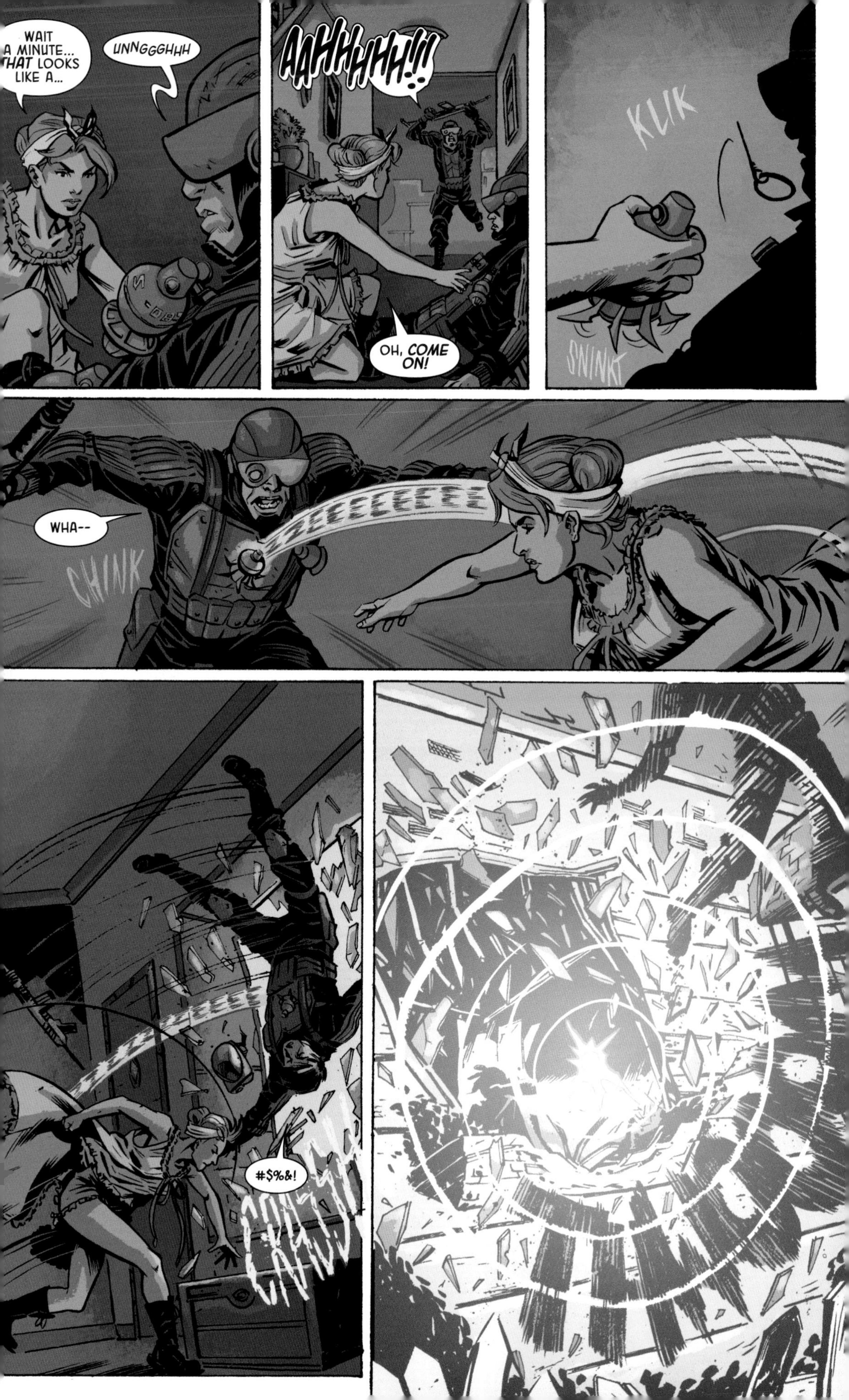
WAIT A MINUTE... THAT LOOKS LIKE A...
UNNGGGHHH
AAHHHHHH!!!
OH, COME ON!
KLIK
SNIKT
WHA--
CHINK
#$%&!

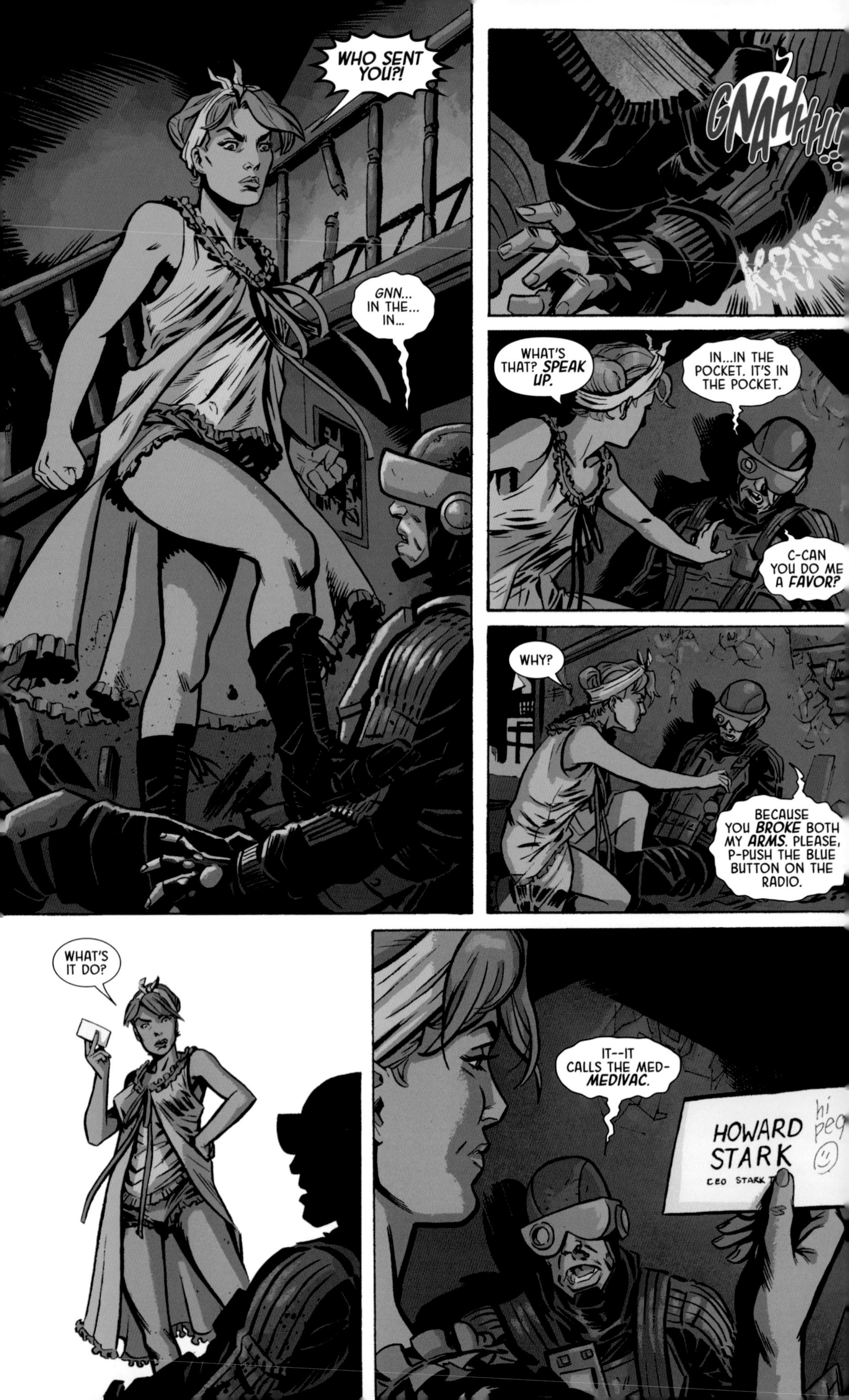
WHO SENT YOU?!
GNN... IN THE... IN...
GNAHHH!!
KRASH
WHAT'S THAT? SPEAK UP.
IN...IN THE POCKET. IT'S IN THE POCKET.
C-CAN YOU DO ME A FAVOR?
WHY?
BECAUSE YOU BROKE BOTH MY ARMS. PLEASE, P-PUSH THE BLUE BUTTON ON THE RADIO.
WHAT'S IT DO?
IT--IT CALLS THE MED-MEDIVAC.
HOWARD STARK
hi peg
CEO STARK

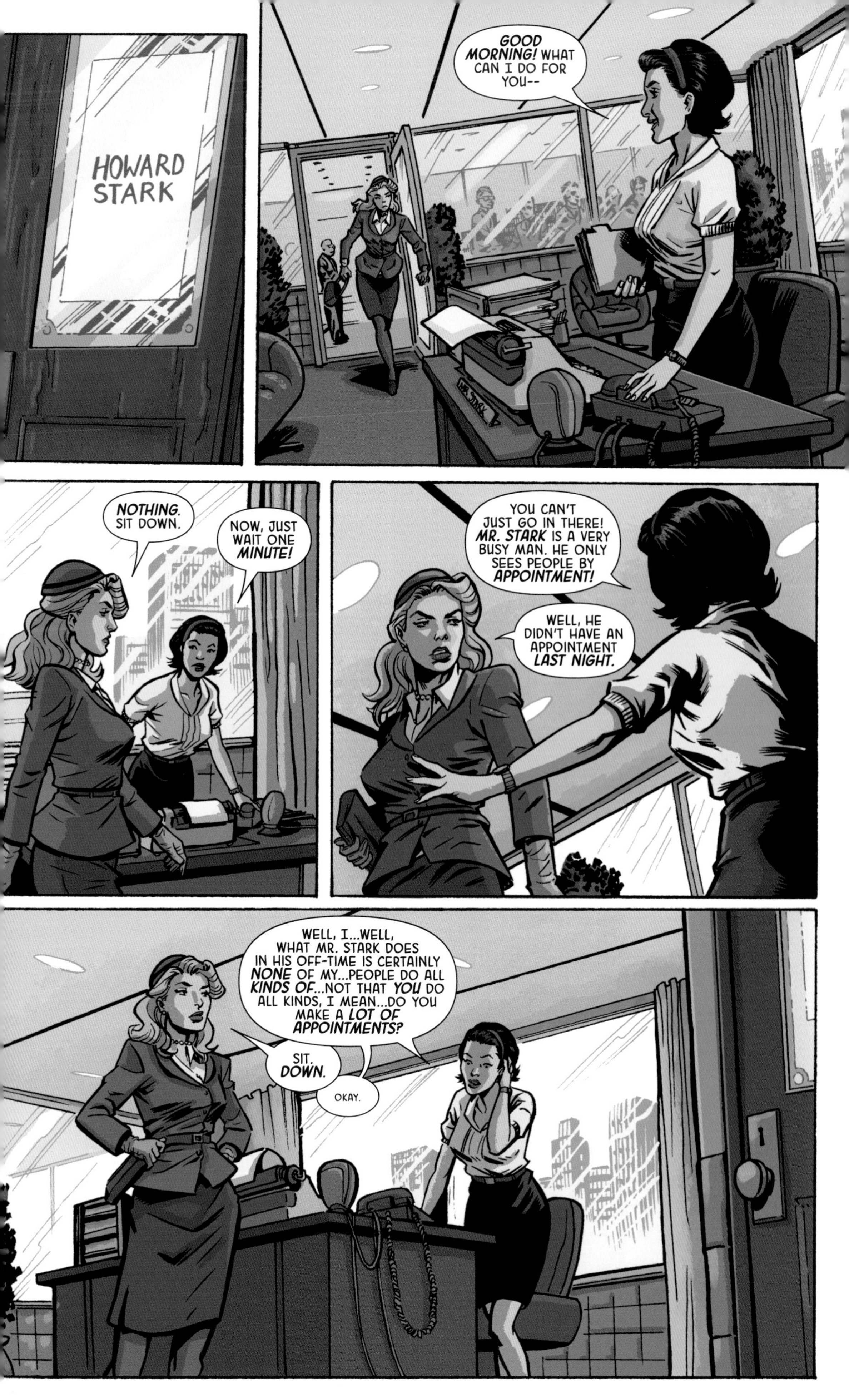
HOWARD STARK
GOOD MORNING! WHAT CAN I DO FOR YOU--
MR. STARK
NOTHING. SIT DOWN.
NOW, JUST WAIT ONE MINUTE!
YOU CAN'T JUST GO IN THERE! MR. STARK IS A VERY BUSY MAN. HE ONLY SEES PEOPLE BY APPOINTMENT!
WELL, HE DIDN'T HAVE AN APPOINTMENT LAST NIGHT.
WELL, I...WELL, WHAT MR. STARK DOES IN HIS OFF-TIME IS CERTAINLY NONE OF MY...PEOPLE DO ALL KINDS OF...NOT THAT YOU DO ALL KINDS, I MEAN...DO YOU MAKE A LOT OF APPOINTMENTS?
SIT. DOWN.
OKAY.

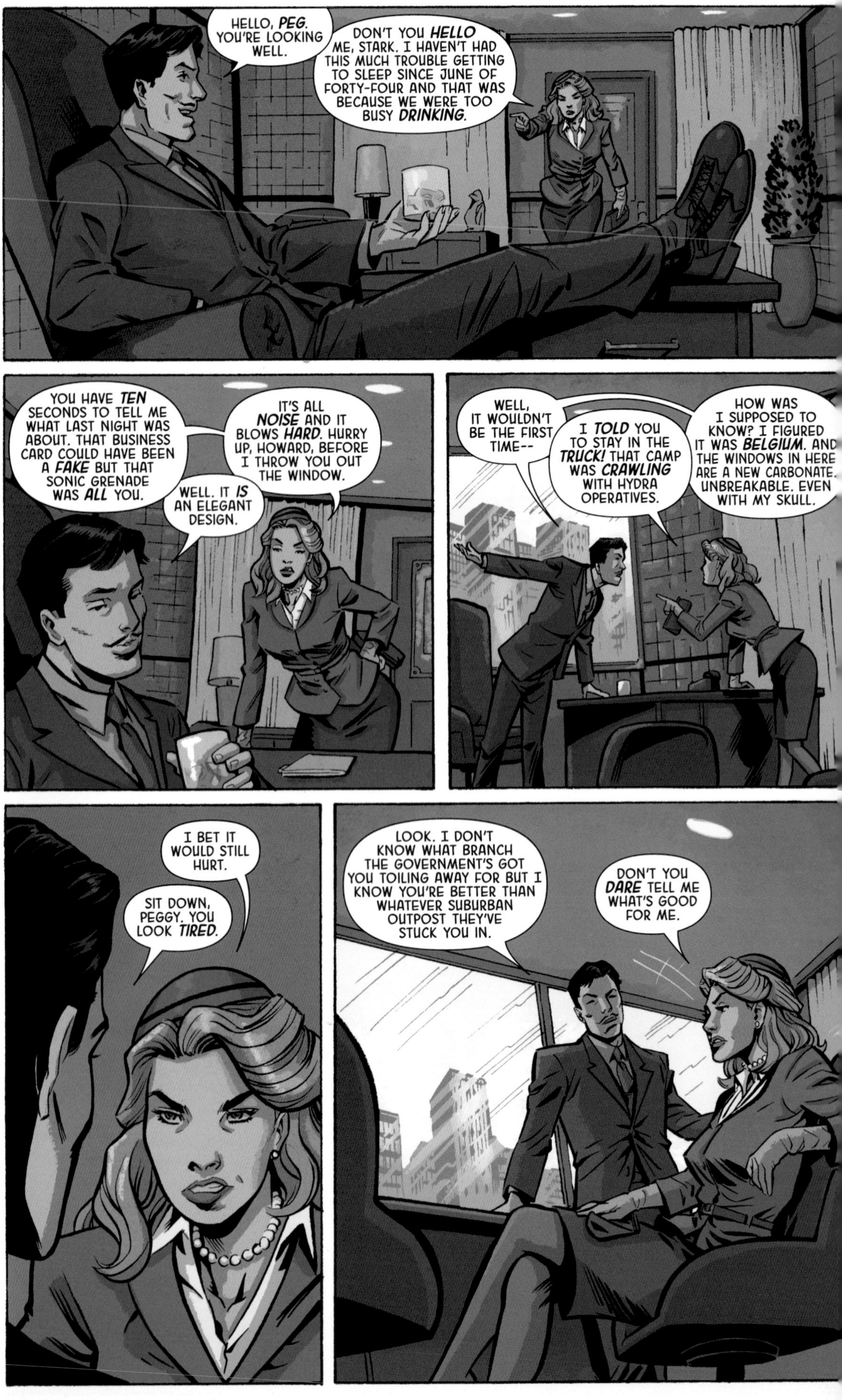
HELLO, PEG. YOU'RE LOOKING WELL.
DON'T YOU HELLO ME, STARK. I HAVEN'T HAD THIS MUCH TROUBLE GETTING TO SLEEP SINCE JUNE OF FORTY-FOUR AND THAT WAS BECAUSE WE WERE TOO BUSY DRINKING.
YOU HAVE TEN SECONDS TO TELL ME WHAT LAST NIGHT WAS ABOUT. THAT BUSINESS CARD COULD HAVE BEEN A FAKE BUT THAT SONIC GRENADE WAS ALL YOU.
WELL. IT IS AN ELEGANT DESIGN.
IT'S ALL NOISE AND IT BLOWS HARD. HURRY UP, HOWARD, BEFORE I THROW YOU OUT THE WINDOW.
WELL, IT WOULDN'T BE THE FIRST TIME--
I TOLD YOU TO STAY IN THE TRUCK! THAT CAMP WAS CRAWLING WITH HYDRA OPERATIVES.
HOW WAS I SUPPOSED TO KNOW? I FIGURED IT WAS BELGIUM. AND THE WINDOWS IN HERE ARE A NEW CARBONATE. UNBREAKABLE. EVEN WITH MY SKULL.
I BET IT WOULD STILL HURT.
SIT DOWN, PEGGY. YOU LOOK TIRED.
LOOK. I DON'T KNOW WHAT BRANCH THE GOVERNMENT'S GOT YOU TOILING AWAY FOR BUT I KNOW YOU'RE BETTER THAN WHATEVER SUBURBAN OUTPOST THEY'VE STUCK YOU IN.
DON'T YOU DARE TELL ME WHAT'S GOOD FOR ME.

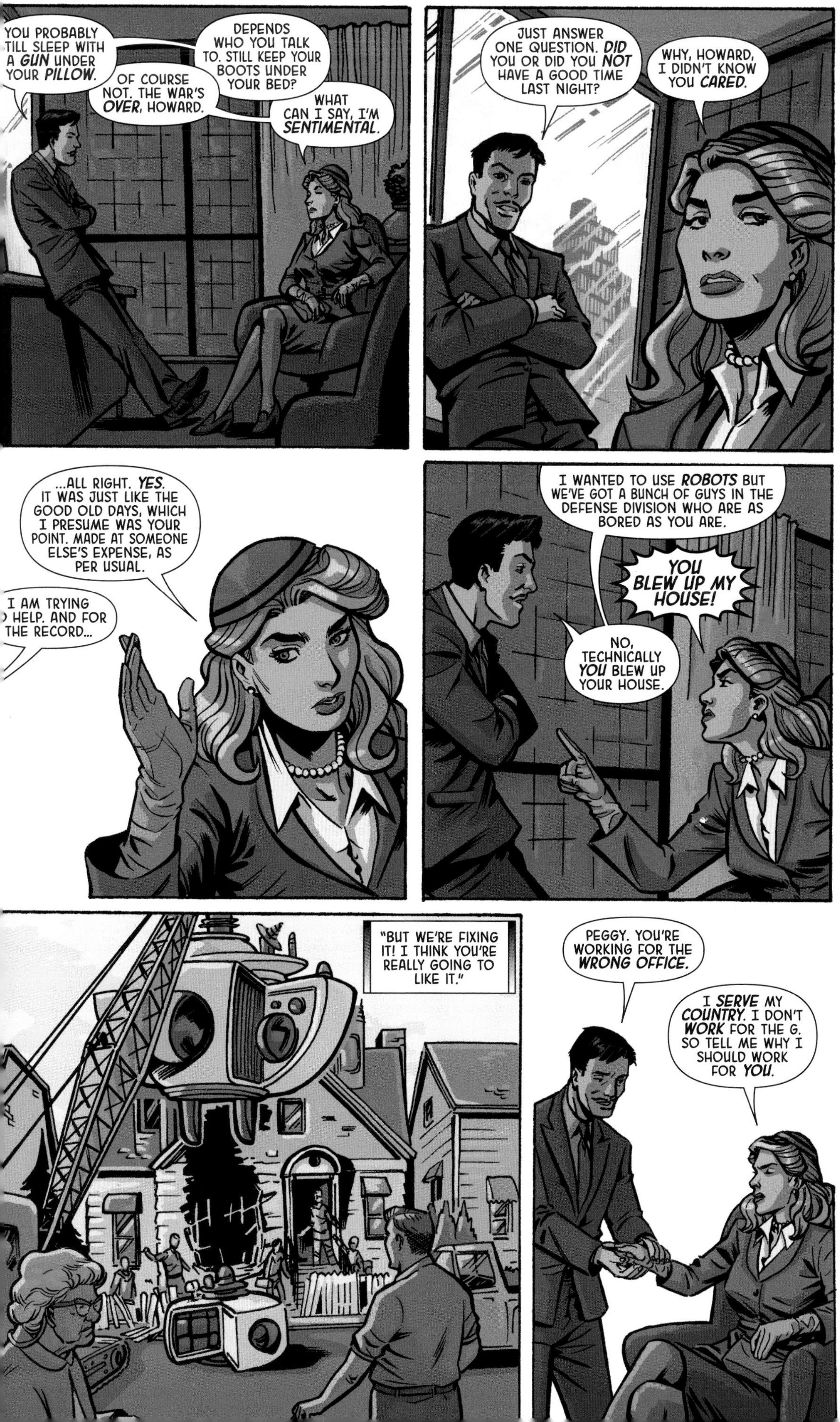
YOU PROBABLY STILL SLEEP WITH A GUN UNDER YOUR PILLOW.
DEPENDS WHO YOU TALK TO. STILL KEEP YOUR BOOTS UNDER YOUR BED?
OF COURSE NOT. THE WAR'S OVER, HOWARD.
WHAT CAN I SAY, I'M SENTIMENTAL.
JUST ANSWER ONE QUESTION. DID YOU OR DID YOU NOT HAVE A GOOD TIME LAST NIGHT?
WHY, HOWARD, I DIDN'T KNOW YOU CARED.
...ALL RIGHT. YES. IT WAS JUST LIKE THE GOOD OLD DAYS, WHICH I PRESUME WAS YOUR POINT. MADE AT SOMEONE ELSE'S EXPENSE, AS PER USUAL.
I AM TRYING TO HELP. AND FOR THE RECORD...
I WANTED TO USE ROBOTS BUT WE'VE GOT A BUNCH OF GUYS IN THE DEFENSE DIVISION WHO ARE AS BORED AS YOU ARE.
YOU BLEW UP MY HOUSE!
NO, TECHNICALLY YOU BLEW UP YOUR HOUSE.
"BUT WE'RE FIXING IT! I THINK YOU'RE REALLY GOING TO LIKE IT."
PEGGY. YOU'RE WORKING FOR THE WRONG OFFICE.
I SERVE MY COUNTRY. I DON'T WORK FOR THE G. SO TELL ME WHY I SHOULD WORK FOR YOU.

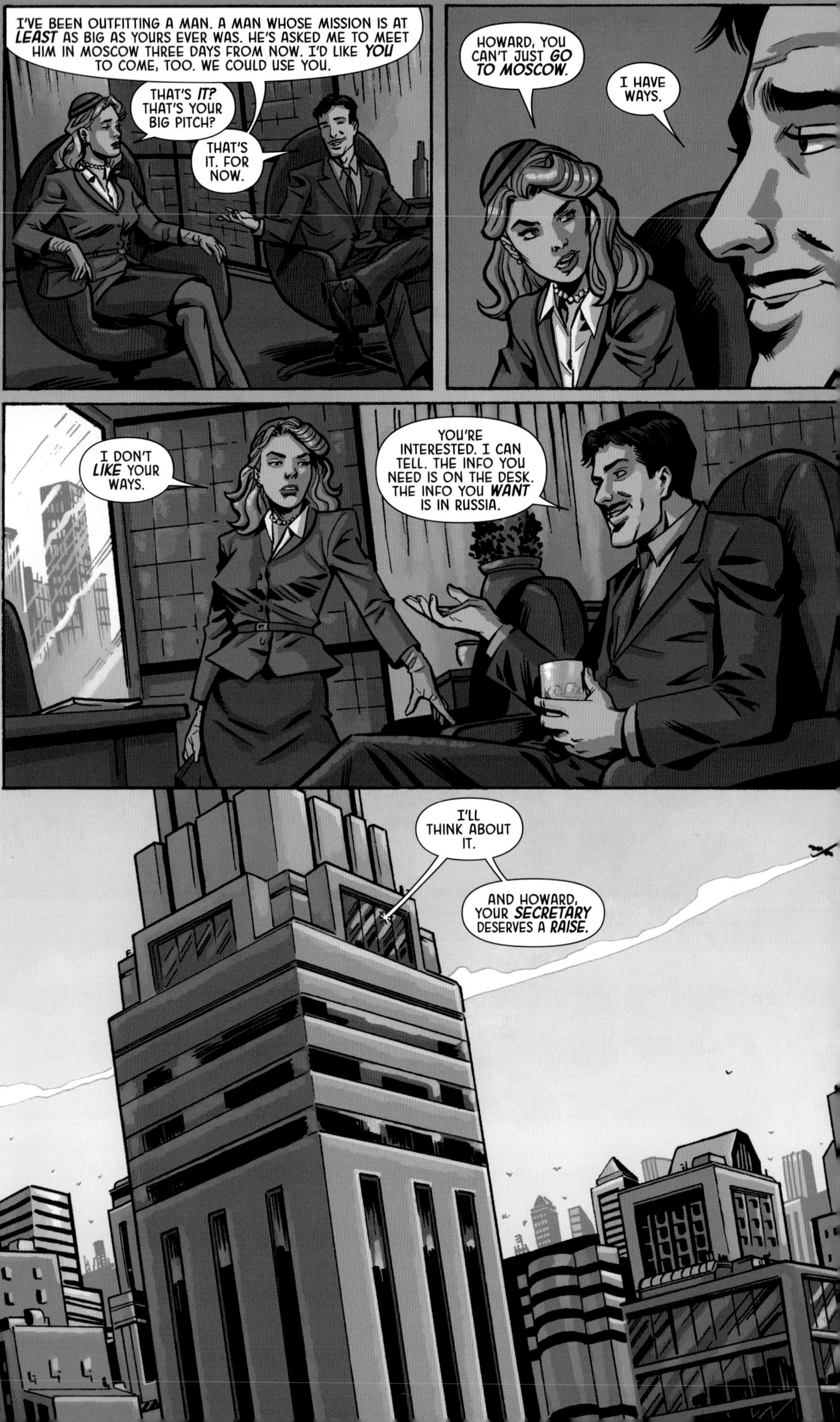
I'VE BEEN OUTFITTING A MAN. A MAN WHOSE MISSION IS AT LEAST AS BIG AS YOURS EVER WAS. HE'S ASKED ME TO MEET HIM IN MOSCOW THREE DAYS FROM NOW. I'D LIKE YOU TO COME, TOO. WE COULD USE YOU.
THAT'S IT? THAT'S YOUR BIG PITCH?
THAT'S IT. FOR NOW.
HOWARD, YOU CAN'T JUST GO TO MOSCOW.
I HAVE WAYS.
I DON'T LIKE YOUR WAYS.
YOU'RE INTERESTED. I CAN TELL. THE INFO YOU NEED IS ON THE DESK. THE INFO YOU WANT IS IN RUSSIA.
I'LL THINK ABOUT IT.
AND HOWARD, YOUR SECRETARY DESERVES A RAISE.

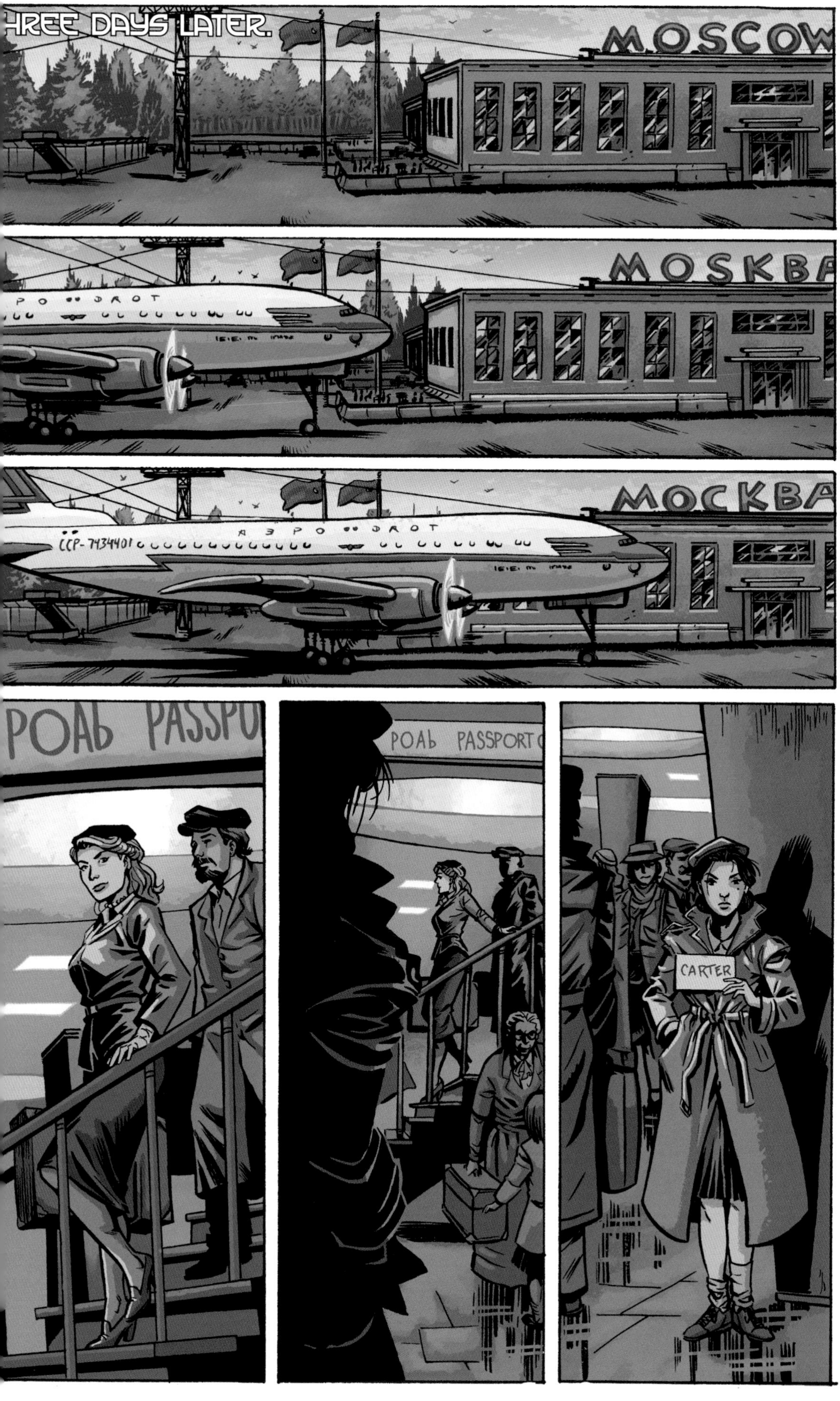
HREE DAYS LATER.
MOSCOW
MOSKBA
MOCKBA
CCP-7434401
POAЬ PASSPORT
CARTER

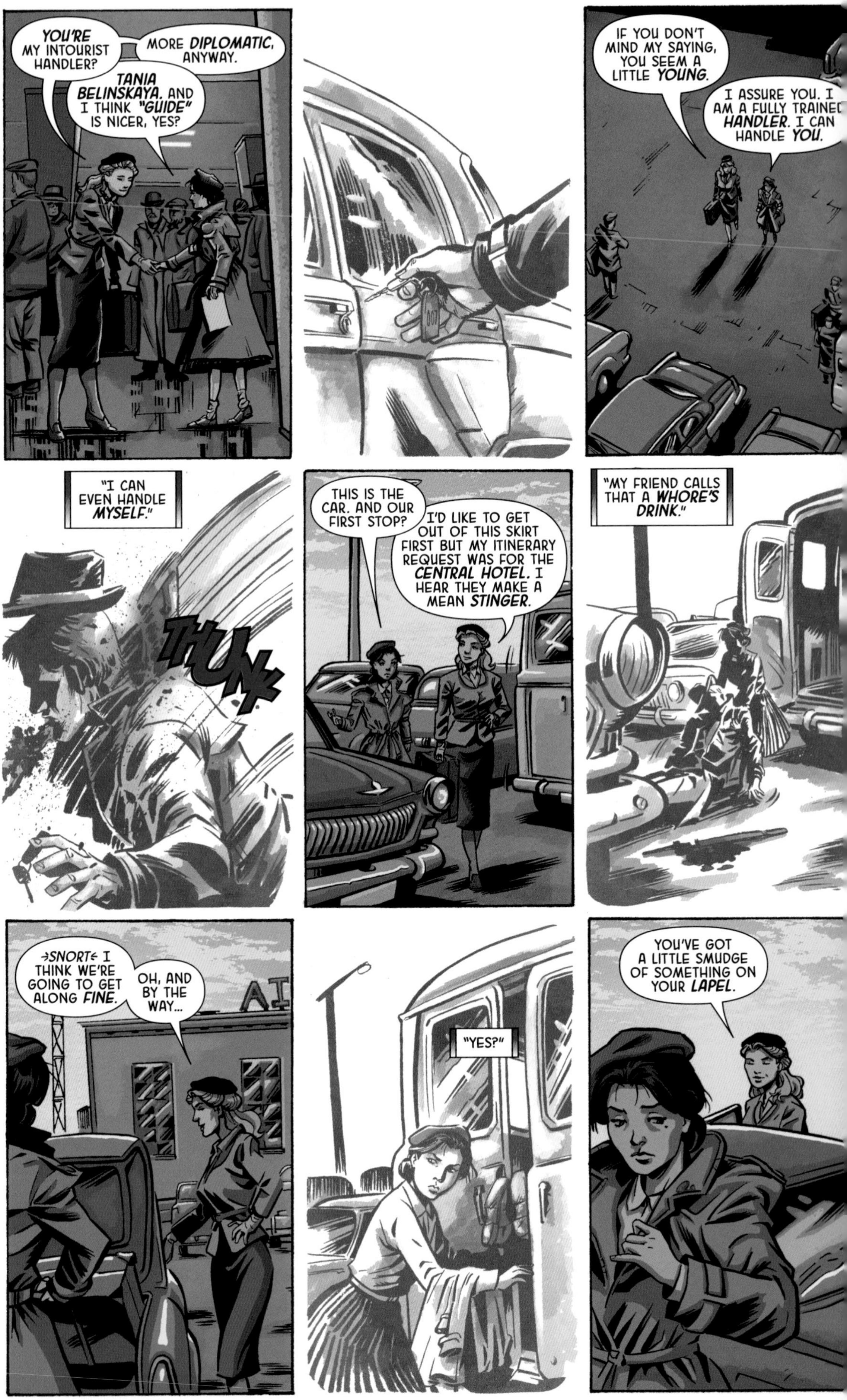
YOU'RE MY INTOURIST HANDLER?
MORE DIPLOMATIC, ANYWAY.
TANIA BELINSKAYA. AND I THINK "GUIDE" IS NICER, YES?
IF YOU DON'T MIND MY SAYING, YOU SEEM A LITTLE YOUNG.
I ASSURE YOU. I AM A FULLY TRAINED HANDLER. I CAN HANDLE YOU.
"I CAN EVEN HANDLE MYSELF."
THUNK
THIS IS THE CAR. AND OUR FIRST STOP?
I'D LIKE TO GET OUT OF THIS SKIRT FIRST BUT MY ITINERARY REQUEST WAS FOR THE CENTRAL HOTEL. I HEAR THEY MAKE A MEAN STINGER.
"MY FRIEND CALLS THAT A WHORE'S DRINK."
SNORT I THINK WE'RE GOING TO GET ALONG FINE.
OH, AND BY THE WAY...
"YES?"
YOU'VE GOT A LITTLE SMUDGE OF SOMETHING ON YOUR LAPEL.

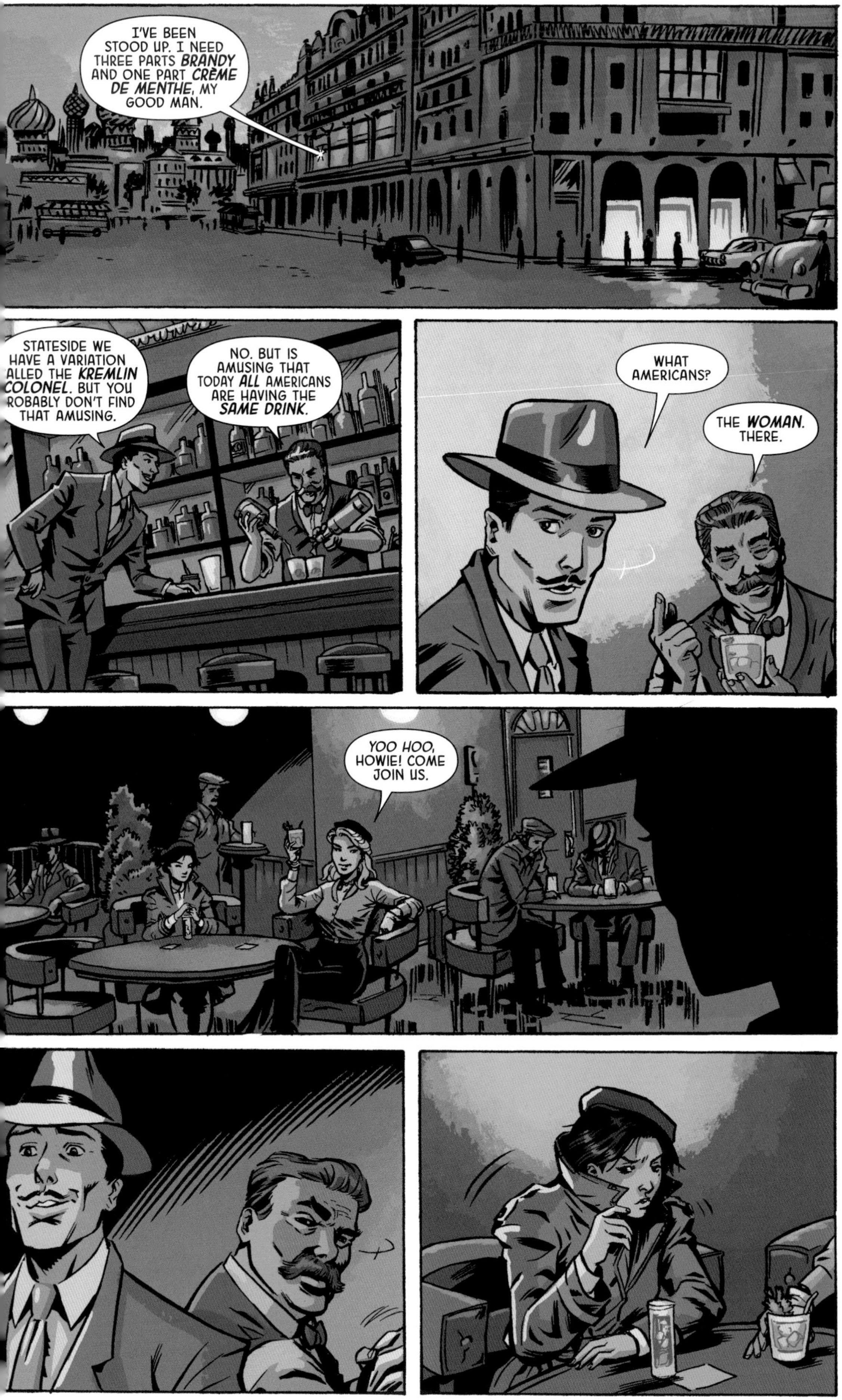

I'VE BEEN STOOD UP. I NEED THREE PARTS BRANDY AND ONE PART CRÈME DE MENTHE, MY GOOD MAN.
STATESIDE WE HAVE A VARIATION ALLED THE KREMLIN COLONEL. BUT YOU ROBABLY DON'T FIND THAT AMUSING.
NO. BUT IS AMUSING THAT TODAY ALL AMERICANS ARE HAVING THE SAME DRINK.
WHAT AMERICANS?
THE WOMAN. THERE.
YOO HOO, HOWIE! COME JOIN US.

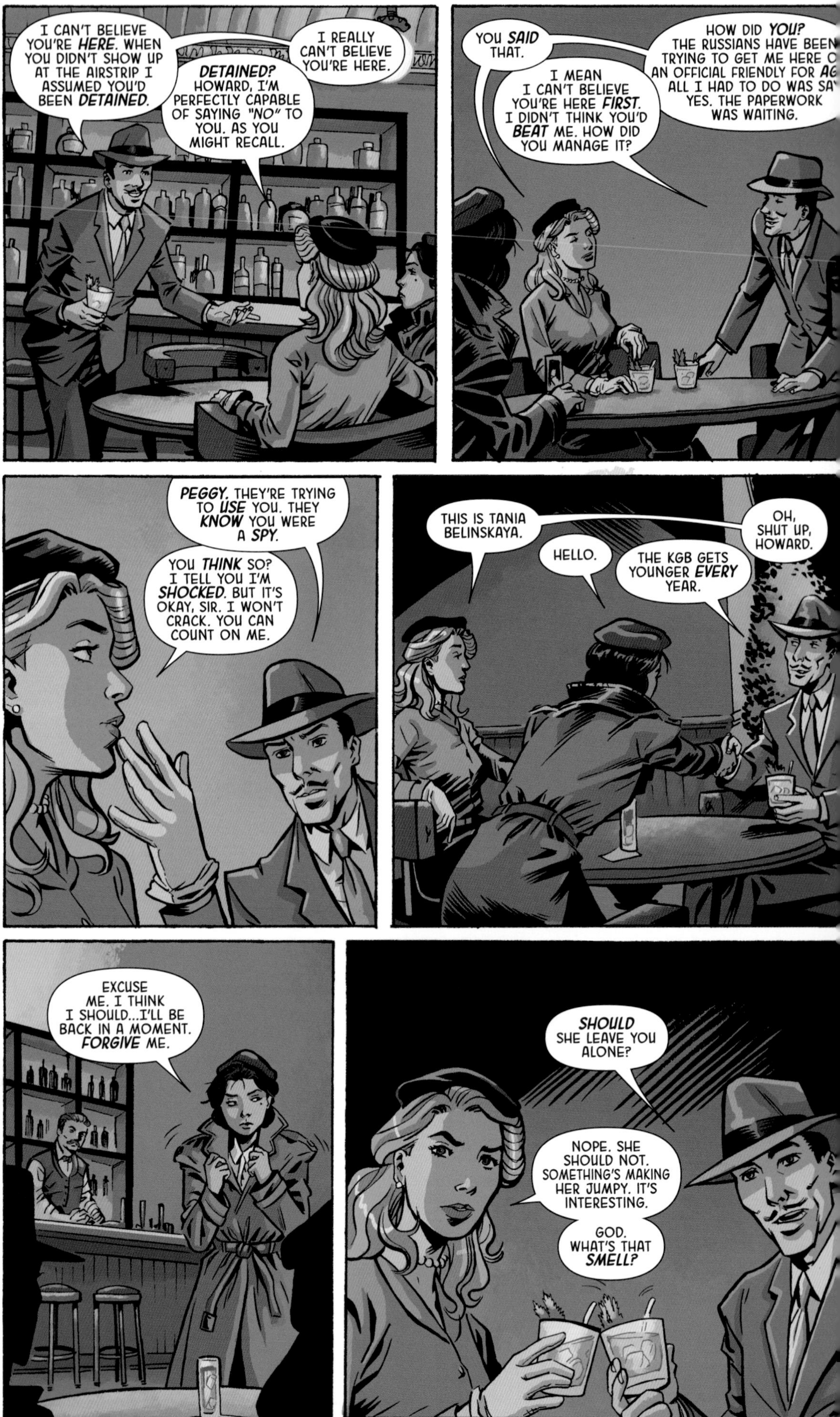
I CAN'T BELIEVE YOU'RE HERE. WHEN YOU DIDN'T SHOW UP AT THE AIRSTRIP I ASSUMED YOU'D BEEN DETAINED.
I REALLY CAN'T BELIEVE YOU'RE HERE.
DETAINED? HOWARD, I'M PERFECTLY CAPABLE OF SAYING "NO" TO YOU. AS YOU MIGHT RECALL.
YOU SAID THAT.
I MEAN I CAN'T BELIEVE YOU'RE HERE FIRST. I DIDN'T THINK YOU'D BEAT ME. HOW DID YOU MANAGE IT?
HOW DID YOU? THE RUSSIANS HAVE BEEN TRYING TO GET ME HERE O AN OFFICIAL FRIENDLY FOR AG ALL I HAD TO DO WAS SA YES. THE PAPERWORK WAS WAITING.
PEGGY. THEY'RE TRYING TO USE YOU. THEY KNOW YOU WERE A SPY.
YOU THINK SO? I TELL YOU I'M SHOCKED. BUT IT'S OKAY, SIR. I WON'T CRACK. YOU CAN COUNT ON ME.
THIS IS TANIA BELINSKAYA.
OH, SHUT UP, HOWARD.
HELLO.
THE KGB GETS YOUNGER EVERY YEAR.
EXCUSE ME. I THINK I SHOULD...I'LL BE BACK IN A MOMENT. FORGIVE ME.
SHOULD SHE LEAVE YOU ALONE?
NOPE. SHE SHOULD NOT. SOMETHING'S MAKING HER JUMPY. IT'S INTERESTING.
GOD. WHAT'S THAT SMELL?

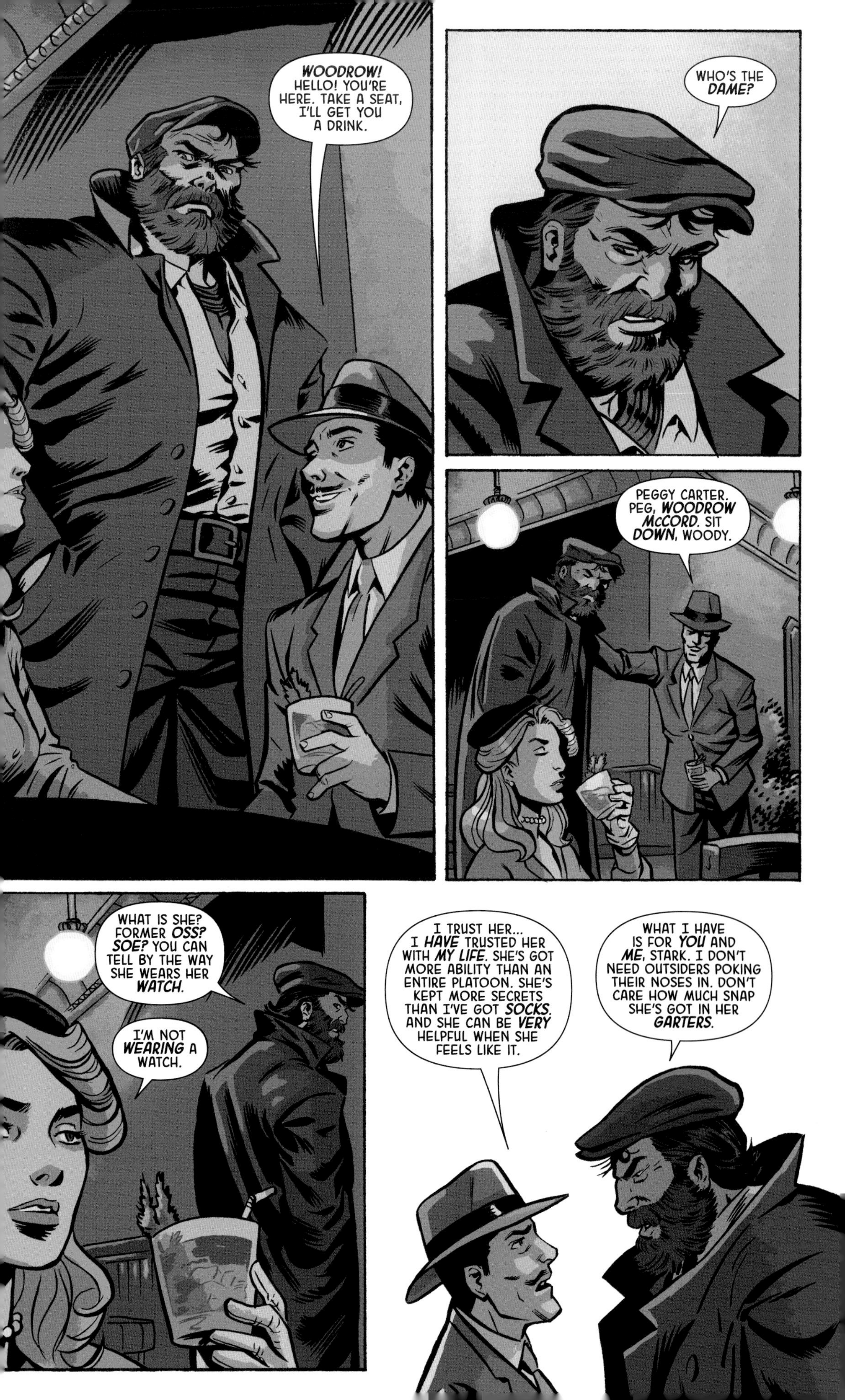
WOODROW! HELLO! YOU'RE HERE. TAKE A SEAT, I'LL GET YOU A DRINK.
WHO'S THE DAME?
PEGGY CARTER. PEG, WOODROW McCORD. SIT DOWN, WOODY.
WHAT IS SHE? FORMER OSS? SOE? YOU CAN TELL BY THE WAY SHE WEARS HER WATCH.
I'M NOT WEARING A WATCH.
I TRUST HER... I HAVE TRUSTED HER WITH MY LIFE. SHE'S GOT MORE ABILITY THAN AN ENTIRE PLATOON. SHE'S KEPT MORE SECRETS THAN I'VE GOT SOCKS. AND SHE CAN BE VERY HELPFUL WHEN SHE FEELS LIKE IT.
WHAT I HAVE IS FOR YOU AND ME, STARK. I DON'T NEED OUTSIDERS POKING THEIR NOSES IN. DON'T CARE HOW MUCH SNAP SHE'S GOT IN HER GARTERS.

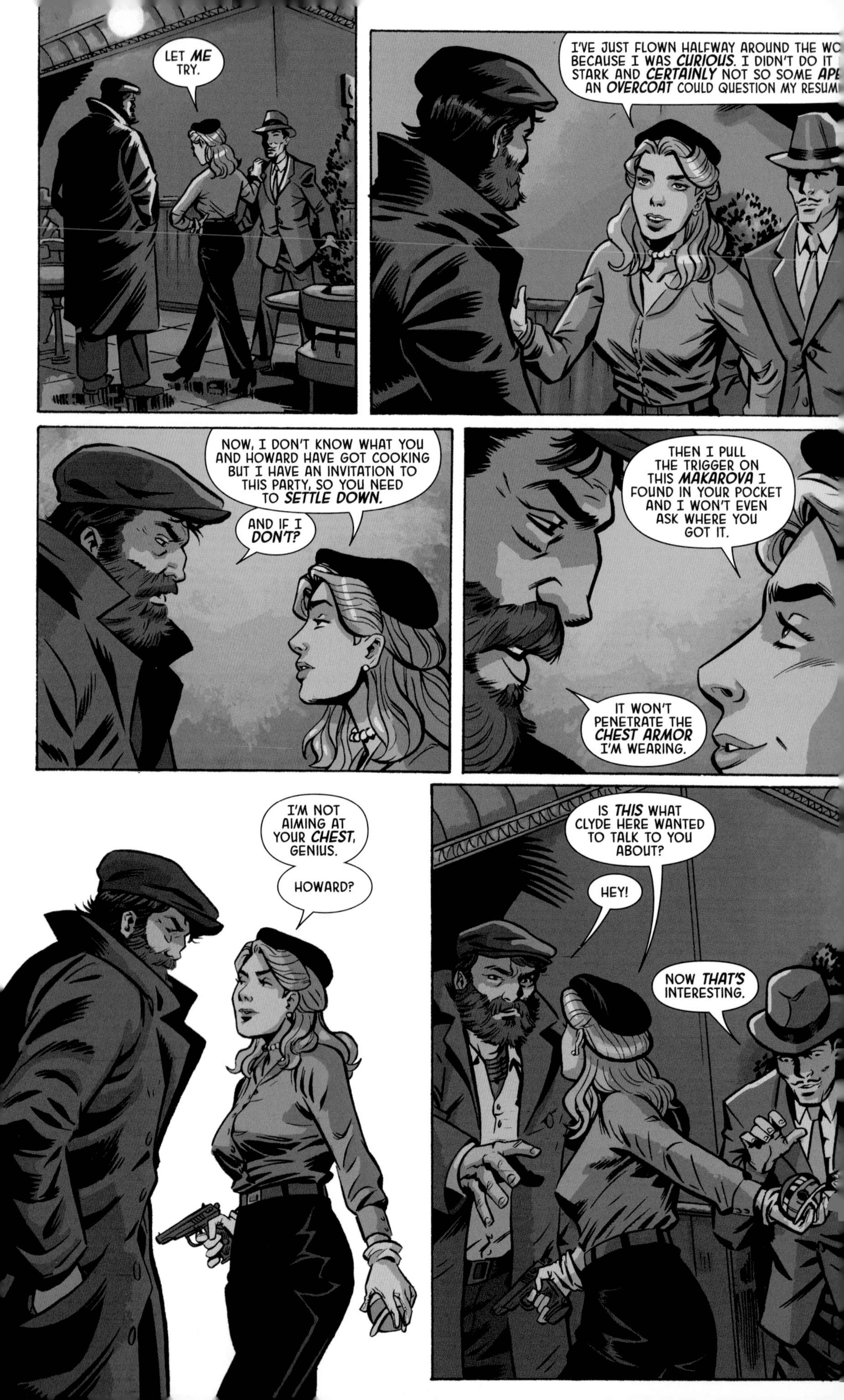
LET ME TRY.
I'VE JUST FLOWN HALFWAY AROUND THE WO
BECAUSE I WAS CURIOUS. I DIDN'T DO IT
STARK AND CERTAINLY NOT SO SOME APE
AN OVERCOAT COULD QUESTION MY RESUM
NOW, I DON'T KNOW WHAT YOU AND HOWARD HAVE GOT COOKING BUT I HAVE AN INVITATION TO THIS PARTY, SO YOU NEED TO SETTLE DOWN.
AND IF I DON'T?
THEN I PULL THE TRIGGER ON THIS MAKAROVA I FOUND IN YOUR POCKET AND I WON'T EVEN ASK WHERE YOU GOT IT.
IT WON'T PENETRATE THE CHEST ARMOR I'M WEARING.
I'M NOT AIMING AT YOUR CHEST, GENIUS.
HOWARD?
IS THIS WHAT CLYDE HERE WANTED TO TALK TO YOU ABOUT?
HEY!
NOW THAT'S INTERESTING.

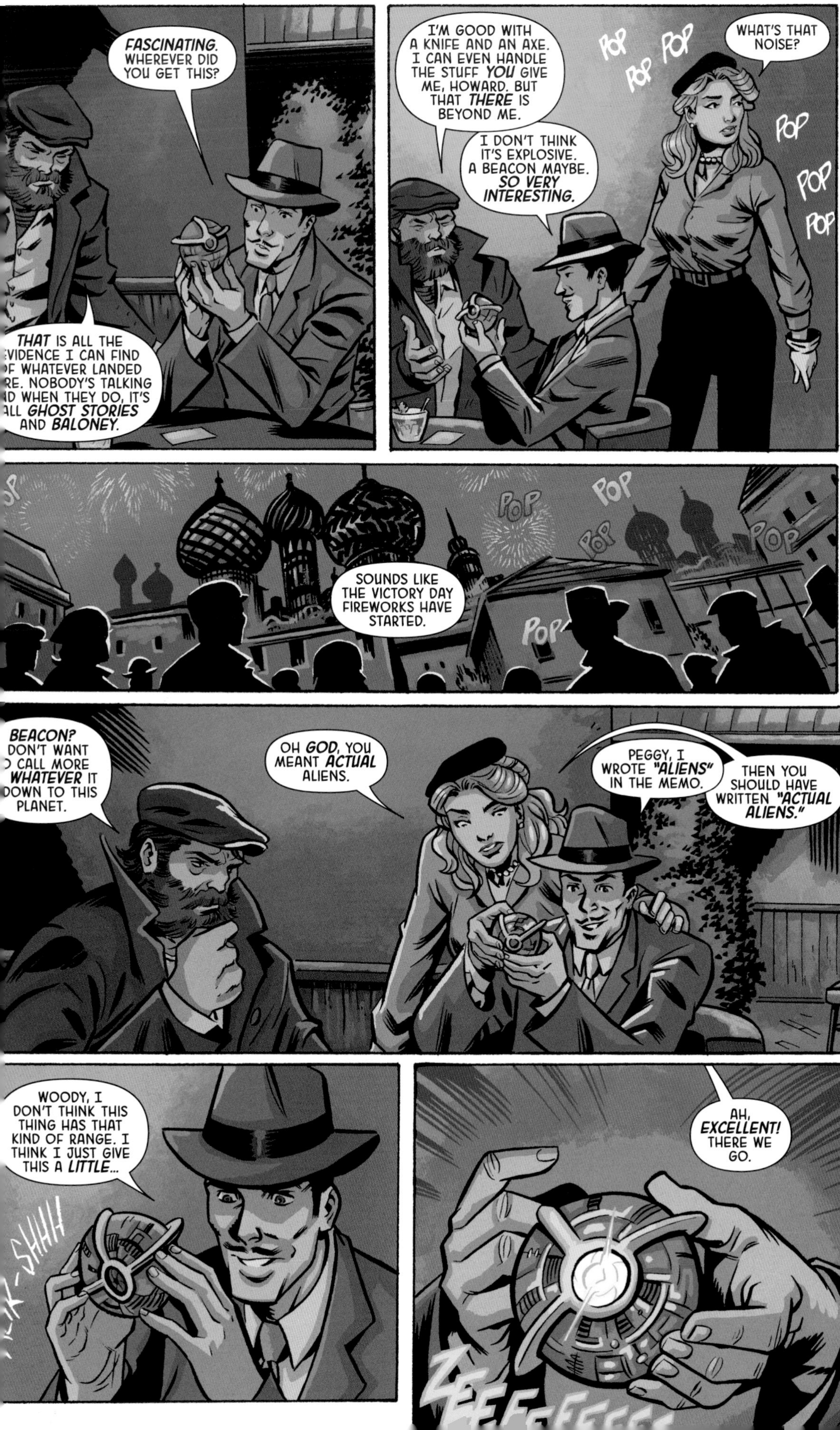
FASCINATING. WHEREVER DID YOU GET THIS?
THAT IS ALL THE EVIDENCE I CAN FIND OF WHATEVER LANDED HERE. NOBODY'S TALKING AND WHEN THEY DO, IT'S ALL GHOST STORIES AND BALONEY.
I'M GOOD WITH A KNIFE AND AN AXE. I CAN EVEN HANDLE THE STUFF YOU GIVE ME, HOWARD. BUT THAT THERE IS BEYOND ME.
I DON'T THINK IT'S EXPLOSIVE. A BEACON MAYBE. SO VERY INTERESTING.
POP POP POP
WHAT'S THAT NOISE?
POP POP POP
POP POP POP POP
SOUNDS LIKE THE VICTORY DAY FIREWORKS HAVE STARTED.
POP
BEACON? I DON'T WANT TO CALL MORE OF WHATEVER IT IS DOWN TO THIS PLANET.
OH GOD, YOU MEANT ACTUAL ALIENS.
PEGGY, I WROTE "ALIENS" IN THE MEMO.
THEN YOU SHOULD HAVE WRITTEN "ACTUAL ALIENS."
WOODY, I DON'T THINK THIS THING HAS THAT KIND OF RANGE. I THINK I JUST GIVE THIS A LITTLE...
SHHH
AH, EXCELLENT! THERE WE GO.
ZEEEEEEEE

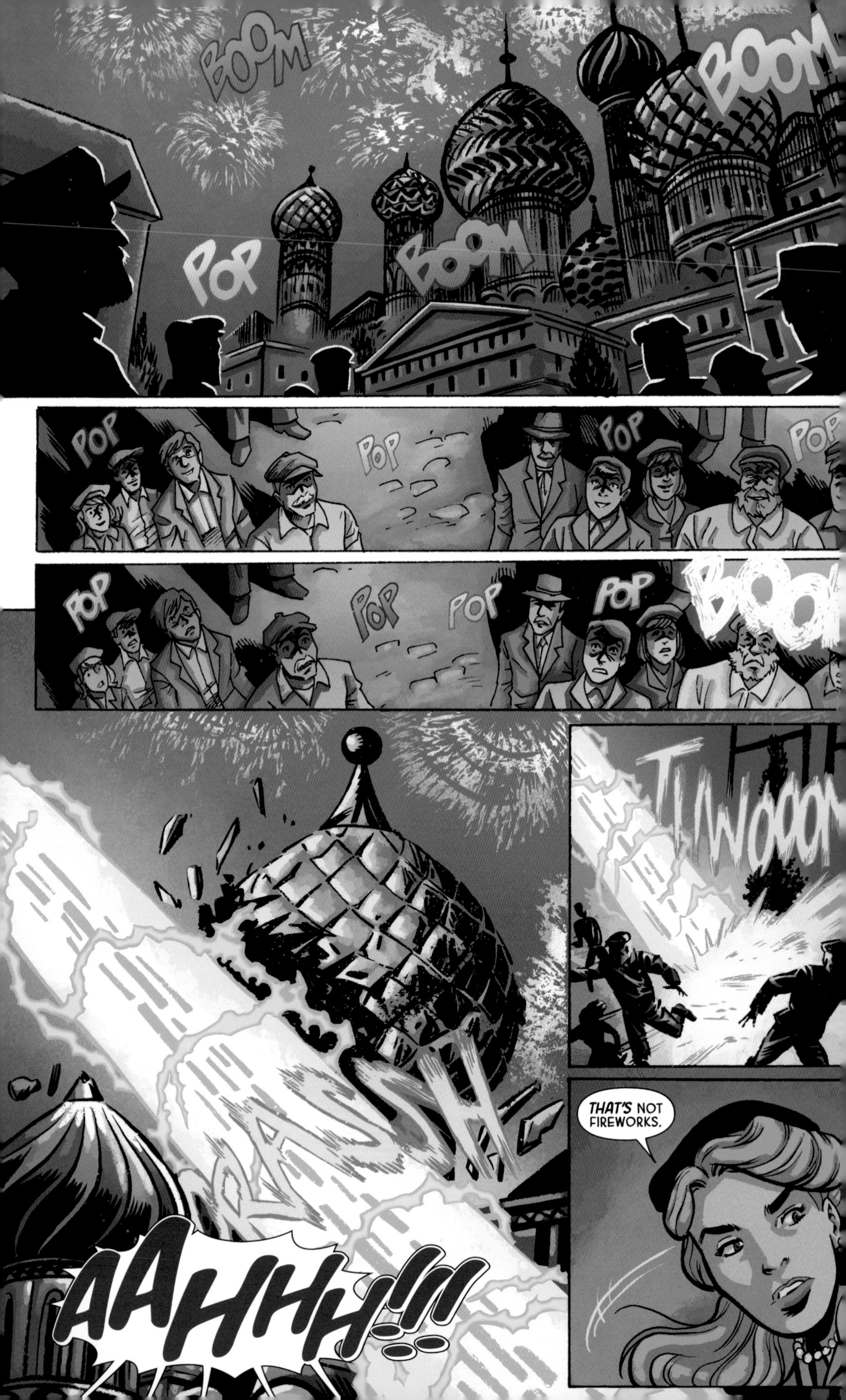

BOOM
BOOM
POP
BOOM
POP
POP
POP
POP
POP
POP
POP
POP
BOO
TWOOM
CRUSH
AAHHH!!!
THAT'S NOT FIREWORKS.

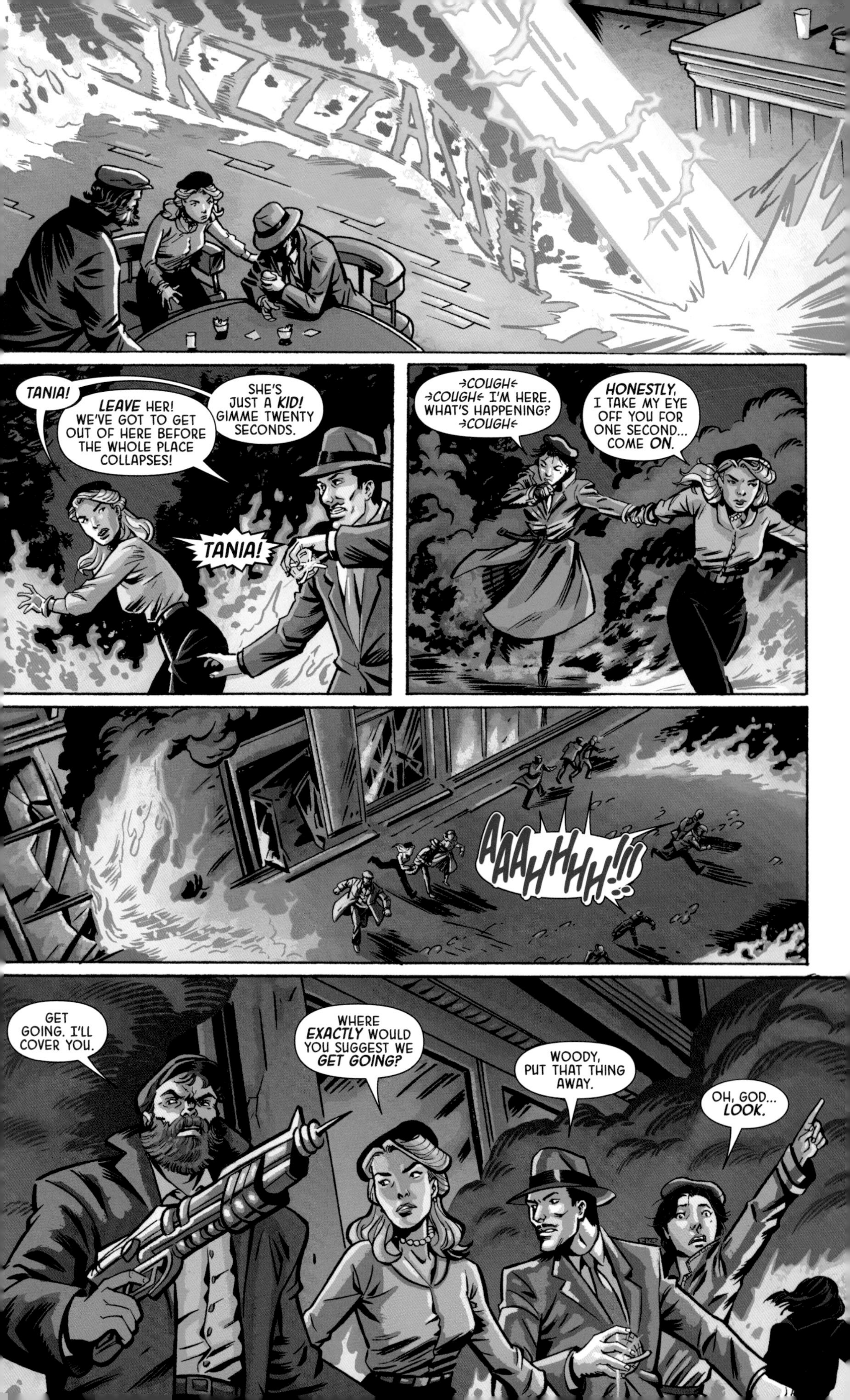

SKZZZZAAASSHH
TANIA!
LEAVE HER! WE'VE GOT TO GET OUT OF HERE BEFORE THE WHOLE PLACE COLLAPSES!
SHE'S JUST A KID! GIMME TWENTY SECONDS.
TANIA!
>COUGH< >COUGH< I'M HERE. WHAT'S HAPPENING? >COUGH<
HONESTLY, I TAKE MY EYE OFF YOU FOR ONE SECOND... COME ON.
AAAHHHH!!!
GET GOING. I'LL COVER YOU.
WHERE EXACTLY WOULD YOU SUGGEST WE GET GOING?
WOODY, PUT THAT THING AWAY.
OH, GOD... LOOK.

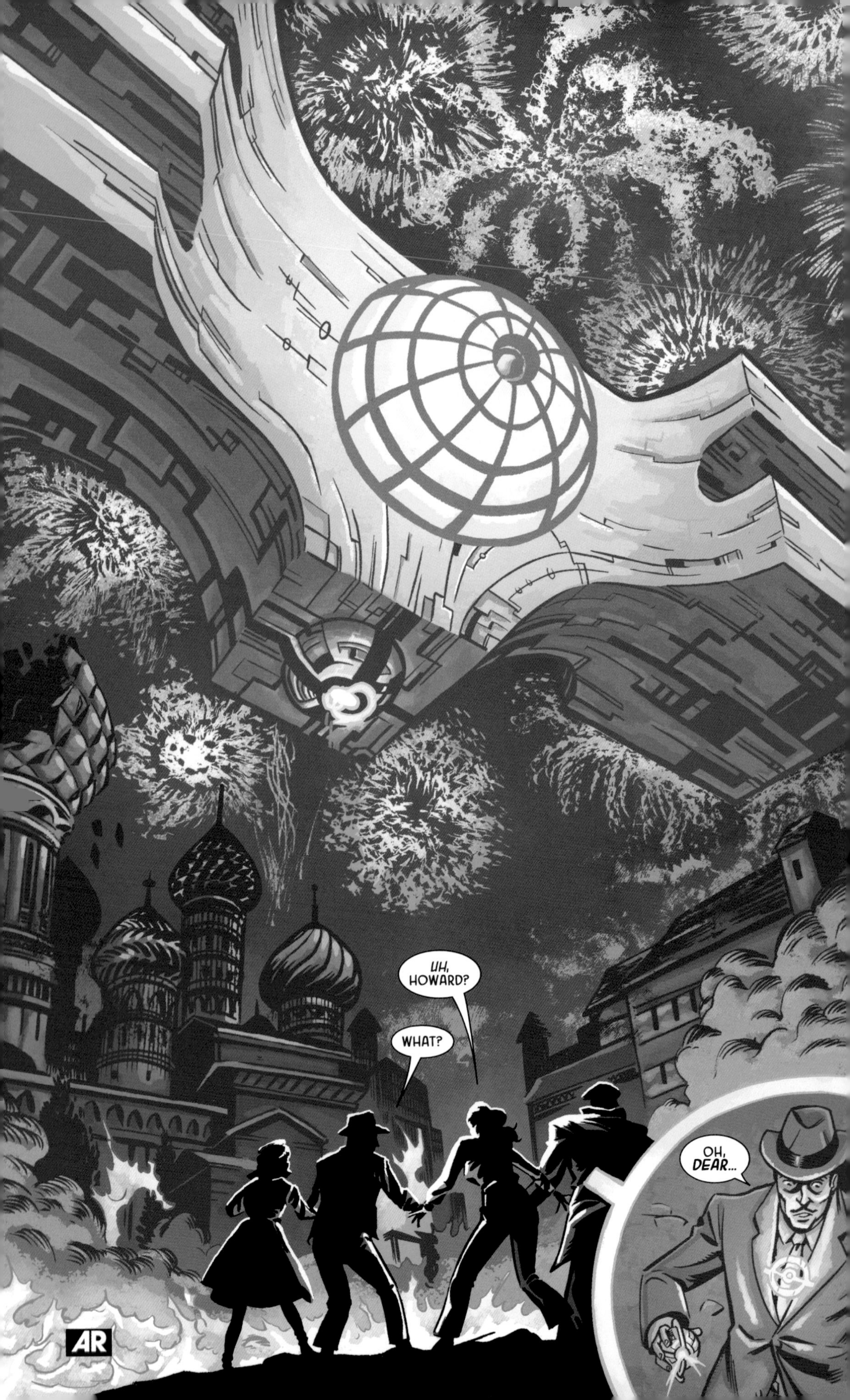
UH, HOWARD?
WHAT?
OH, DEAR...

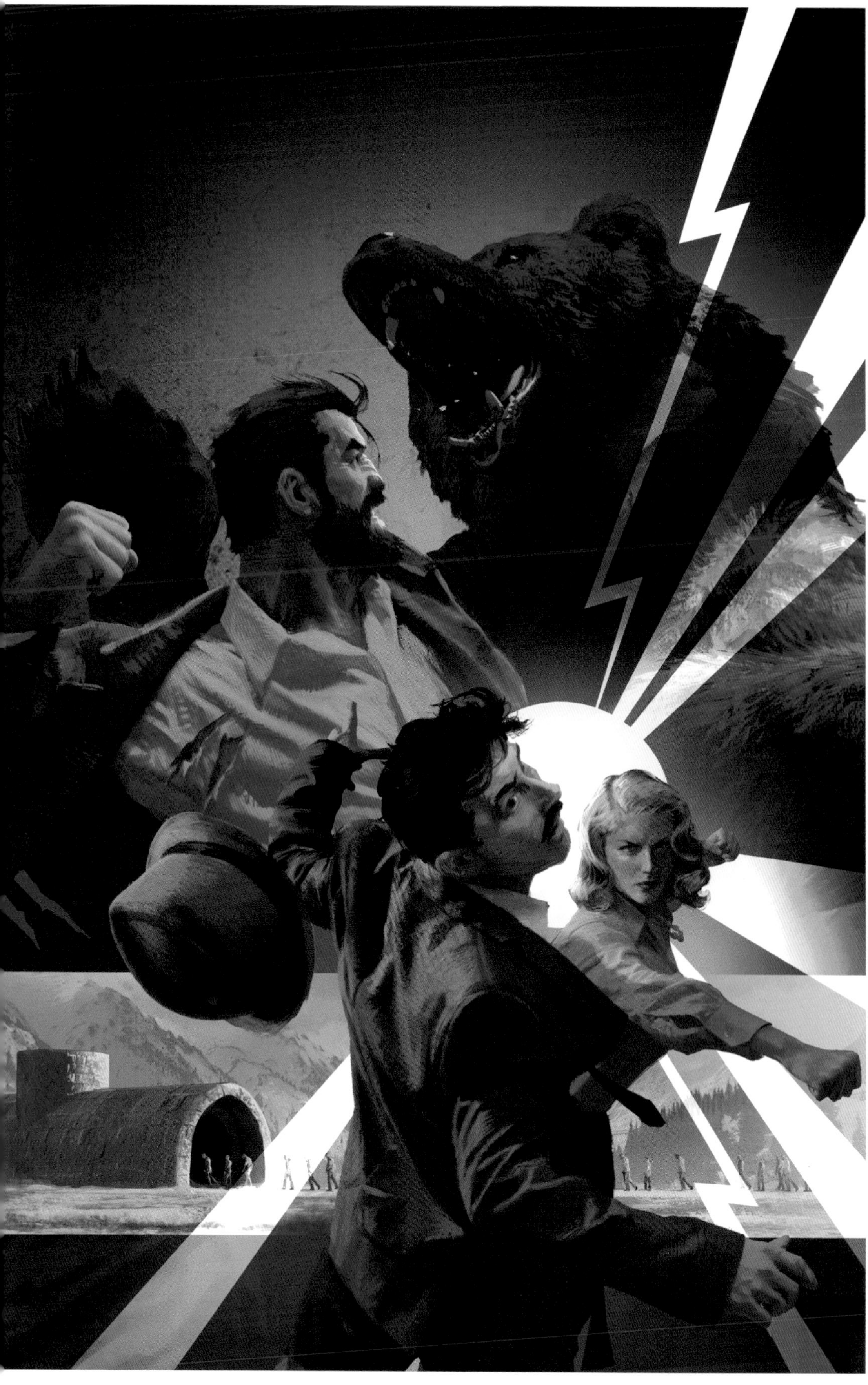

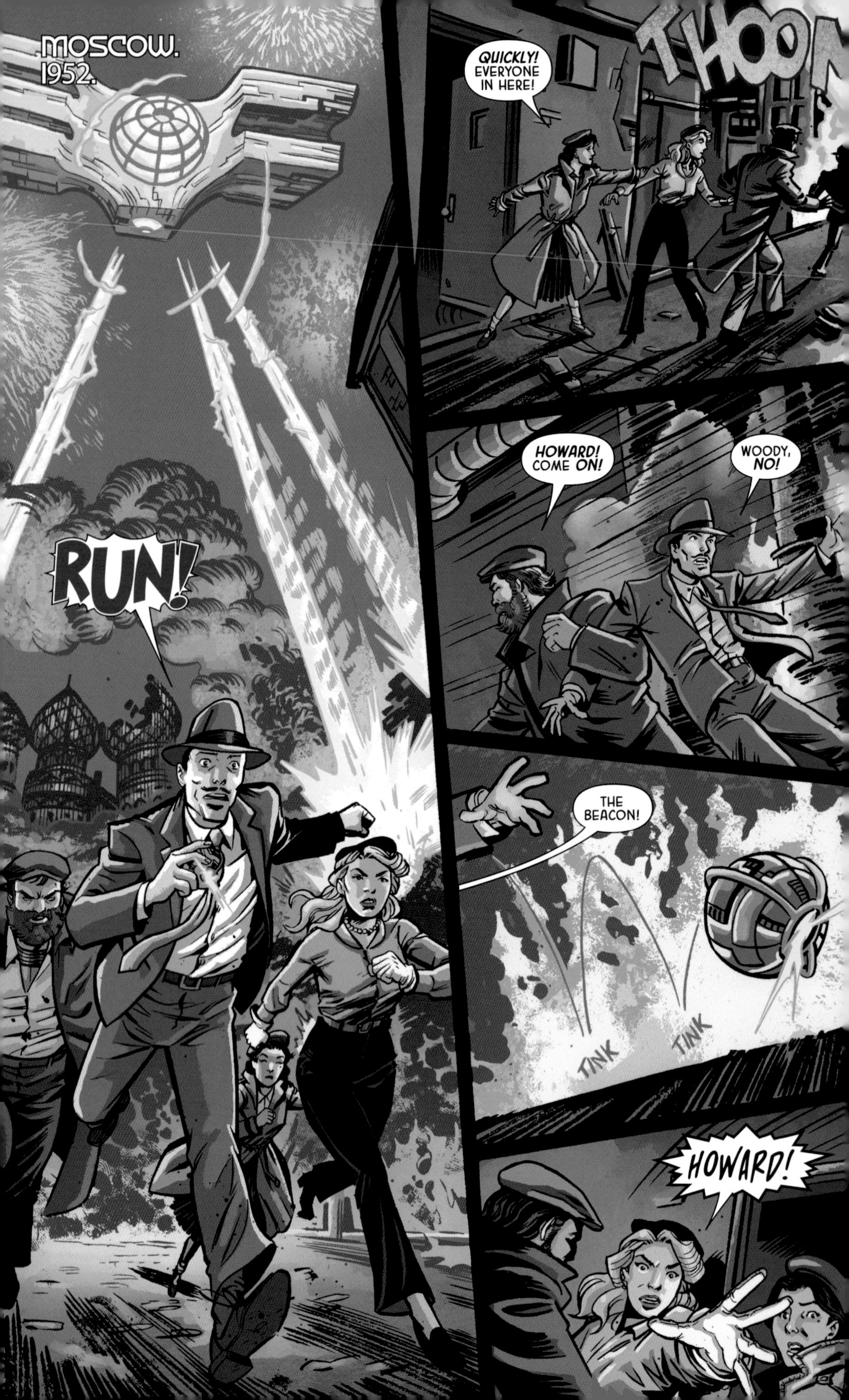
MOSCOW.
1952.
RUN!
QUICKLY! EVERYONE IN HERE!
THOOM
HOWARD! COME ON!
WOODY, NO!
THE BEACON!
TINK
TINK
HOWARD!

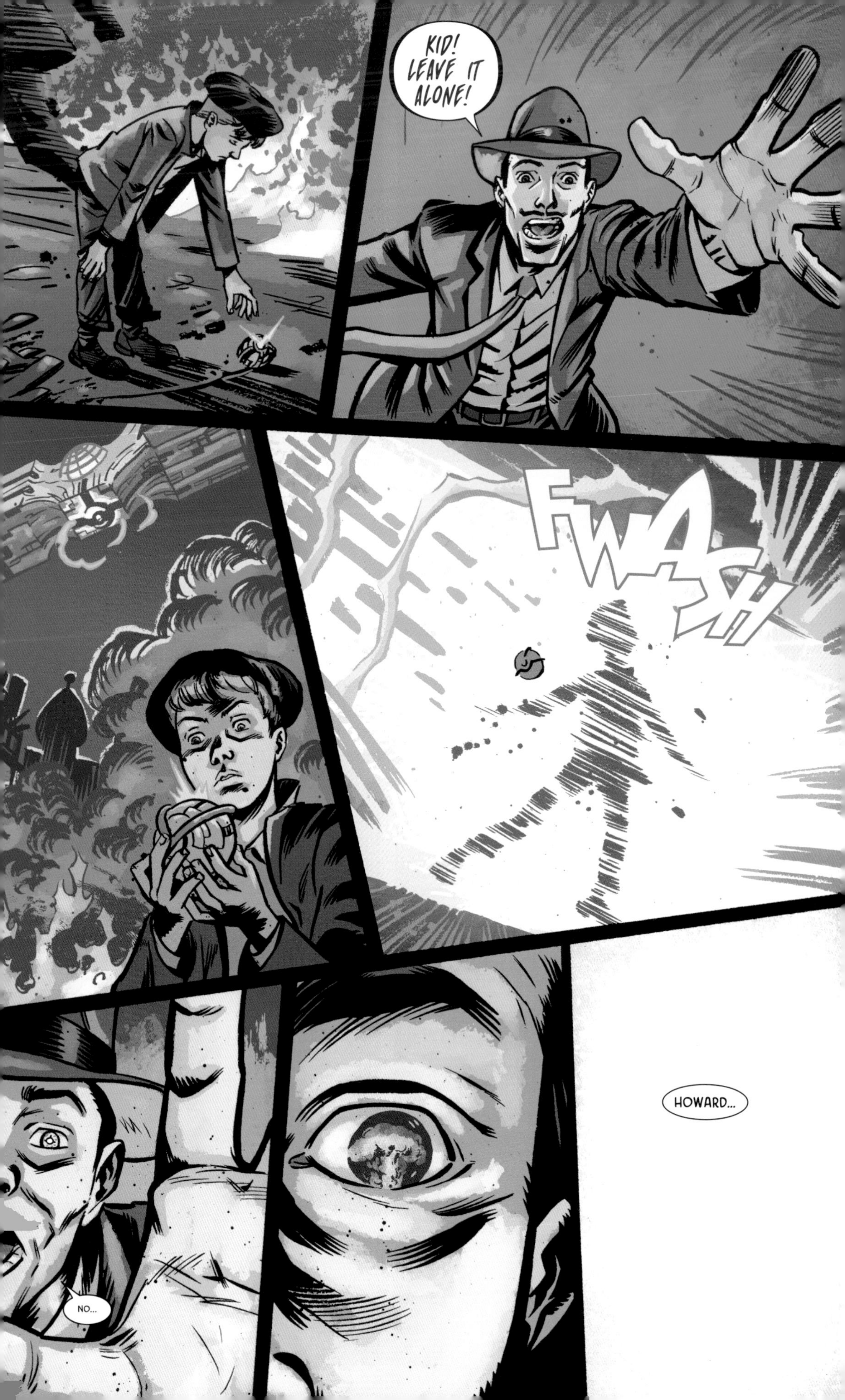
KID! LEAVE IT ALONE!
FWASH
HOWARD...
NO...

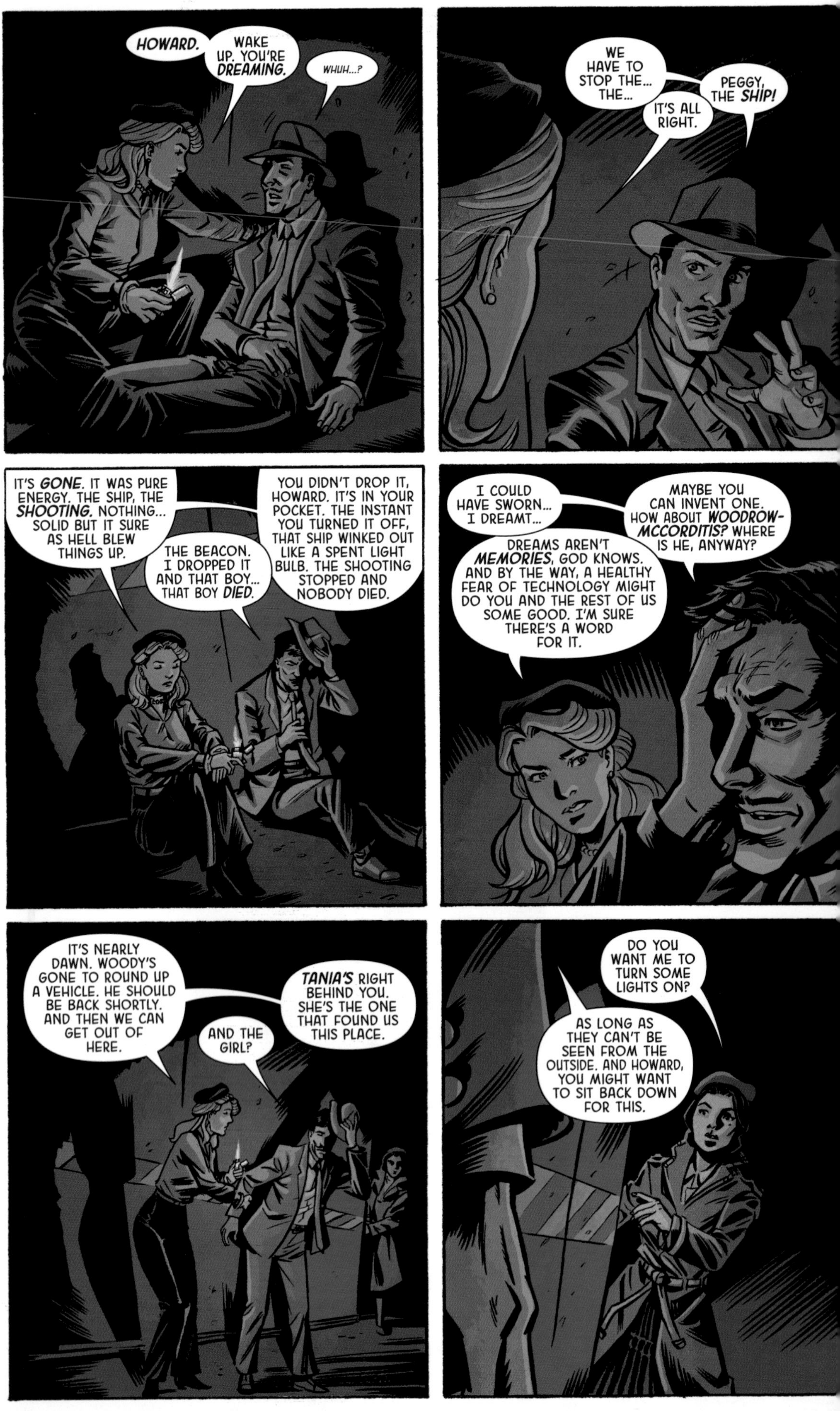
HOWARD.
WAKE UP. YOU'RE DREAMING.
WHUH...?
WE HAVE TO STOP THE... THE...
IT'S ALL RIGHT.
PEGGY, THE SHIP!
IT'S GONE. IT WAS PURE ENERGY. THE SHIP, THE SHOOTING. NOTHING... SOLID BUT IT SURE AS HELL BLEW THINGS UP.
THE BEACON. I DROPPED IT AND THAT BOY... THAT BOY DIED.
YOU DIDN'T DROP IT, HOWARD. IT'S IN YOUR POCKET. THE INSTANT YOU TURNED IT OFF, THAT SHIP WINKED OUT LIKE A SPENT LIGHT BULB. THE SHOOTING STOPPED AND NOBODY DIED.
I COULD HAVE SWORN... I DREAMT...
DREAMS AREN'T MEMORIES, GOD KNOWS. AND BY THE WAY, A HEALTHY FEAR OF TECHNOLOGY MIGHT DO YOU AND THE REST OF US SOME GOOD. I'M SURE THERE'S A WORD FOR IT.
MAYBE YOU CAN INVENT ONE. HOW ABOUT WOODROW-MCCORDITIS? WHERE IS HE, ANYWAY?
IT'S NEARLY DAWN. WOODY'S GONE TO ROUND UP A VEHICLE. HE SHOULD BE BACK SHORTLY. AND THEN WE CAN GET OUT OF HERE.
AND THE GIRL?
TANIA'S RIGHT BEHIND YOU. SHE'S THE ONE THAT FOUND US THIS PLACE.
DO YOU WANT ME TO TURN SOME LIGHTS ON?
AS LONG AS THEY CAN'T BE SEEN FROM THE OUTSIDE. AND HOWARD, YOU MIGHT WANT TO SIT BACK DOWN FOR THIS.

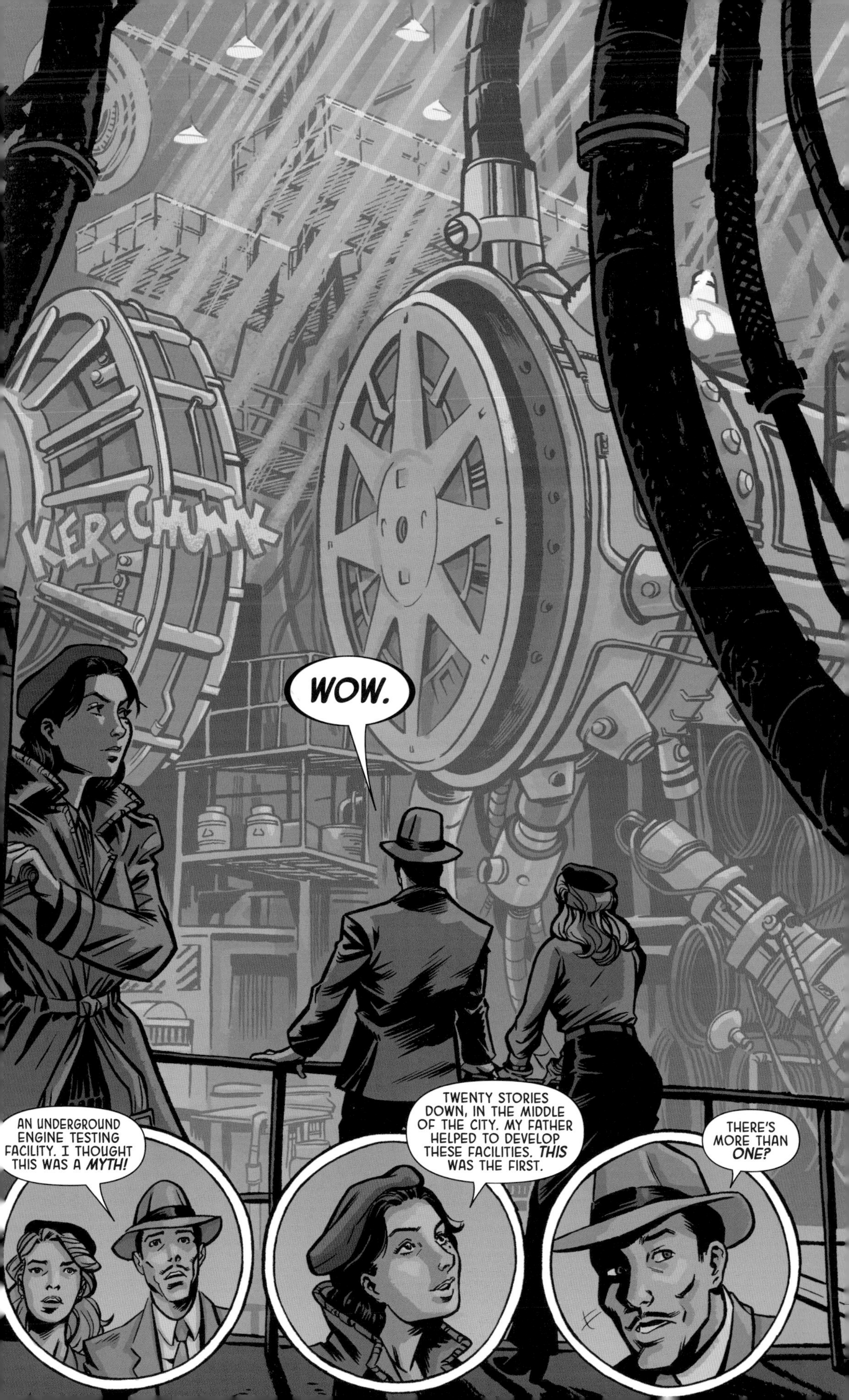
KER-CHUNK
WOW.
AN UNDERGROUND ENGINE TESTING FACILITY. I THOUGHT THIS WAS A *MYTH!*
TWENTY STORIES DOWN, IN THE MIDDLE OF THE CITY. MY FATHER HELPED TO DEVELOP THESE FACILITIES. *THIS* WAS THE FIRST.
THERE'S MORE THAN *ONE?*

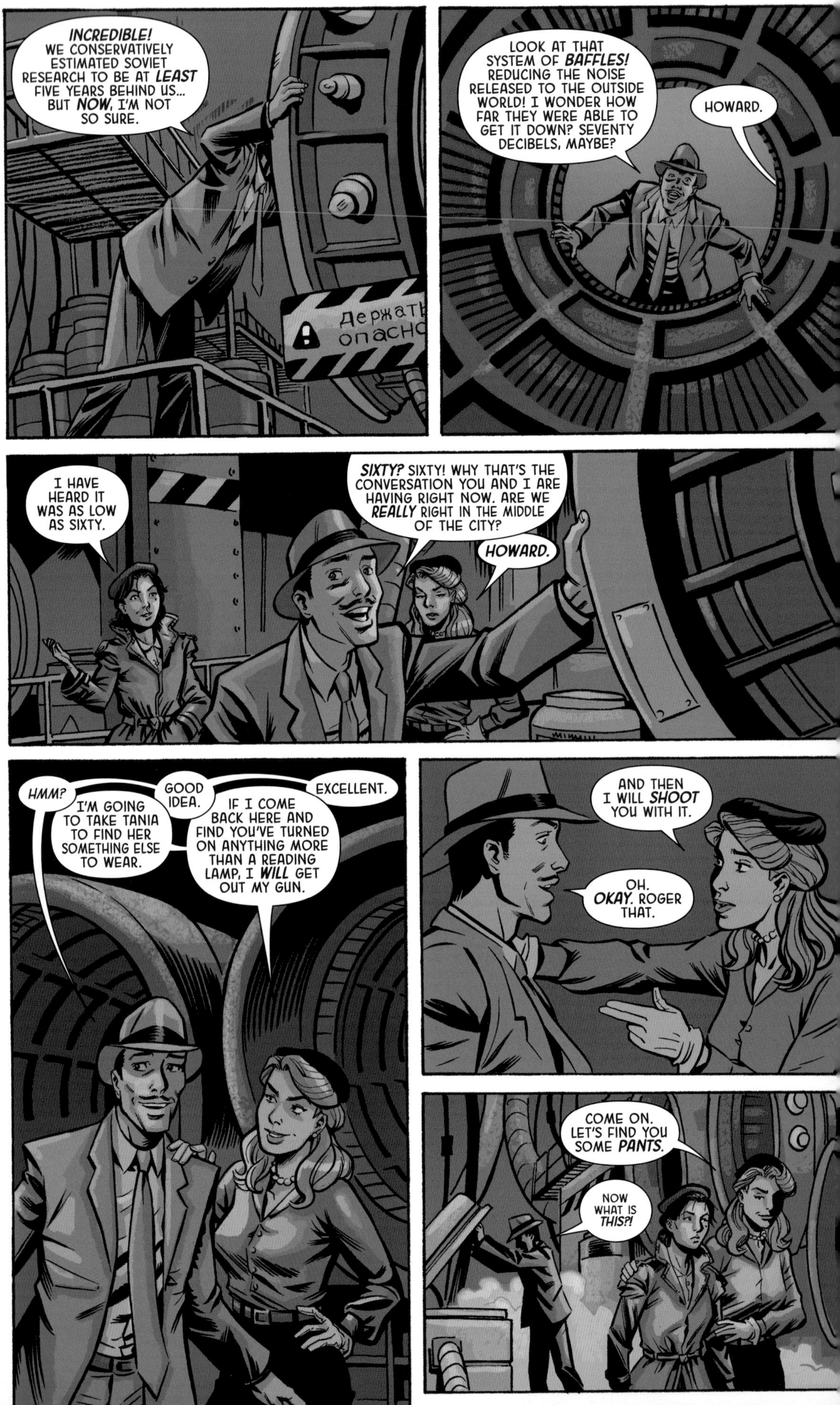
INCREDIBLE! WE CONSERVATIVELY ESTIMATED SOVIET RESEARCH TO BE AT LEAST FIVE YEARS BEHIND US... BUT NOW, I'M NOT SO SURE.
LOOK AT THAT SYSTEM OF BAFFLES! REDUCING THE NOISE RELEASED TO THE OUTSIDE WORLD! I WONDER HOW FAR THEY WERE ABLE TO GET IT DOWN? SEVENTY DECIBELS, MAYBE?
HOWARD.
I HAVE HEARD IT WAS AS LOW AS SIXTY.
SIXTY? SIXTY! WHY THAT'S THE CONVERSATION YOU AND I ARE HAVING RIGHT NOW. ARE WE REALLY RIGHT IN THE MIDDLE OF THE CITY?
HOWARD.
HMM?
I'M GOING TO TAKE TANIA TO FIND HER SOMETHING ELSE TO WEAR.
GOOD IDEA.
IF I COME BACK HERE AND FIND YOU'VE TURNED ON ANYTHING MORE THAN A READING LAMP, I WILL GET OUT MY GUN.
EXCELLENT.
AND THEN I WILL SHOOT YOU WITH IT.
OH. OKAY. ROGER THAT.
COME ON. LET'S FIND YOU SOME PANTS.
NOW WHAT IS THIS?!

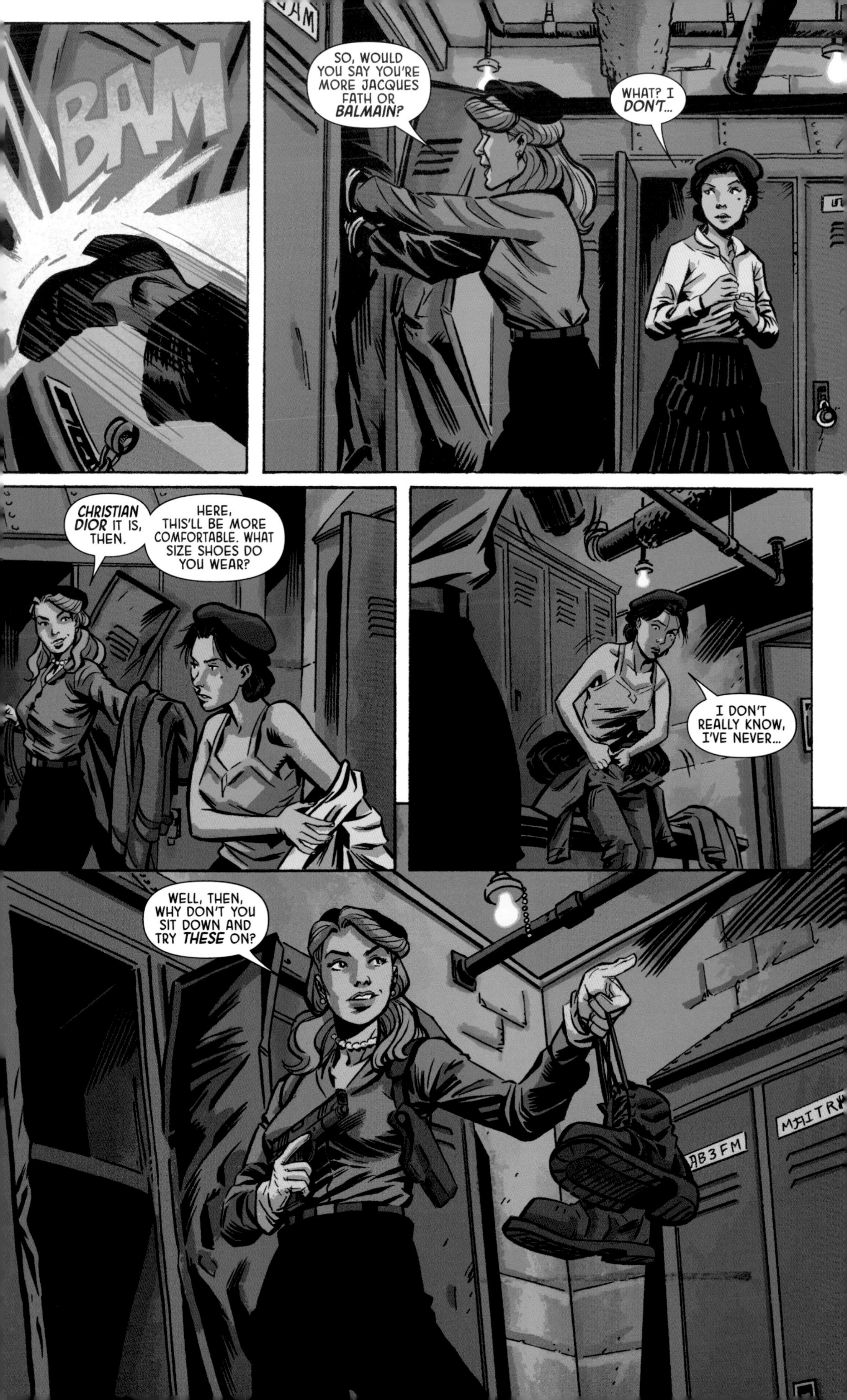
BAM
SO, WOULD YOU SAY YOU'RE MORE JACQUES FATH OR BALMAIN?
WHAT? I DON'T...
CHRISTIAN DIOR IT IS, THEN.
HERE, THIS'LL BE MORE COMFORTABLE. WHAT SIZE SHOES DO YOU WEAR?
I DON'T REALLY KNOW, I'VE NEVER...
WELL, THEN, WHY DON'T YOU SIT DOWN AND TRY THESE ON?

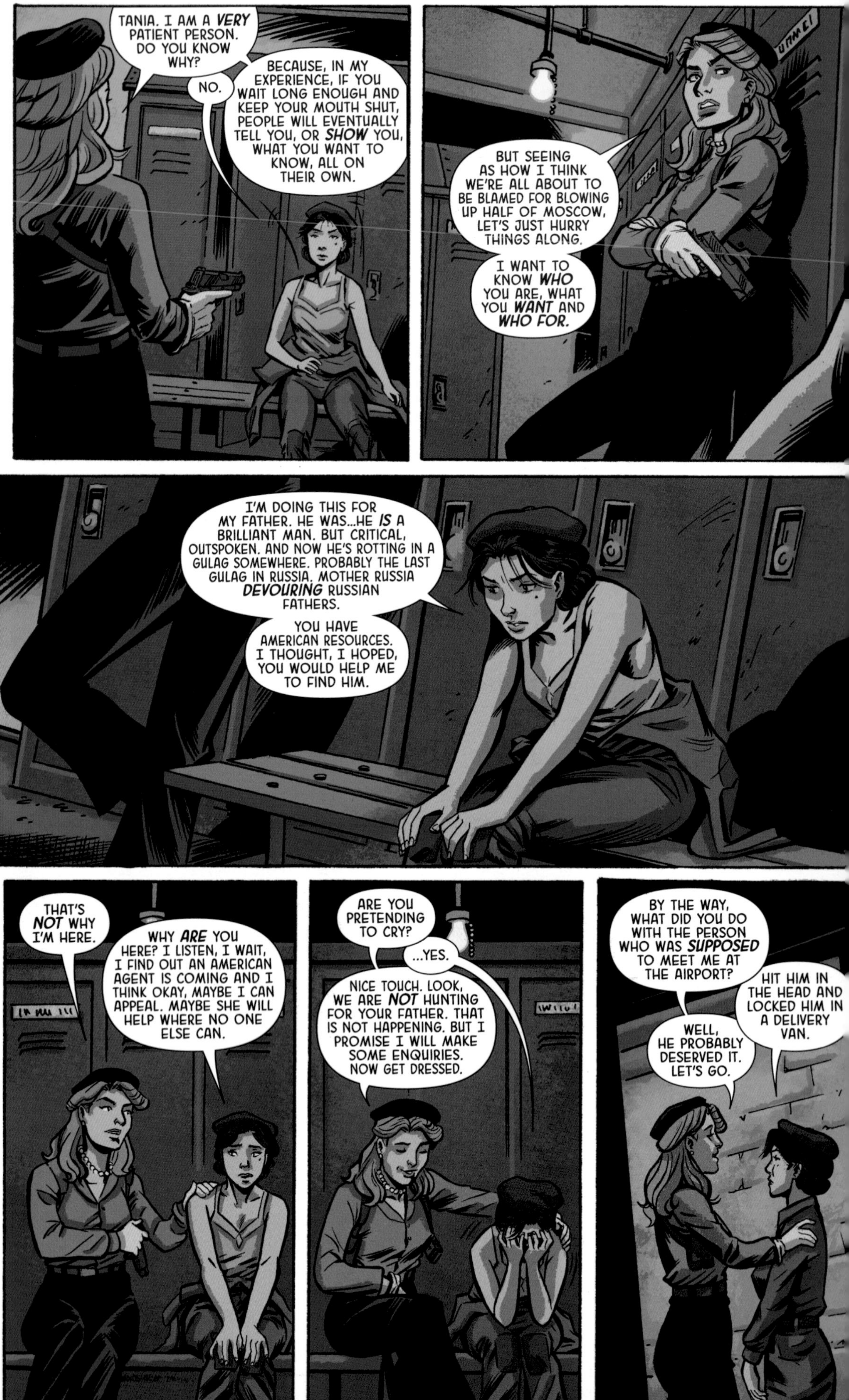

TANIA. I AM A VERY PATIENT PERSON. DO YOU KNOW WHY?
NO.
BECAUSE, IN MY EXPERIENCE, IF YOU WAIT LONG ENOUGH AND KEEP YOUR MOUTH SHUT, PEOPLE WILL EVENTUALLY TELL YOU, OR SHOW YOU, WHAT YOU WANT TO KNOW, ALL ON THEIR OWN.
BUT SEEING AS HOW I THINK WE'RE ALL ABOUT TO BE BLAMED FOR BLOWING UP HALF OF MOSCOW, LET'S JUST HURRY THINGS ALONG.
I WANT TO KNOW WHO YOU ARE, WHAT YOU WANT AND WHO FOR.
I'M DOING THIS FOR MY FATHER. HE WAS...HE IS A BRILLIANT MAN. BUT CRITICAL, OUTSPOKEN. AND NOW HE'S ROTTING IN A GULAG SOMEWHERE. PROBABLY THE LAST GULAG IN RUSSIA. MOTHER RUSSIA DEVOURING RUSSIAN FATHERS.
YOU HAVE AMERICAN RESOURCES. I THOUGHT, I HOPED, YOU WOULD HELP ME TO FIND HIM.
THAT'S NOT WHY I'M HERE.
WHY ARE YOU HERE? I LISTEN, I WAIT, I FIND OUT AN AMERICAN AGENT IS COMING AND I THINK OKAY, MAYBE I CAN APPEAL. MAYBE SHE WILL HELP WHERE NO ONE ELSE CAN.
ARE YOU PRETENDING TO CRY?
...YES.
NICE TOUCH. LOOK, WE ARE NOT HUNTING FOR YOUR FATHER. THAT IS NOT HAPPENING. BUT I PROMISE I WILL MAKE SOME ENQUIRIES. NOW GET DRESSED.
BY THE WAY, WHAT DID YOU DO WITH THE PERSON WHO WAS SUPPOSED TO MEET ME AT THE AIRPORT?
HIT HIM IN THE HEAD AND LOCKED HIM IN A DELIVERY VAN.
WELL, HE PROBABLY DESERVED IT. LET'S GO.

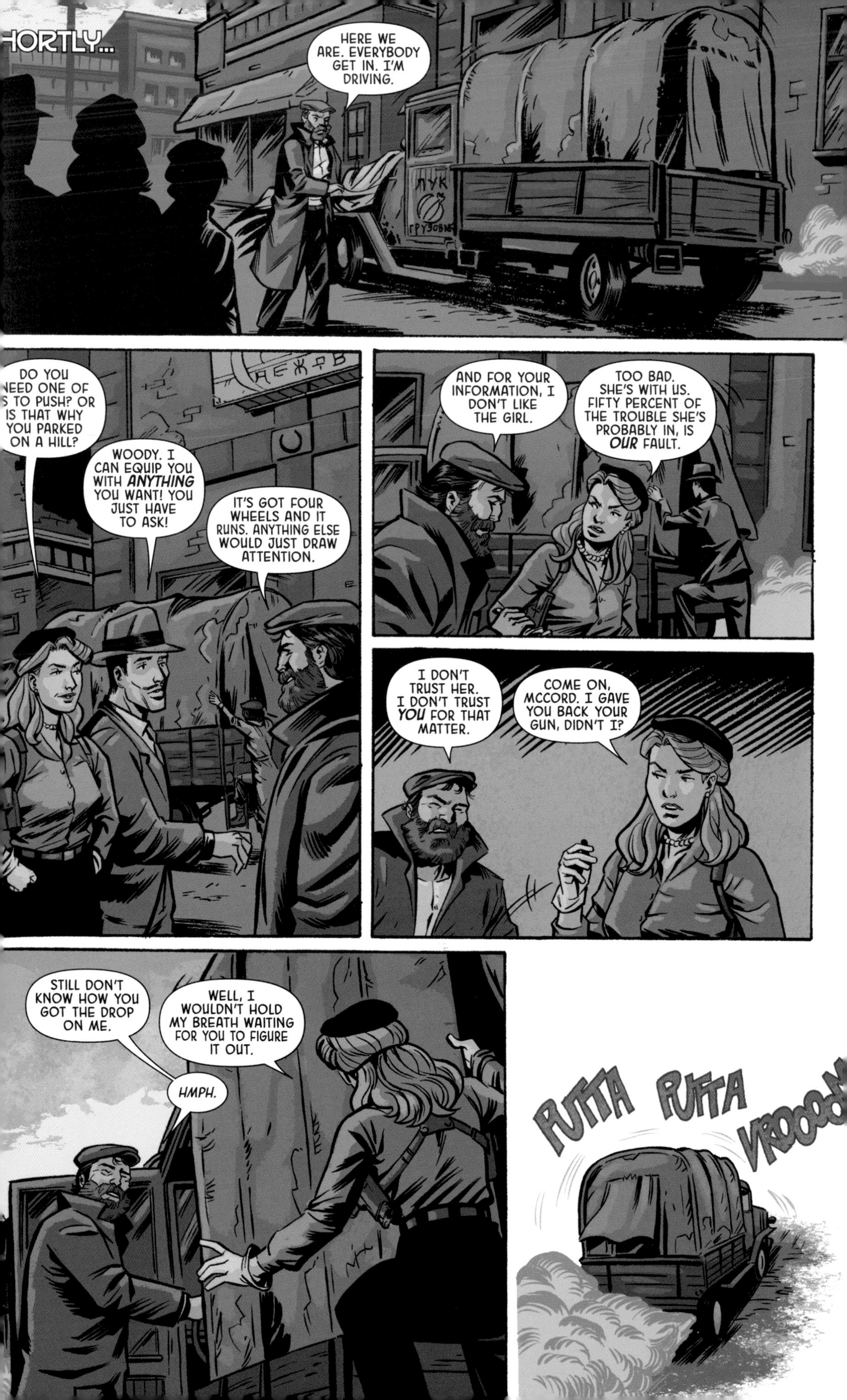
HORTLY...
HERE WE ARE. EVERYBODY GET IN. I'M DRIVING.
ЛУК
ГРУЗОВИК
DO YOU NEED ONE OF S TO PUSH? OR IS THAT WHY YOU PARKED ON A HILL?
WOODY. I CAN EQUIP YOU WITH ANYTHING YOU WANT! YOU JUST HAVE TO ASK!
IT'S GOT FOUR WHEELS AND IT RUNS. ANYTHING ELSE WOULD JUST DRAW ATTENTION.
AND FOR YOUR INFORMATION, I DON'T LIKE THE GIRL.
TOO BAD. SHE'S WITH US. FIFTY PERCENT OF THE TROUBLE SHE'S PROBABLY IN, IS OUR FAULT.
I DON'T TRUST HER. I DON'T TRUST YOU FOR THAT MATTER.
COME ON, MCCORD. I GAVE YOU BACK YOUR GUN, DIDN'T I?
STILL DON'T KNOW HOW YOU GOT THE DROP ON ME.
WELL, I WOULDN'T HOLD MY BREATH WAITING FOR YOU TO FIGURE IT OUT.
HMPH.
PUTTA PUTTA VROOOO

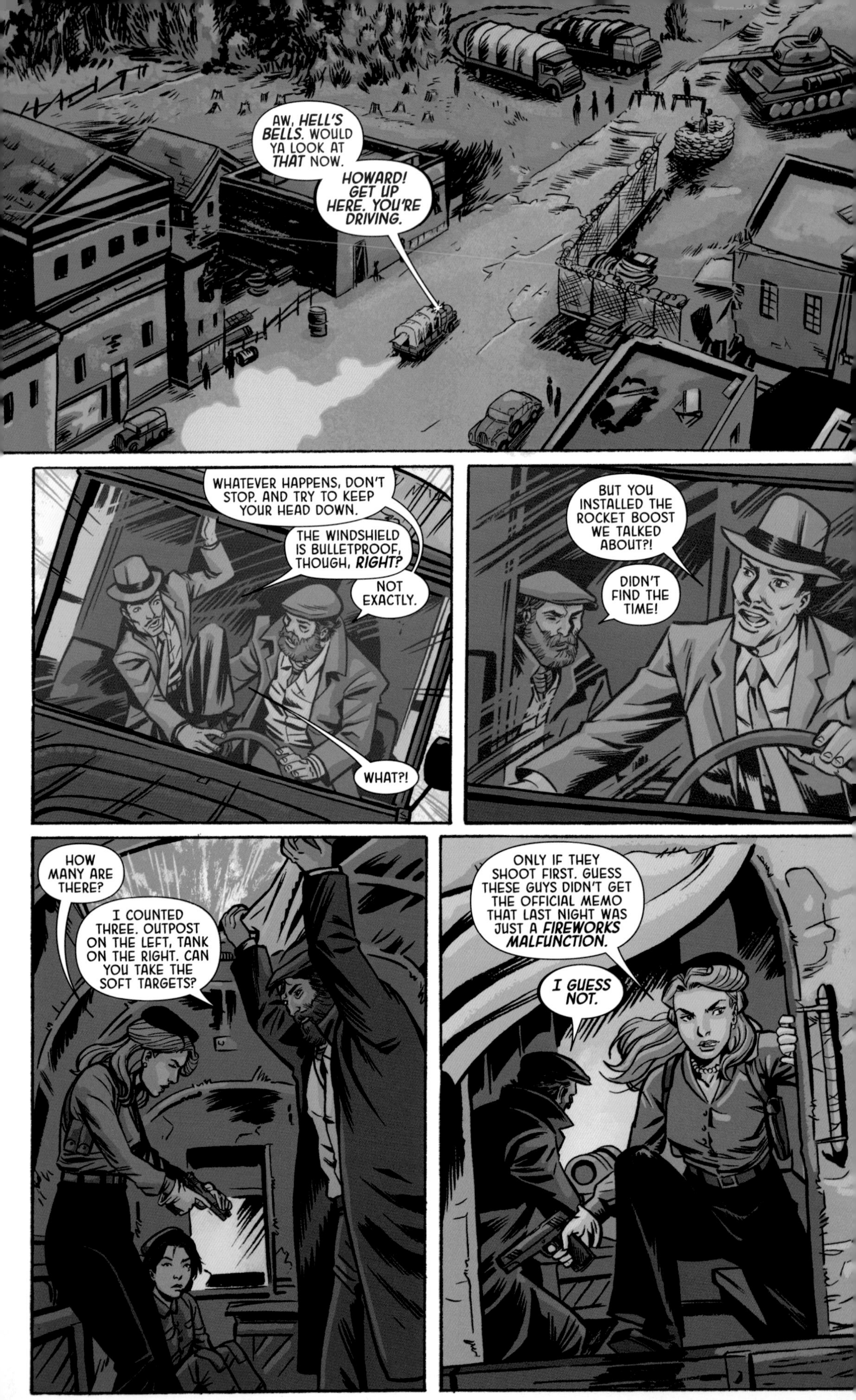
AW, HELL'S BELLS. WOULD YA LOOK AT THAT NOW.
HOWARD! GET UP HERE. YOU'RE DRIVING.
WHATEVER HAPPENS, DON'T STOP. AND TRY TO KEEP YOUR HEAD DOWN.
THE WINDSHIELD IS BULLETPROOF, THOUGH, RIGHT?
NOT EXACTLY.
WHAT?!
BUT YOU INSTALLED THE ROCKET BOOST WE TALKED ABOUT?!
DIDN'T FIND THE TIME!
HOW MANY ARE THERE?
I COUNTED THREE. OUTPOST ON THE LEFT, TANK ON THE RIGHT. CAN YOU TAKE THE SOFT TARGETS?
ONLY IF THEY SHOOT FIRST. GUESS THESE GUYS DIDN'T GET THE OFFICIAL MEMO THAT LAST NIGHT WAS JUST A FIREWORKS MALFUNCTION.
I GUESS NOT.

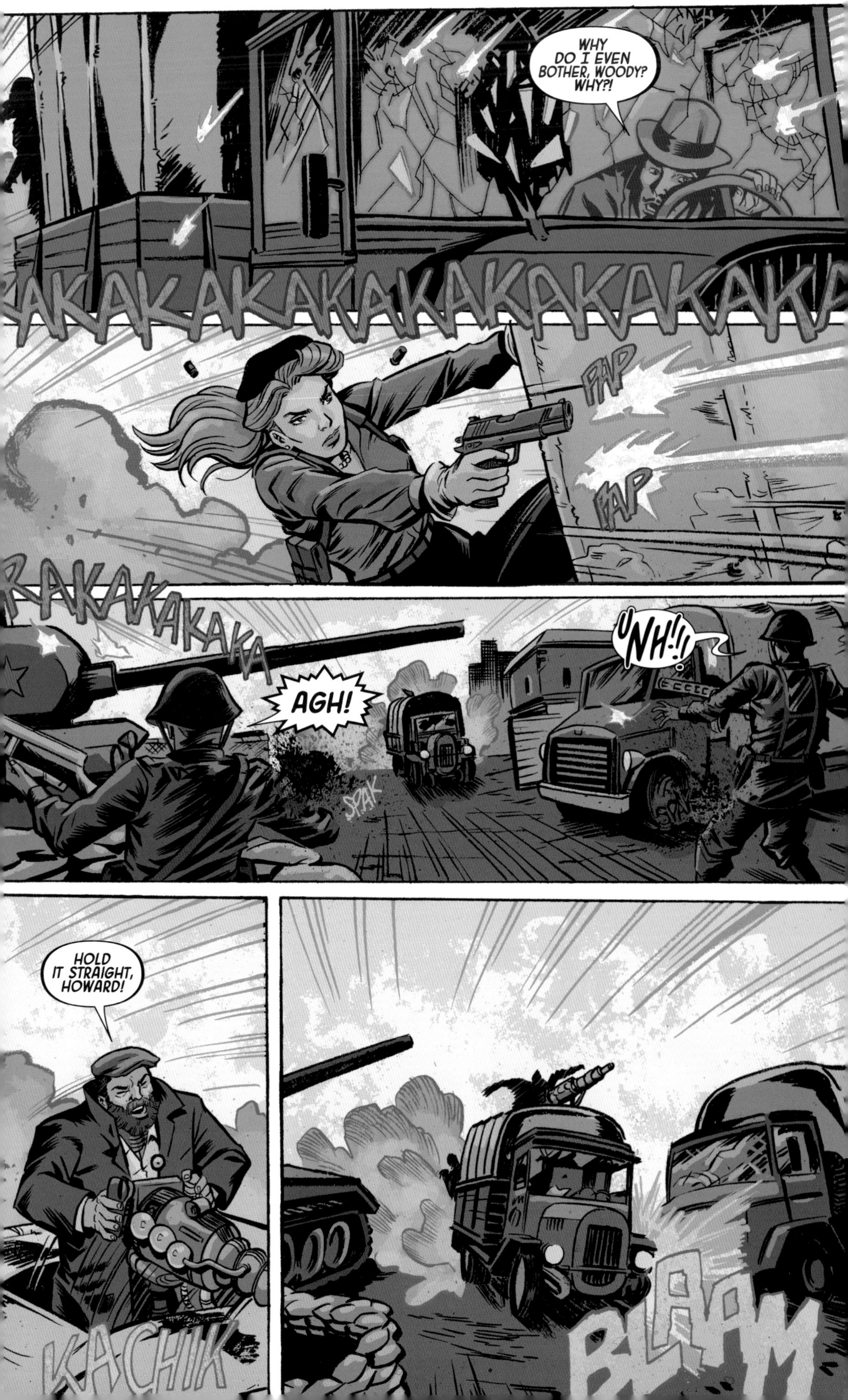
WHY DO I EVEN BOTHER, WOODY? WHY?!
KAKAKAKAKAKAKAKAKAKAKAKA
PAP
PAP
KAKAKAKAKAKA
AGH!
SPAK
UNH!!!
SPAK
HOLD IT STRAIGHT, HOWARD!
KACHIK
BLAM

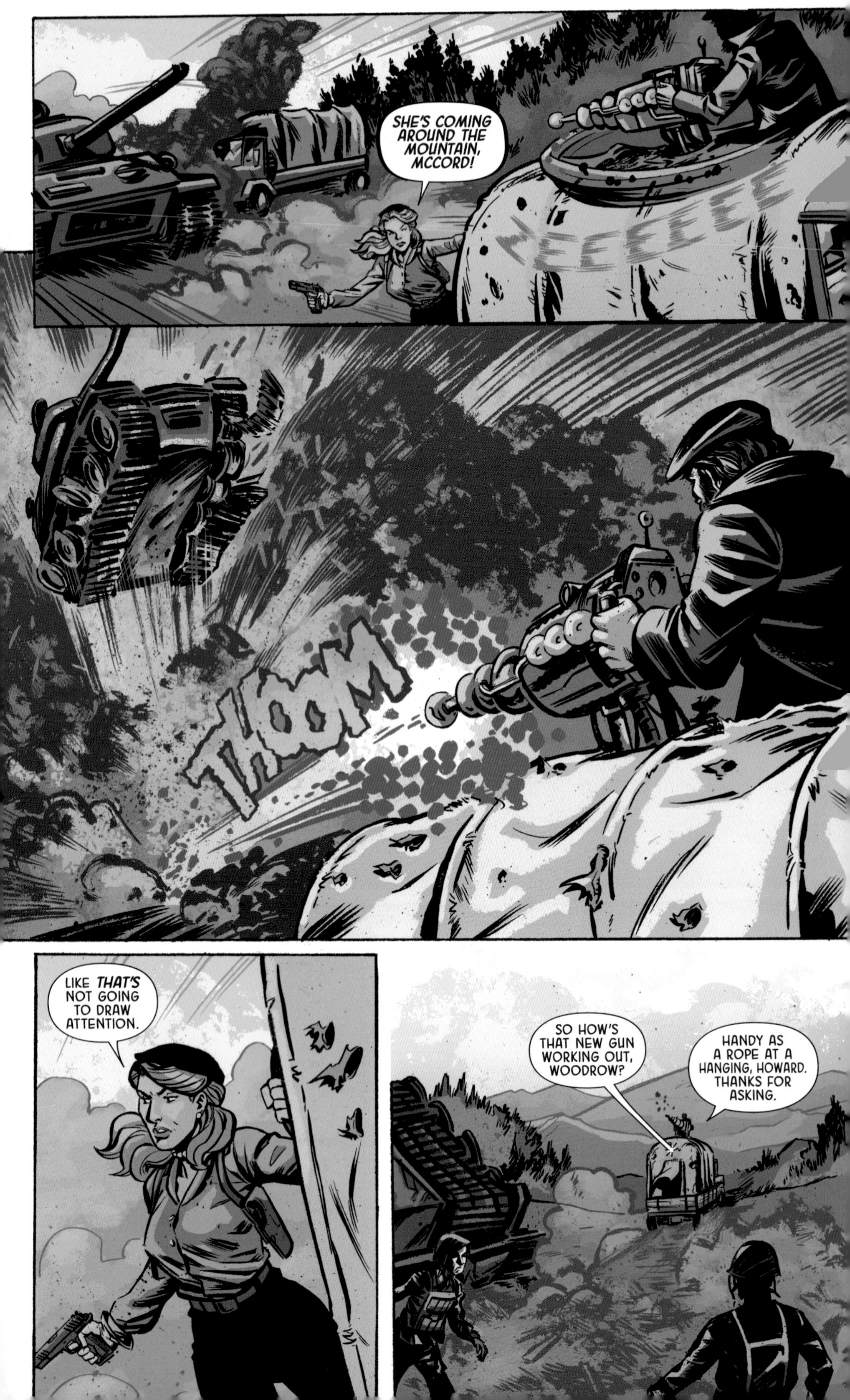
SHE'S COMING AROUND THE MOUNTAIN, MCCORD!
ZEEEEEE
TOOM
LIKE *THAT'S* NOT GOING TO DRAW ATTENTION.
SO HOW'S THAT NEW GUN WORKING OUT, WOODROW?
HANDY AS A ROPE AT A HANGING, HOWARD. THANKS FOR ASKING.

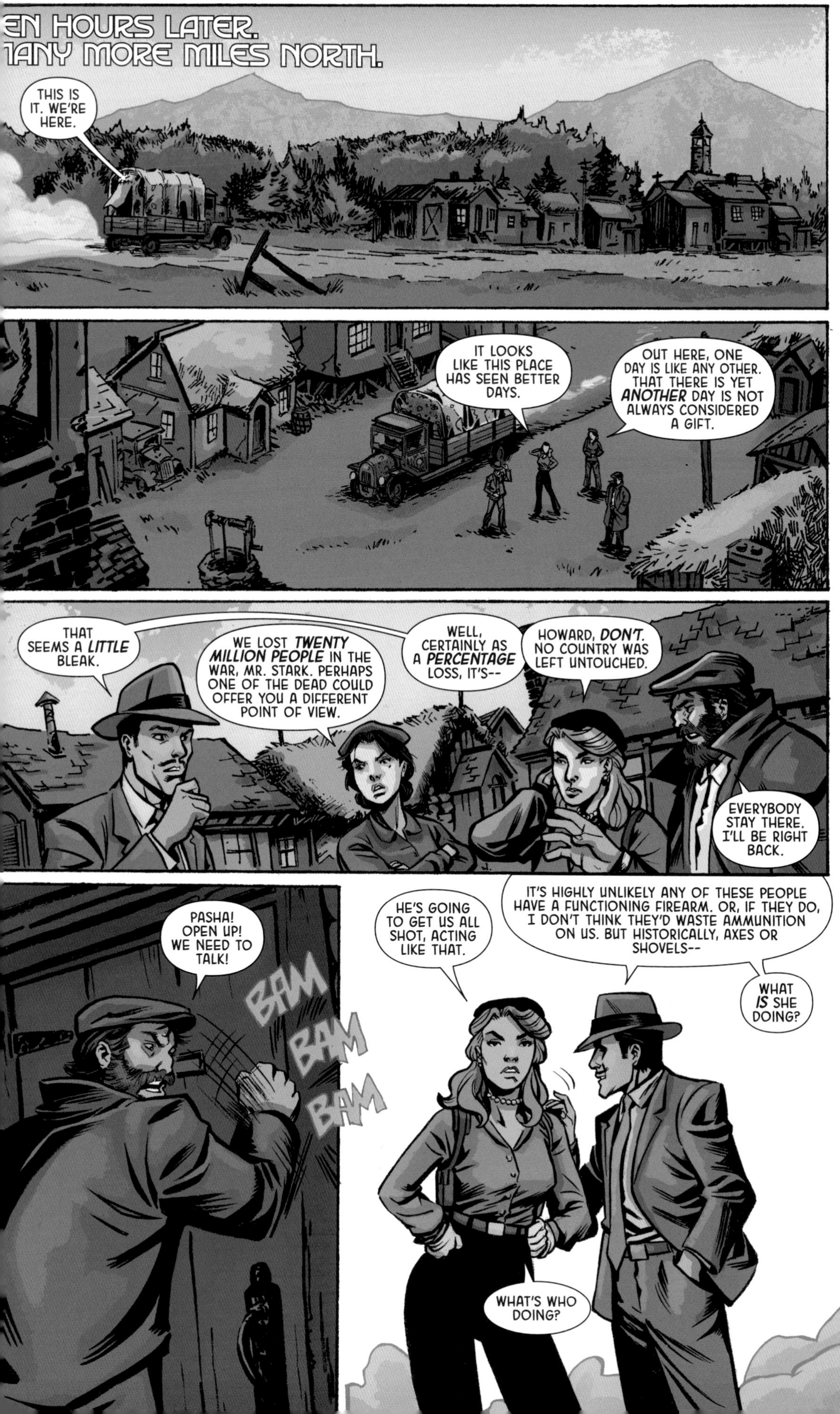
EN HOURS LATER.
IANY MORE MILES NORTH.
THIS IS IT. WE'RE HERE.
IT LOOKS LIKE THIS PLACE HAS SEEN BETTER DAYS.
OUT HERE, ONE DAY IS LIKE ANY OTHER. THAT THERE IS YET ANOTHER DAY IS NOT ALWAYS CONSIDERED A GIFT.
THAT SEEMS A LITTLE BLEAK.
WE LOST TWENTY MILLION PEOPLE IN THE WAR, MR. STARK. PERHAPS ONE OF THE DEAD COULD OFFER YOU A DIFFERENT POINT OF VIEW.
WELL, CERTAINLY AS A PERCENTAGE LOSS, IT'S--
HOWARD, DON'T. NO COUNTRY WAS LEFT UNTOUCHED.
EVERYBODY STAY THERE. I'LL BE RIGHT BACK.
PASHA! OPEN UP! WE NEED TO TALK!
BAM
BAM
BAM
HE'S GOING TO GET US ALL SHOT, ACTING LIKE THAT.
IT'S HIGHLY UNLIKELY ANY OF THESE PEOPLE HAVE A FUNCTIONING FIREARM. OR, IF THEY DO, I DON'T THINK THEY'D WASTE AMMUNITION ON US. BUT HISTORICALLY, AXES OR SHOVELS--
WHAT IS SHE DOING?
WHAT'S WHO DOING?

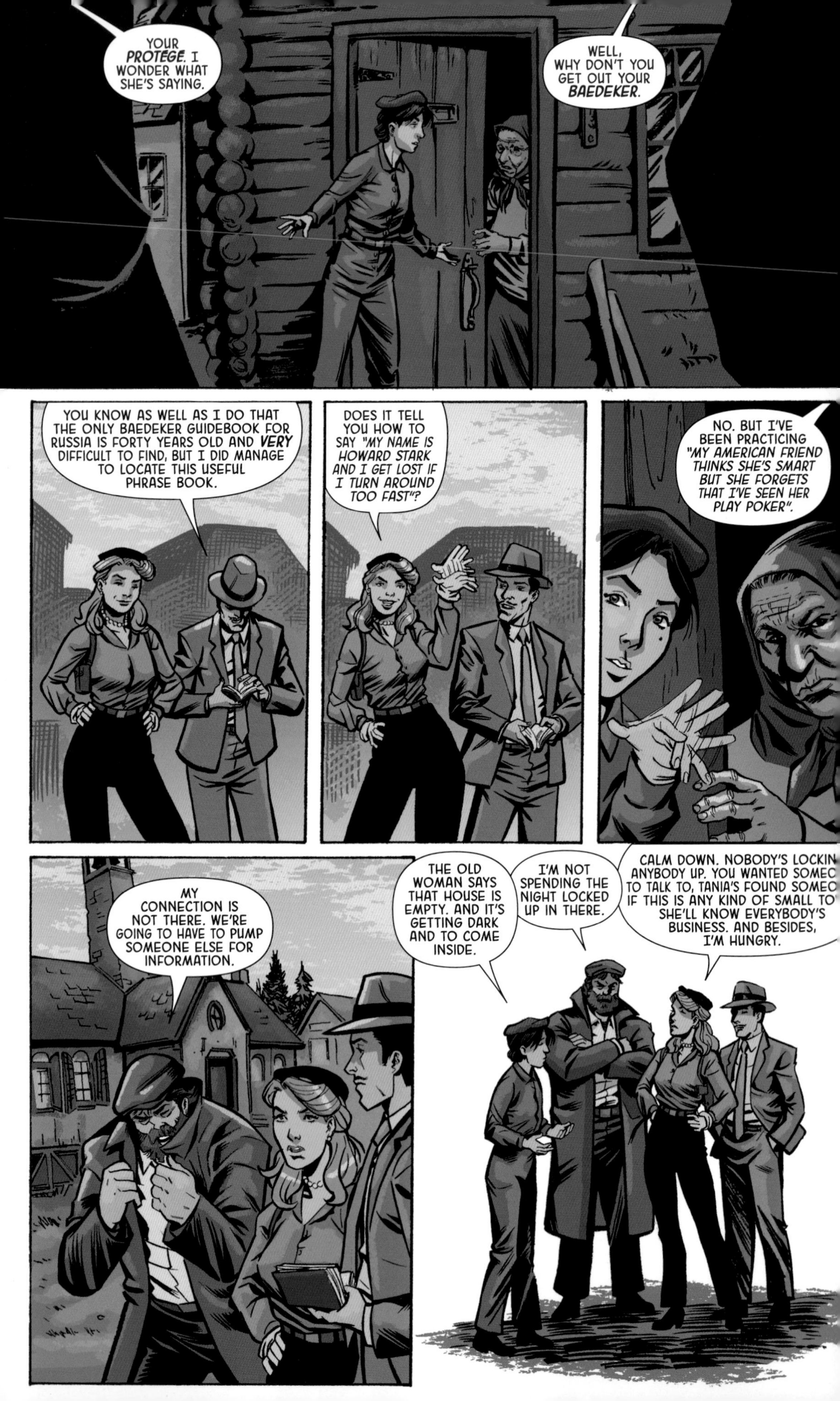
YOUR *PROTEGE*. I WONDER WHAT SHE'S SAYING.
WELL, WHY DON'T YOU GET OUT YOUR *BAEDEKER*.
YOU KNOW AS WELL AS I DO THAT THE ONLY BAEDEKER GUIDEBOOK FOR RUSSIA IS FORTY YEARS OLD AND *VERY* DIFFICULT TO FIND, BUT I DID MANAGE TO LOCATE THIS USEFUL PHRASE BOOK.
DOES IT TELL YOU HOW TO SAY *"MY NAME IS HOWARD STARK AND I GET LOST IF I TURN AROUND TOO FAST"*?
NO. BUT I'VE BEEN PRACTICING *"MY AMERICAN FRIEND THINKS SHE'S SMART BUT SHE FORGETS THAT I'VE SEEN HER PLAY POKER"*.
MY CONNECTION IS NOT THERE. WE'RE GOING TO HAVE TO PUMP SOMEONE ELSE FOR INFORMATION.
THE OLD WOMAN SAYS THAT HOUSE IS EMPTY. AND IT'S GETTING DARK AND TO COME INSIDE.
I'M NOT SPENDING THE NIGHT LOCKED UP IN THERE.
CALM DOWN. NOBODY'S LOCKIN ANYBODY UP. YOU WANTED SOMEO TO TALK TO, TANIA'S FOUND SOMEO IF THIS IS ANY KIND OF SMALL TO SHE'LL KNOW EVERYBODY'S BUSINESS. AND BESIDES, I'M HUNGRY.

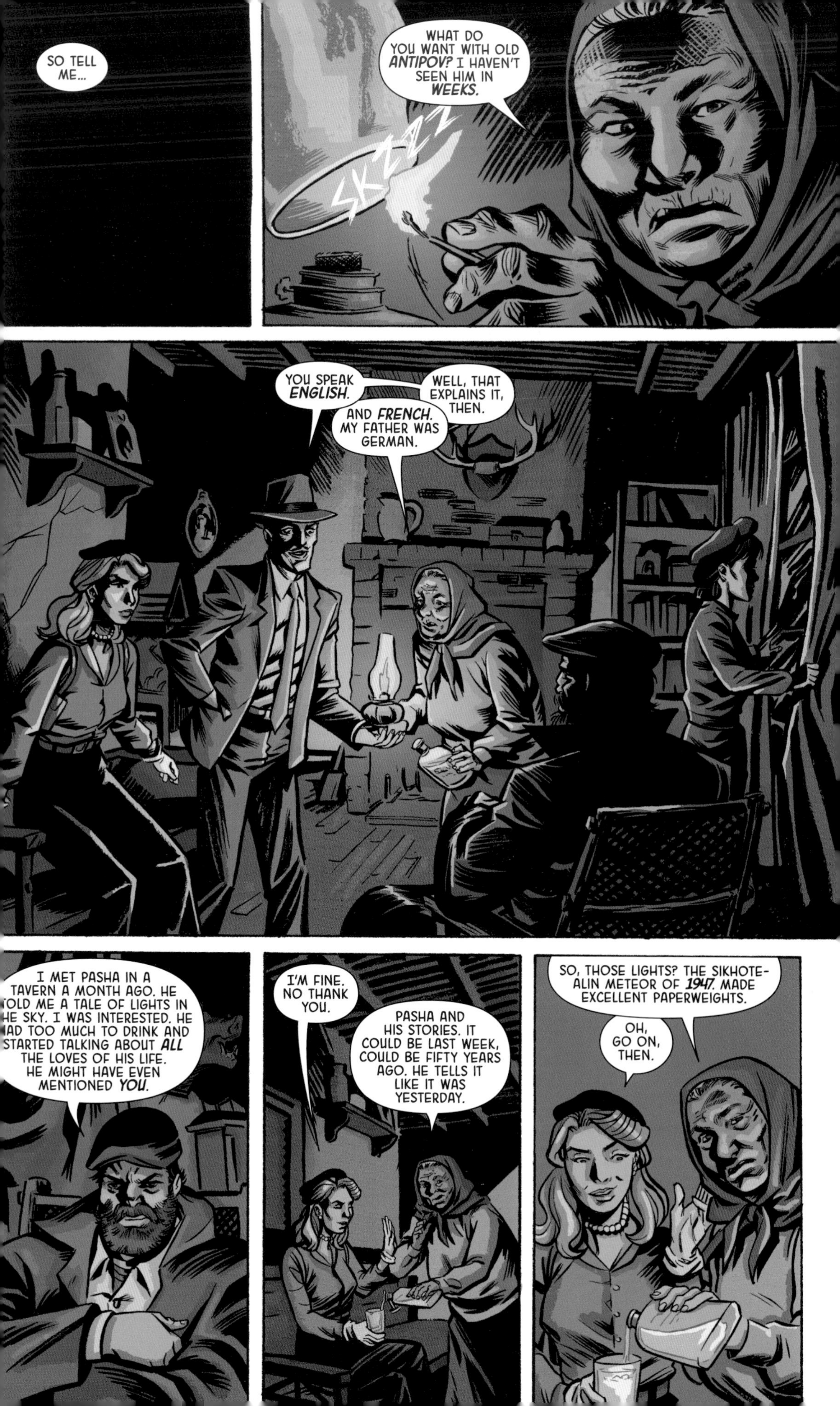
SO TELL ME...
WHAT DO YOU WANT WITH OLD ANTIPOV? I HAVEN'T SEEN HIM IN WEEKS.
SKZZZZ
YOU SPEAK ENGLISH.
AND FRENCH. MY FATHER WAS GERMAN.
WELL, THAT EXPLAINS IT, THEN.
I MET PASHA IN A TAVERN A MONTH AGO. HE TOLD ME A TALE OF LIGHTS IN THE SKY. I WAS INTERESTED. HE HAD TOO MUCH TO DRINK AND STARTED TALKING ABOUT ALL THE LOVES OF HIS LIFE. HE MIGHT HAVE EVEN MENTIONED YOU.
I'M FINE. NO THANK YOU.
PASHA AND HIS STORIES. IT COULD BE LAST WEEK, COULD BE FIFTY YEARS AGO. HE TELLS IT LIKE IT WAS YESTERDAY.
SO, THOSE LIGHTS? THE SIKHOTE-ALIN METEOR OF 1947. MADE EXCELLENT PAPERWEIGHTS.
OH, GO ON, THEN.

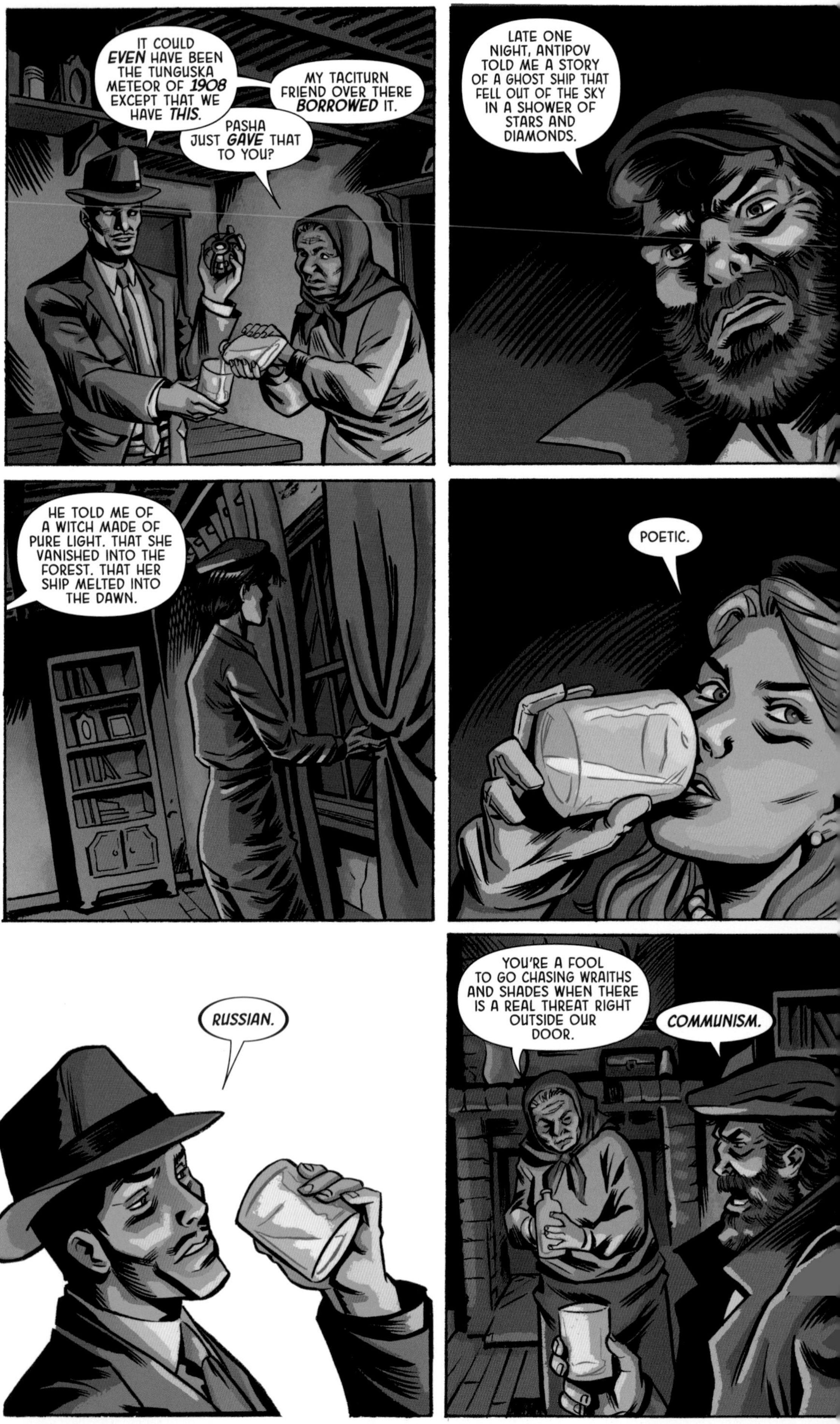
IT COULD EVEN HAVE BEEN THE TUNGUSKA METEOR OF 1908 EXCEPT THAT WE HAVE THIS.
MY TACITURN FRIEND OVER THERE BORROWED IT.
PASHA JUST GAVE THAT TO YOU?
LATE ONE NIGHT, ANTIPOV TOLD ME A STORY OF A GHOST SHIP THAT FELL OUT OF THE SKY IN A SHOWER OF STARS AND DIAMONDS.
HE TOLD ME OF A WITCH MADE OF PURE LIGHT. THAT SHE VANISHED INTO THE FOREST. THAT HER SHIP MELTED INTO THE DAWN.
POETIC.
RUSSIAN.
YOU'RE A FOOL TO GO CHASING WRAITHS AND SHADES WHEN THERE IS A REAL THREAT RIGHT OUTSIDE OUR DOOR.
COMMUNISM.

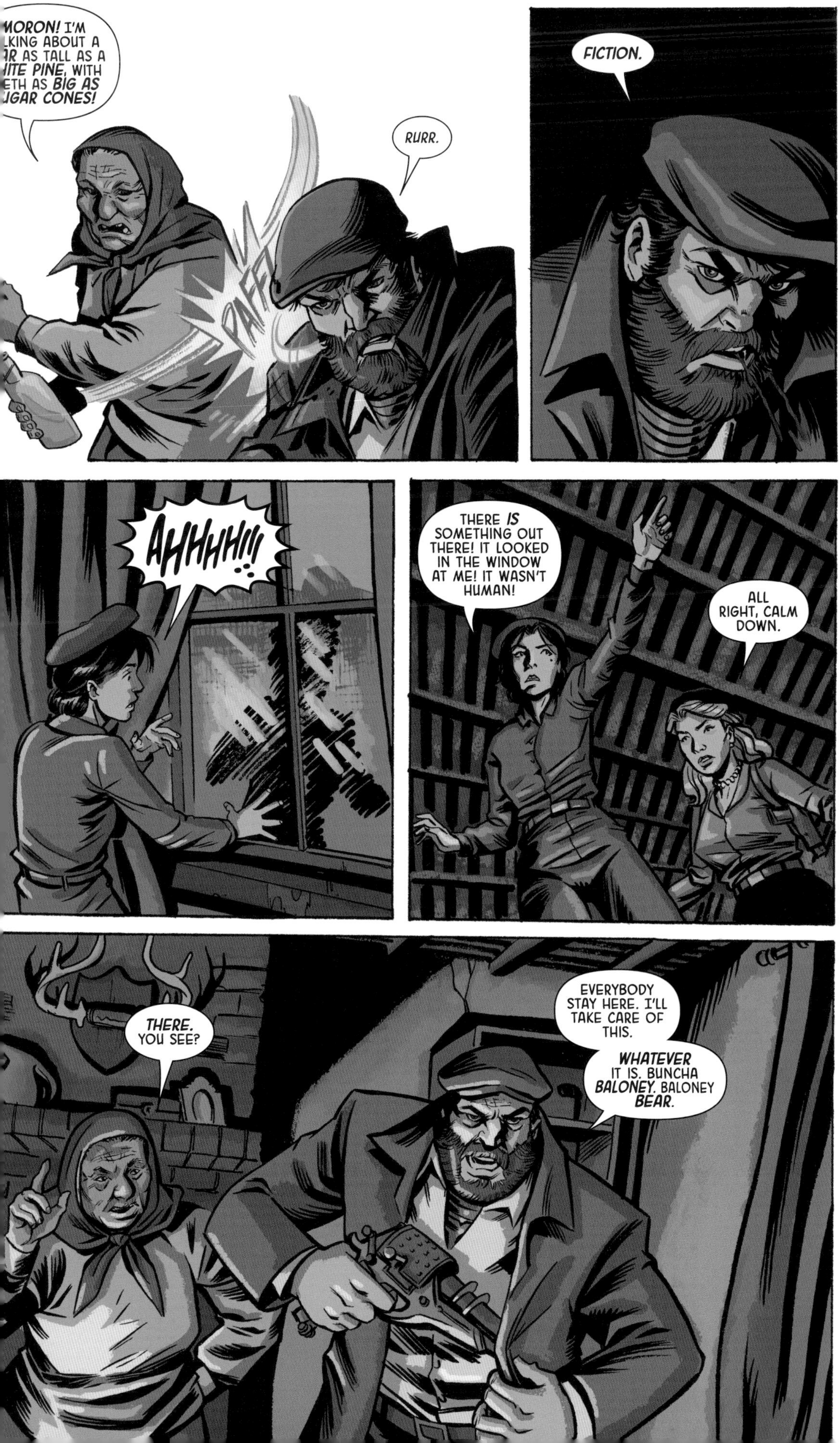

MORON! I'M
LKING ABOUT A
R AS TALL AS A
ITE PINE, WITH
ETH AS BIG AS
JGAR CONES!
PAFF!
RURR.
FICTION.
AHHHH!!!
THERE IS SOMETHING OUT THERE! IT LOOKED IN THE WINDOW AT ME! IT WASN'T HUMAN!
ALL RIGHT, CALM DOWN.
THERE. YOU SEE?
EVERYBODY STAY HERE. I'LL TAKE CARE OF THIS.
WHATEVER IT IS. BUNCHA BALONEY. BALONEY BEAR.

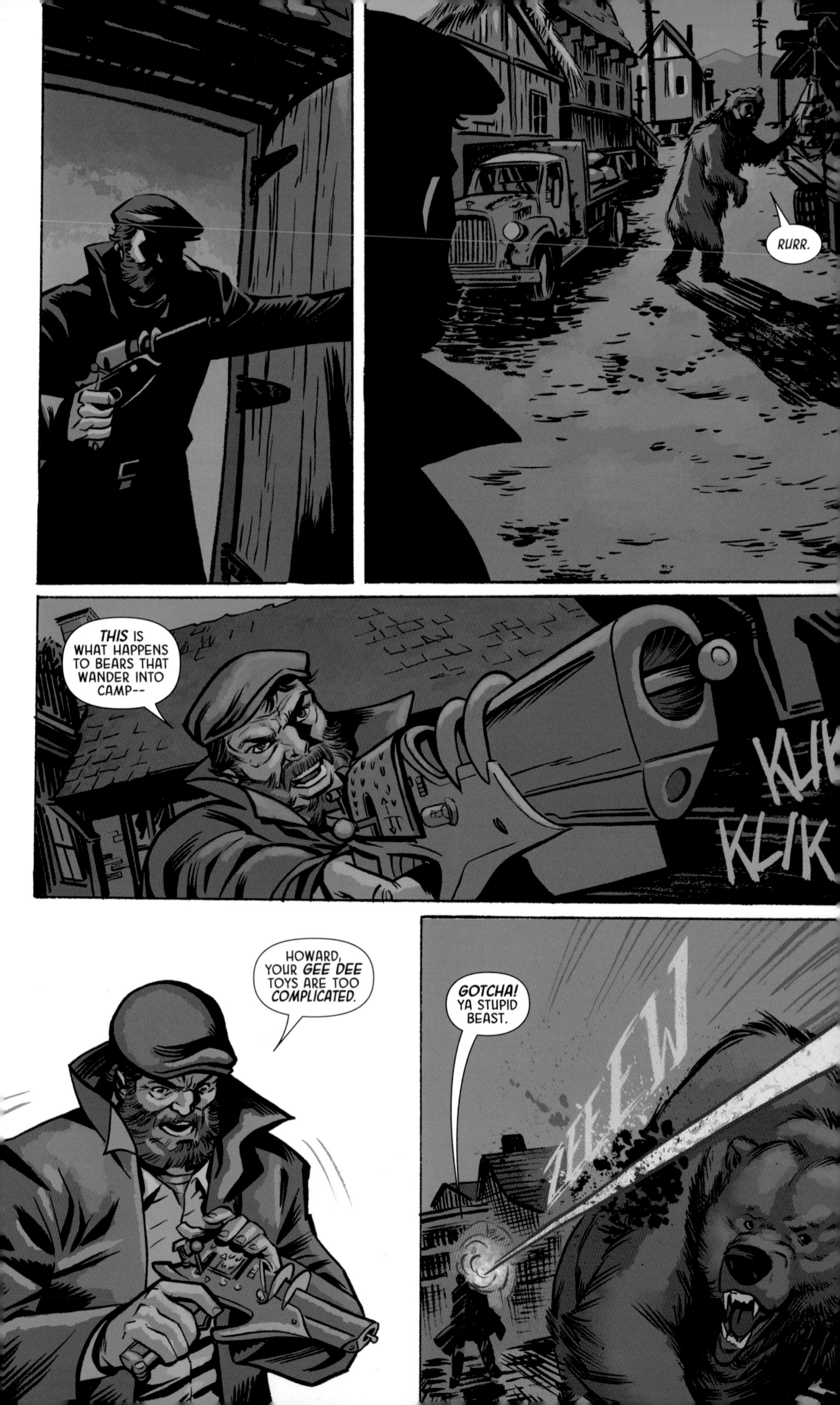
RURR.
THIS IS WHAT HAPPENS TO BEARS THAT WANDER INTO CAMP--
KLIK
KLIK
HOWARD, YOUR GEE DEE TOYS ARE TOO COMPLICATED.
GOTCHA! YA STUPID BEAST.
ZEEEW

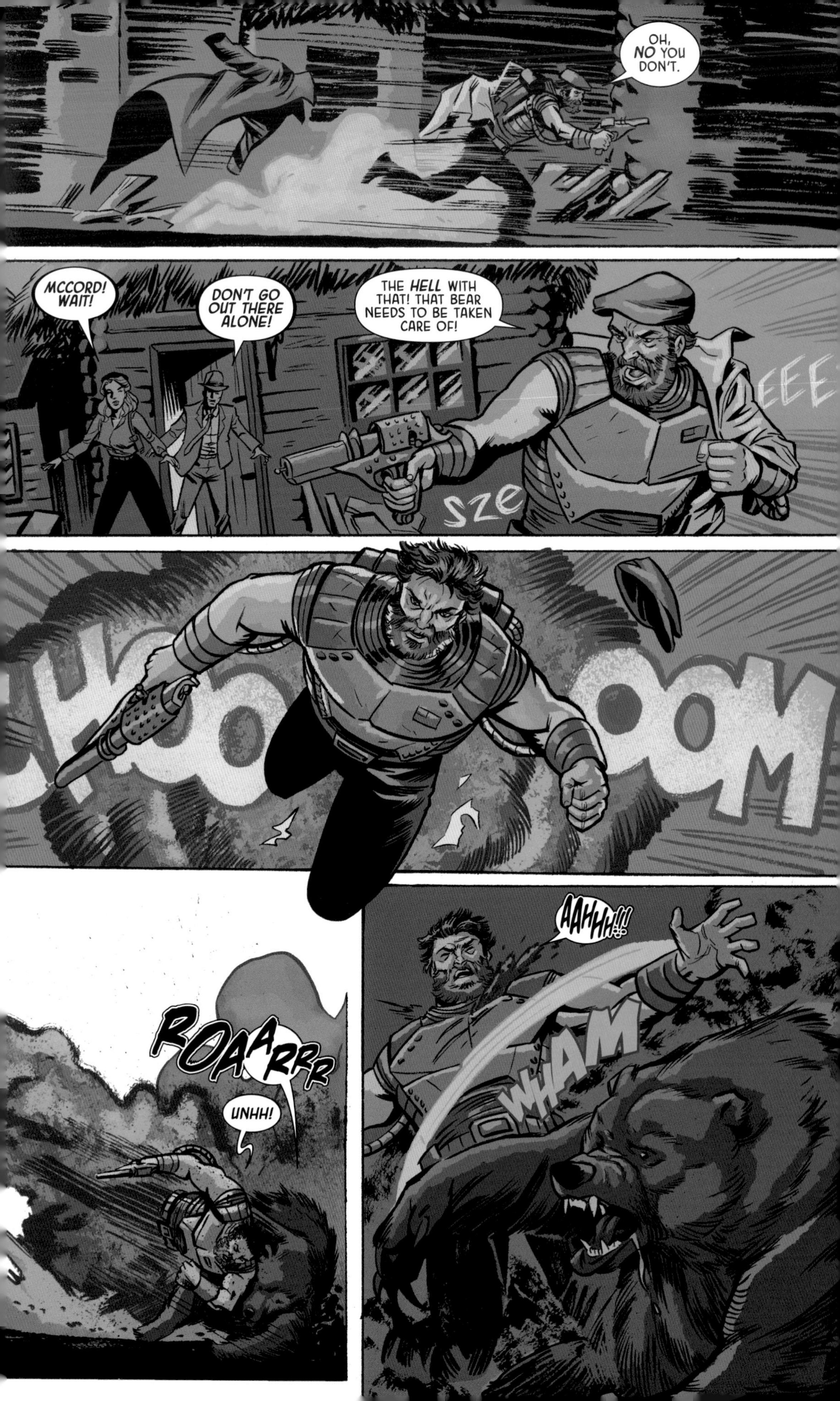
OH, NO YOU DON'T.
MCCORD! WAIT!
DON'T GO OUT THERE ALONE!
THE HELL WITH THAT! THAT BEAR NEEDS TO BE TAKEN CARE OF!
EEEE
SZE
CHOOOOM
ROAARRR
UNHH!
AAHHH!!!
WHAM

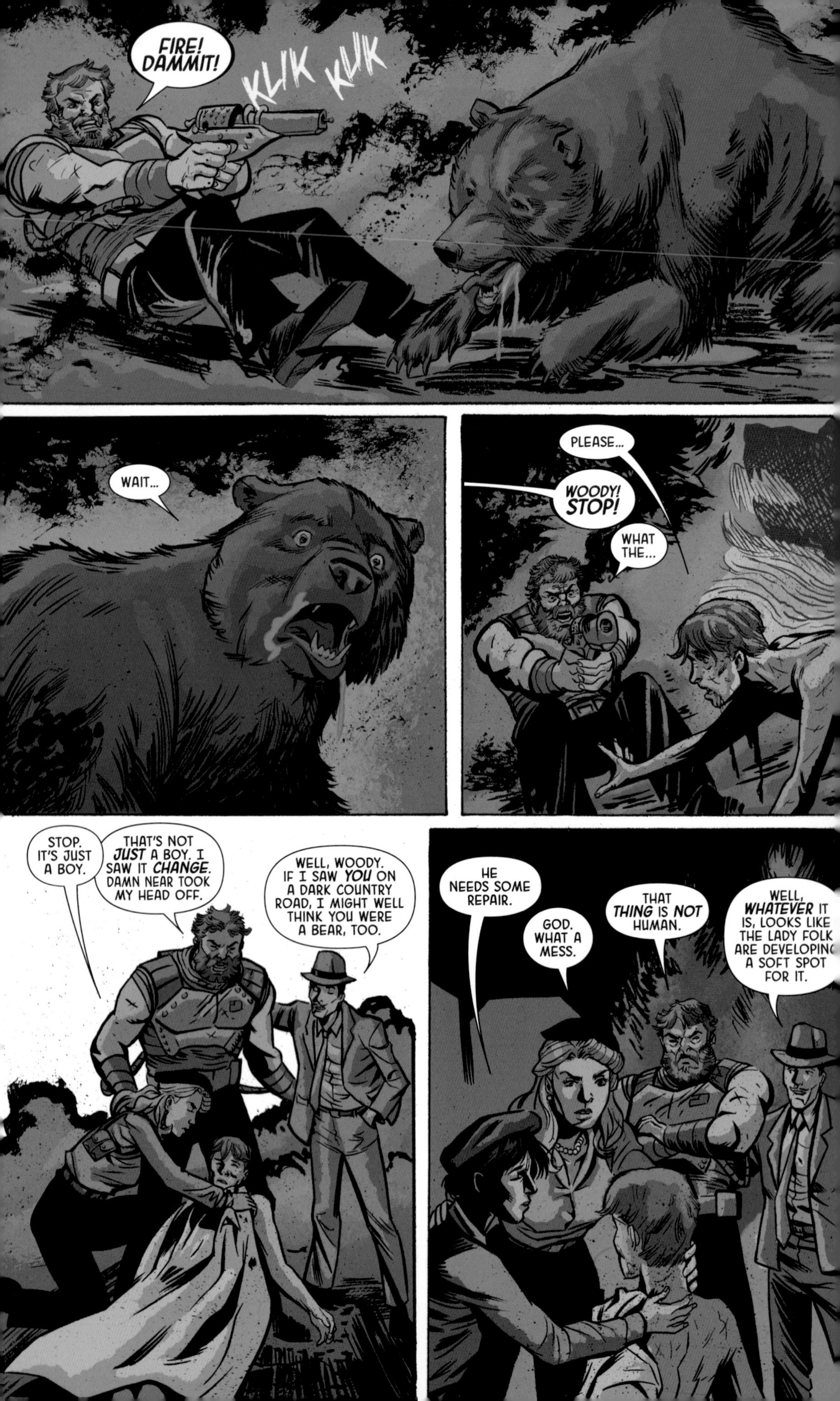
FIRE! DAMMIT!
KLIK KLIK
WAIT...
PLEASE...
WOODY! STOP!
WHAT THE...
STOP. IT'S JUST A BOY.
THAT'S NOT JUST A BOY. I SAW IT CHANGE. DAMN NEAR TOOK MY HEAD OFF.
WELL, WOODY. IF I SAW YOU ON A DARK COUNTRY ROAD, I MIGHT WELL THINK YOU WERE A BEAR, TOO.
HE NEEDS SOME REPAIR.
GOD. WHAT A MESS.
THAT THING IS NOT HUMAN.
WELL, WHATEVER IT IS, LOOKS LIKE THE LADY FOLK ARE DEVELOPING A SOFT SPOT FOR IT.

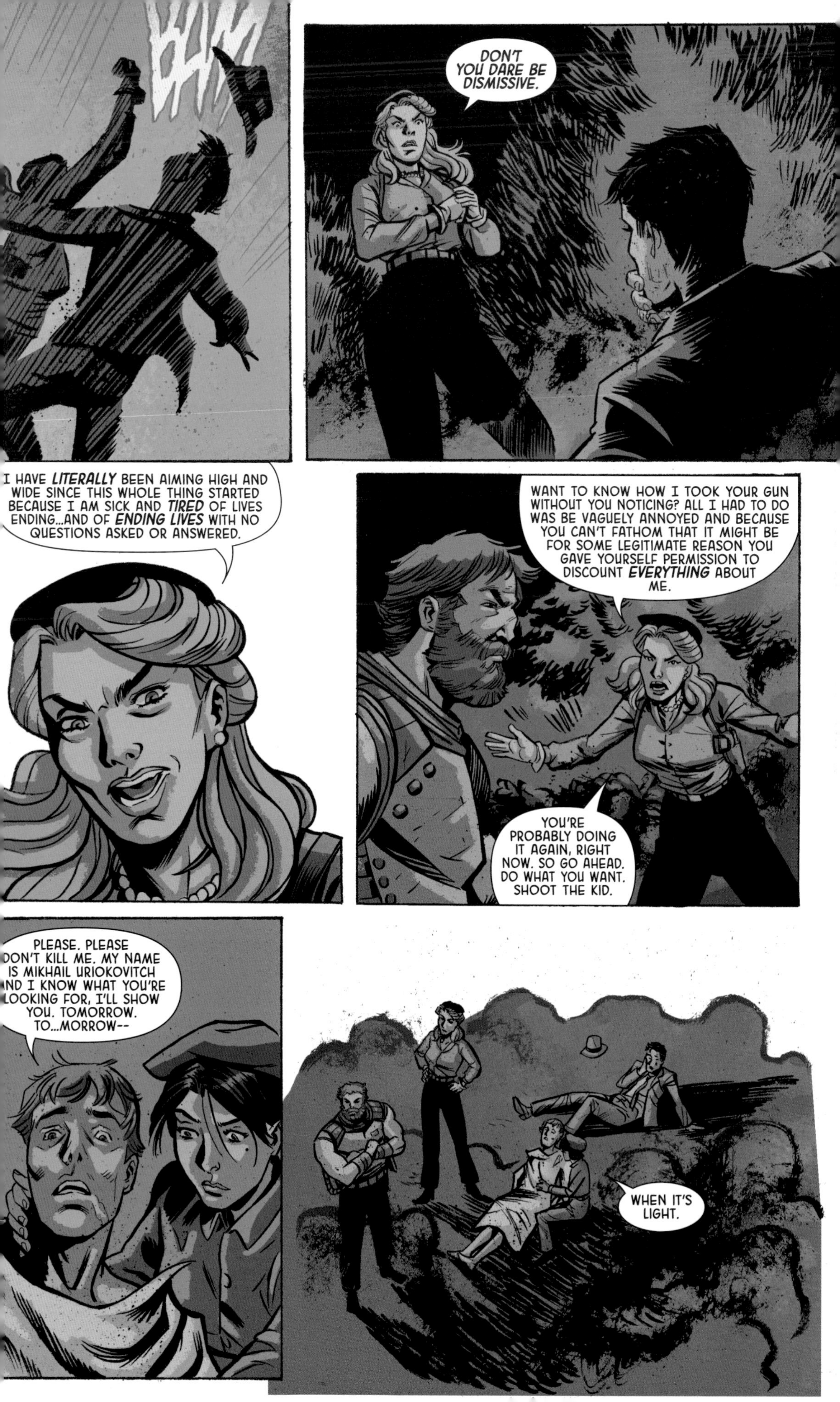
BAM
DON'T YOU DARE BE DISMISSIVE.
I HAVE LITERALLY BEEN AIMING HIGH AND WIDE SINCE THIS WHOLE THING STARTED BECAUSE I AM SICK AND TIRED OF LIVES ENDING...AND OF ENDING LIVES WITH NO QUESTIONS ASKED OR ANSWERED.
WANT TO KNOW HOW I TOOK YOUR GUN WITHOUT YOU NOTICING? ALL I HAD TO DO WAS BE VAGUELY ANNOYED AND BECAUSE YOU CAN'T FATHOM THAT IT MIGHT BE FOR SOME LEGITIMATE REASON YOU GAVE YOURSELF PERMISSION TO DISCOUNT EVERYTHING ABOUT ME.
YOU'RE PROBABLY DOING IT AGAIN, RIGHT NOW. SO GO AHEAD. DO WHAT YOU WANT. SHOOT THE KID.
PLEASE. PLEASE DON'T KILL ME. MY NAME IS MIKHAIL URIOKOVITCH AND I KNOW WHAT YOU'RE LOOKING FOR, I'LL SHOW YOU. TOMORROW. TO...MORROW--
WHEN IT'S LIGHT.

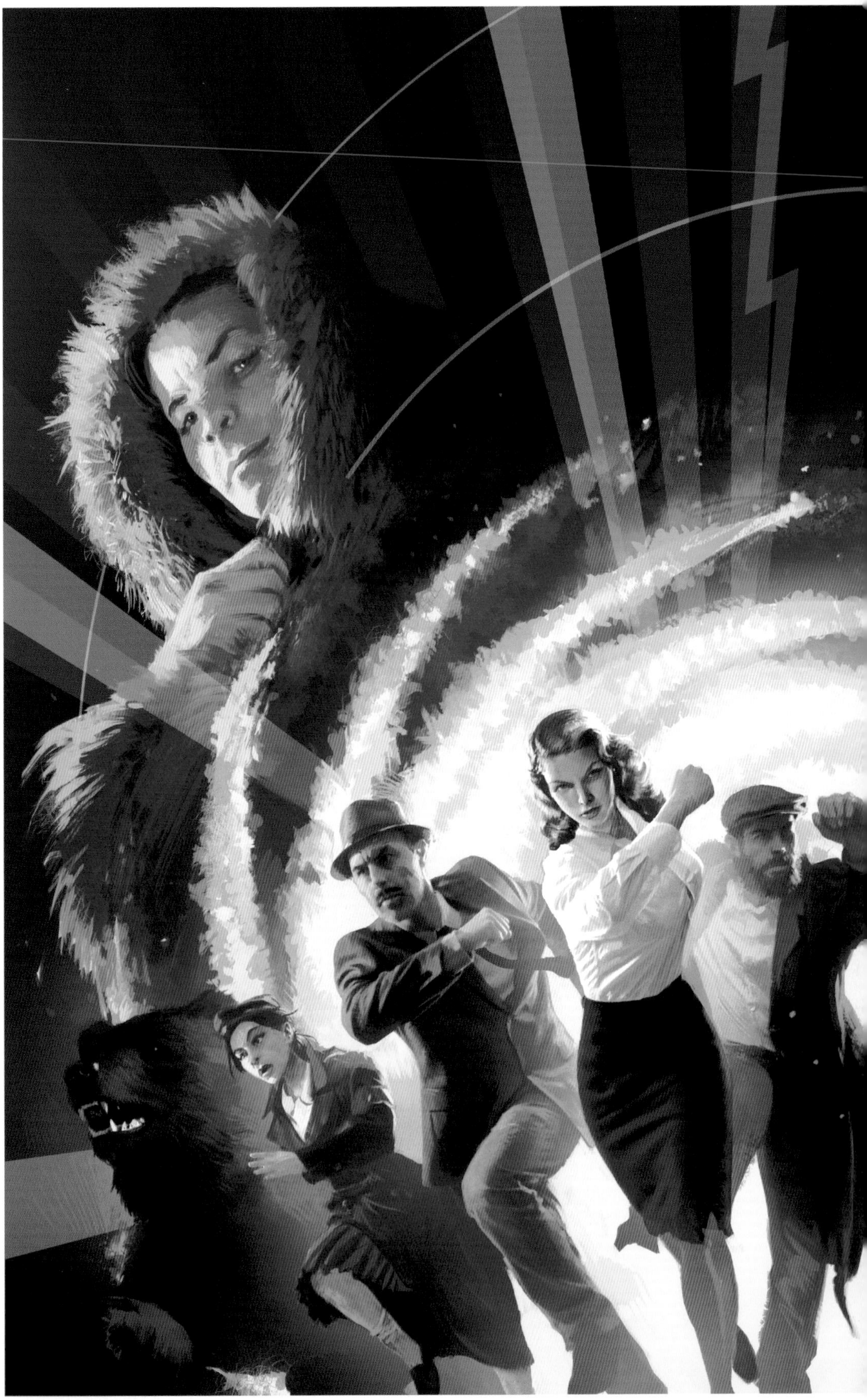

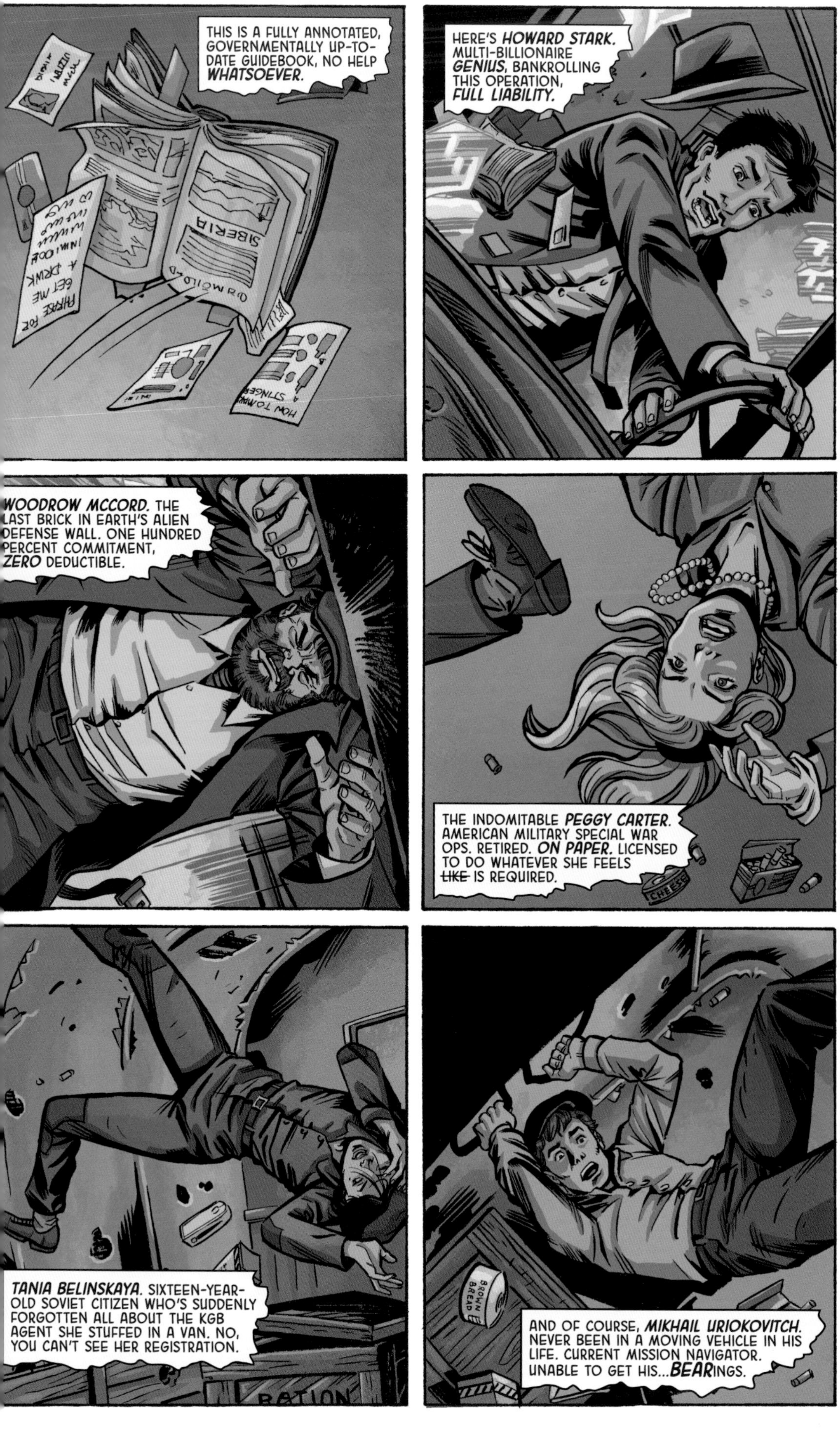
THIS IS A FULLY ANNOTATED, GOVERNMENTALLY UP-TO-DATE GUIDEBOOK, NO HELP **WHATSOEVER.**
SIBERIA
HOW TO MAKE A STINGER
HERE'S **HOWARD STARK.** MULTI-BILLIONAIRE **GENIUS**, BANKROLLING THIS OPERATION, **FULL LIABILITY.**
WOODROW MCCORD. THE LAST BRICK IN EARTH'S ALIEN DEFENSE WALL. ONE HUNDRED PERCENT COMMITMENT, **ZERO** DEDUCTIBLE.
THE INDOMITABLE **PEGGY CARTER.** AMERICAN MILITARY SPECIAL WAR OPS. RETIRED. **ON PAPER.** LICENSED TO DO WHATEVER SHE FEELS ~~LIKE~~ IS REQUIRED.
CHEESE
TANIA BELINSKAYA. SIXTEEN-YEAR-OLD SOVIET CITIZEN WHO'S SUDDENLY FORGOTTEN ALL ABOUT THE KGB AGENT SHE STUFFED IN A VAN. NO, YOU CAN'T SEE HER REGISTRATION.
RATION
BROWN BREAD
AND OF COURSE, **MIKHAIL URIOKOVITCH.** NEVER BEEN IN A MOVING VEHICLE IN HIS LIFE. CURRENT MISSION NAVIGATOR. UNABLE TO GET HIS...**BEAR**INGS.

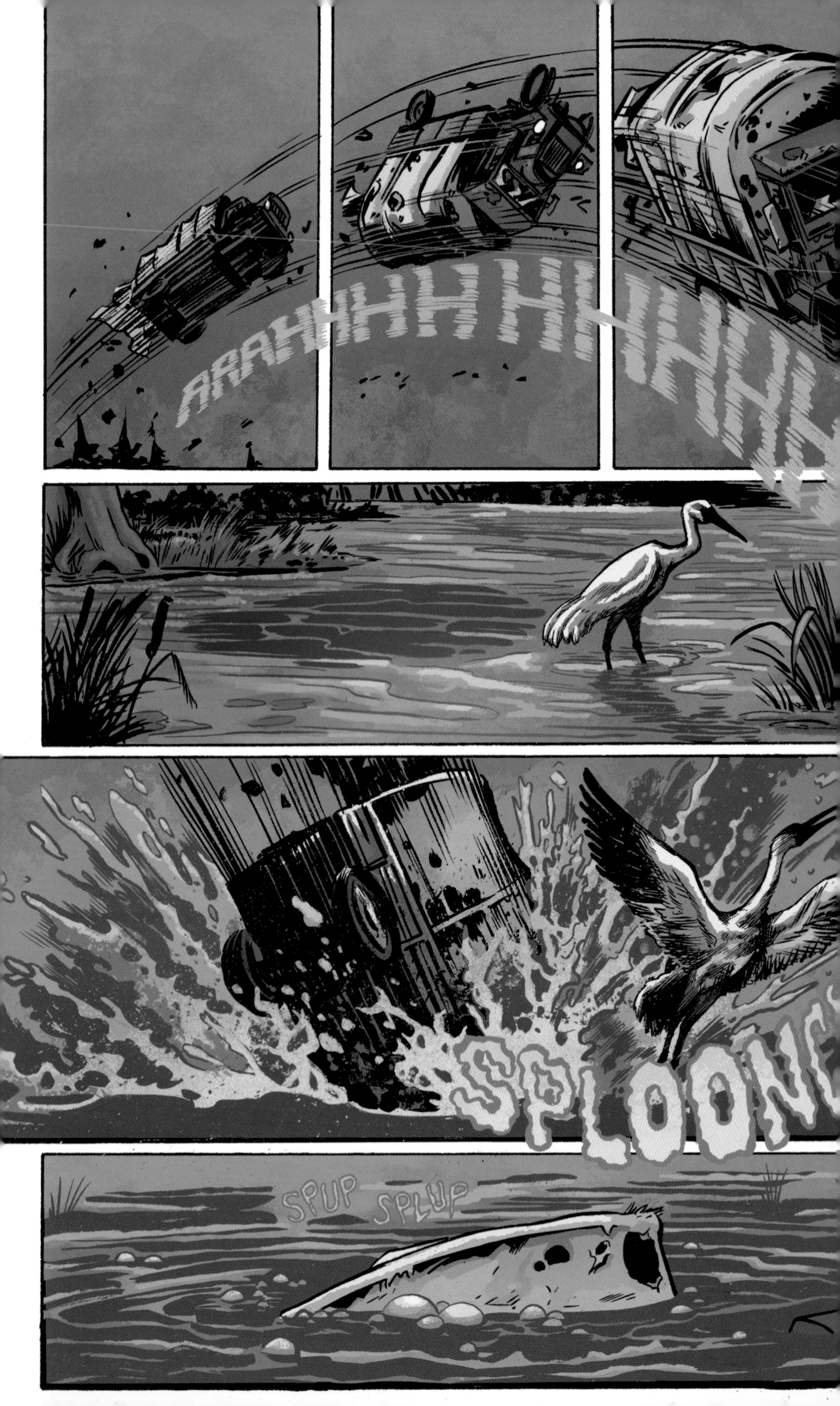

ARRAHHHHHHHHHHHHH
SPLOONG
SPUP SPLUP

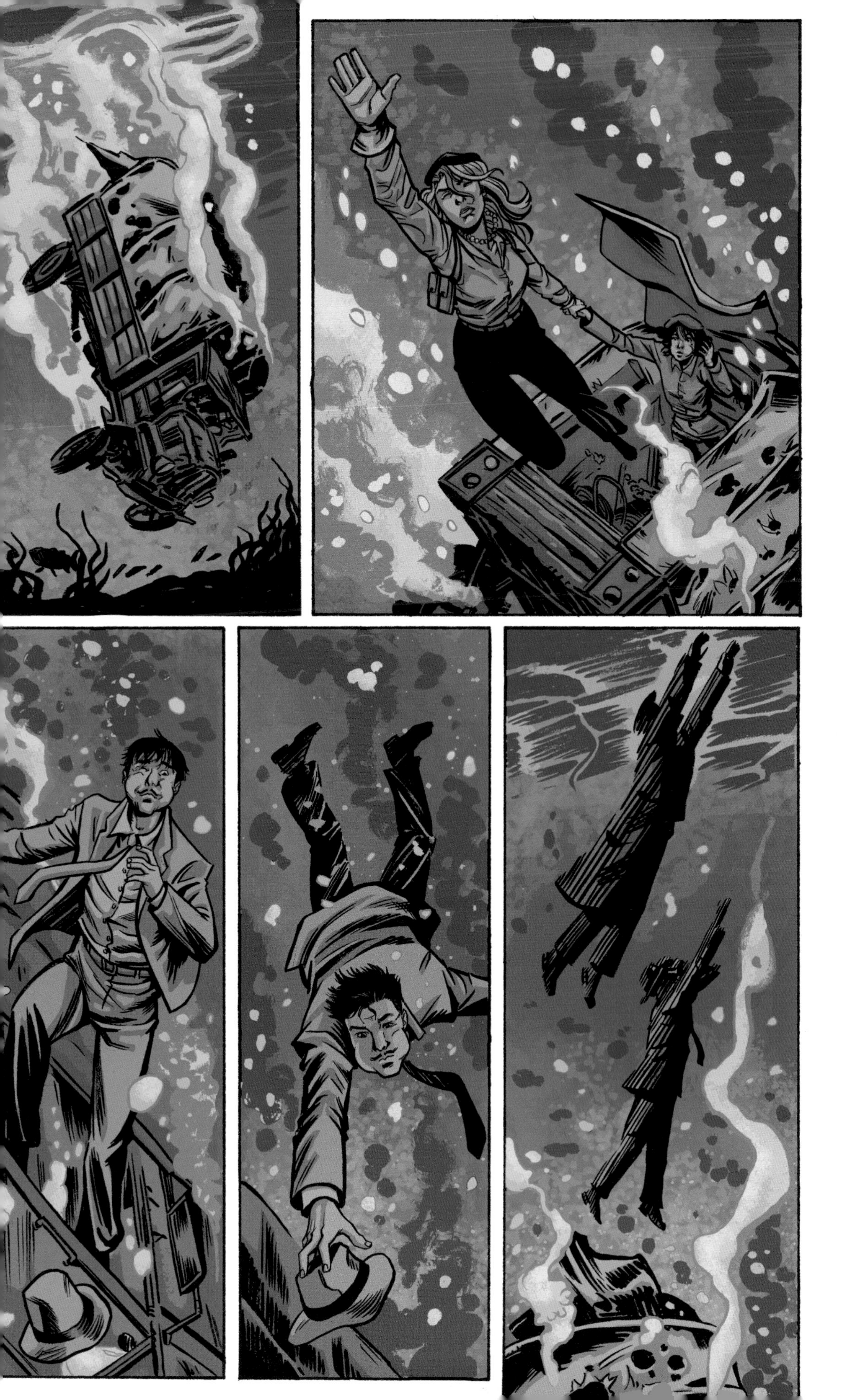

WELL, HOWARD. I'D SAY THAT'S THE *LAST TIME* I LET YOU DRIVE, 'CEPT SEEING AS HOW WE DON'T HAVE A *TRUCK* ANYMORE, I GUESS IT'S A NON-ISSUE.

I *TOLD* YOU IT WAS PULLING TO THE RIGHT!

AND THEN I HAD TO AVOID THAT HERD O' BLOODY REINDEER. NEVER MIND THAT WE'RE FOLLOWIN' A *CATTLE TRACK!* I'LL SAY O' THING IN FAVOR OF THE NA AT LEAST THEY BUILT A *DECENT ROAD!*

NORTHERN RUSSIA. 1952.

WHERE'S THE BOY?

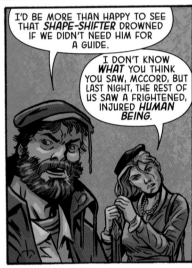

I'D BE MORE THAN HAPPY TO SEE THAT *SHAPE-SHIFTER* DROWNED IF WE DIDN'T NEED HIM FOR A GUIDE.

I DON'T KNOW *WHAT* YOU THINK YOU SAW, MCCORD, BUT LAST NIGHT, THE REST OF US SAW A FRIGHTENED, INJURED *HUMAN BEING.*

CAN'T BE *TOO* HARD TO IMAGINE. YO SEEN A LOT OF STRANGE THINGS, CAN PROBABLY EVEN *KILLED* SOME OF THEM.

MEN CHANGING INTO *BEARS?* NO. INTO *MONSTERS*, ABSOLUTELY. BUT THEY DIED FOR WHAT THEY *DID*, NOT FOR WHAT THEY *LOOKED* LIKE.

YOU *NEVER* SHOT A NAZI ON SIGHT?

YOU DON'T HOLD A GRUDGE, DO YOU, CARTER?

NOPE.

I GUESS THAT'S *LUCKY* FOR ME.

IS THAT YOUR VERSION OF AN APOLOGY?

MIGHT BE. YOU GONNA APOLOGIZE TO STARK FOR PUNCHING HIM IN THE FACE?

WELL, I NEVER HAVE *BEFORE*. WHY BREAK THE HABIT OF A LIFETIME?

HM.

THERE HE IS!

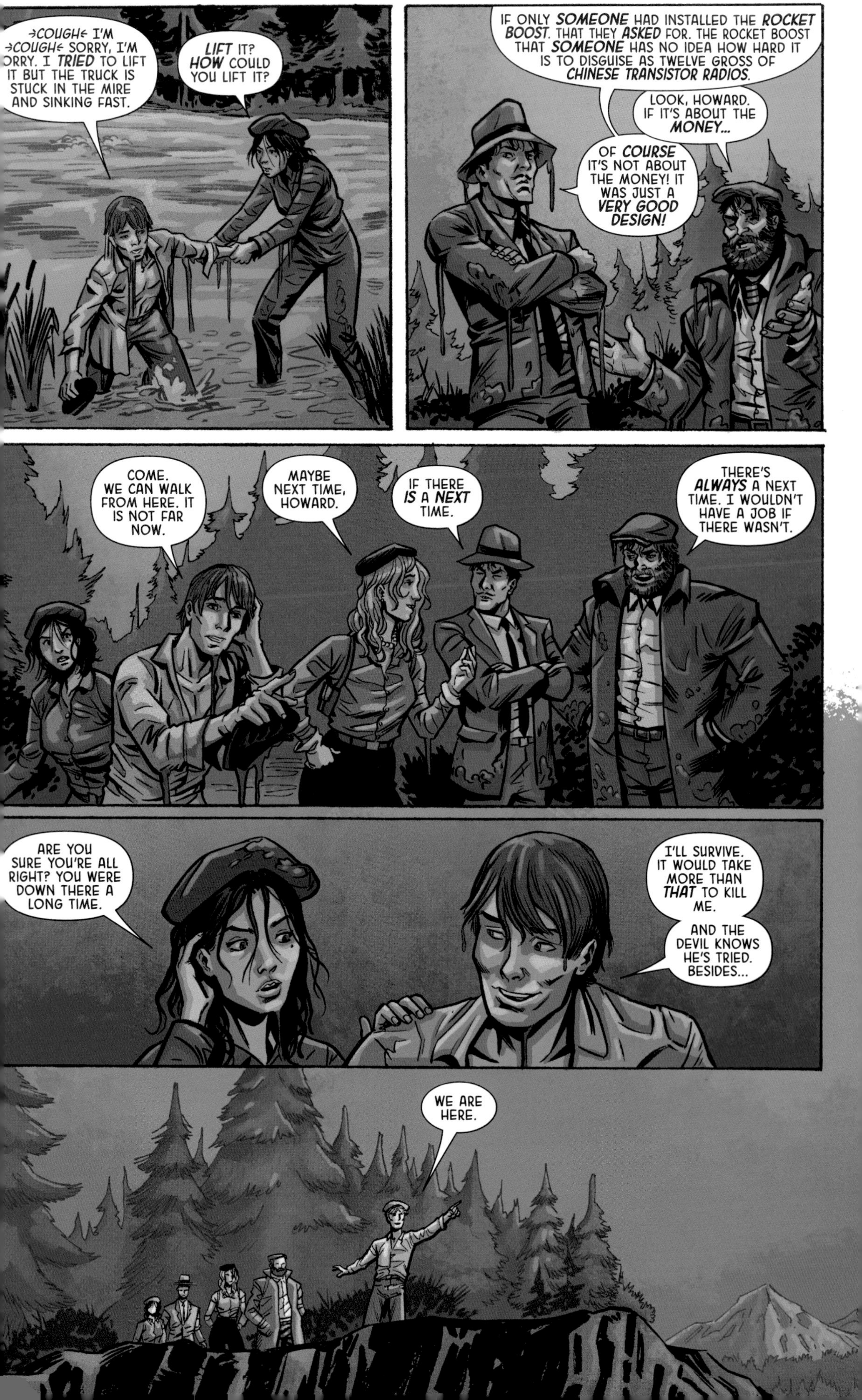

→COUGH← I'M →COUGH← SORRY, I'M SORRY. I TRIED TO LIFT IT BUT THE TRUCK IS STUCK IN THE MIRE AND SINKING FAST.
LIFT IT? HOW COULD YOU LIFT IT?
IF ONLY SOMEONE HAD INSTALLED THE ROCKET BOOST. THAT THEY ASKED FOR. THE ROCKET BOOST THAT SOMEONE HAS NO IDEA HOW HARD IT IS TO DISGUISE AS TWELVE GROSS OF CHINESE TRANSISTOR RADIOS.
LOOK, HOWARD. IF IT'S ABOUT THE MONEY...
OF COURSE IT'S NOT ABOUT THE MONEY! IT WAS JUST A VERY GOOD DESIGN!
COME. WE CAN WALK FROM HERE. IT IS NOT FAR NOW.
MAYBE NEXT TIME, HOWARD.
IF THERE IS A NEXT TIME.
THERE'S ALWAYS A NEXT TIME. I WOULDN'T HAVE A JOB IF THERE WASN'T.
ARE YOU SURE YOU'RE ALL RIGHT? YOU WERE DOWN THERE A LONG TIME.
I'LL SURVIVE. IT WOULD TAKE MORE THAN THAT TO KILL ME.
AND THE DEVIL KNOWS HE'S TRIED. BESIDES...
WE ARE HERE.

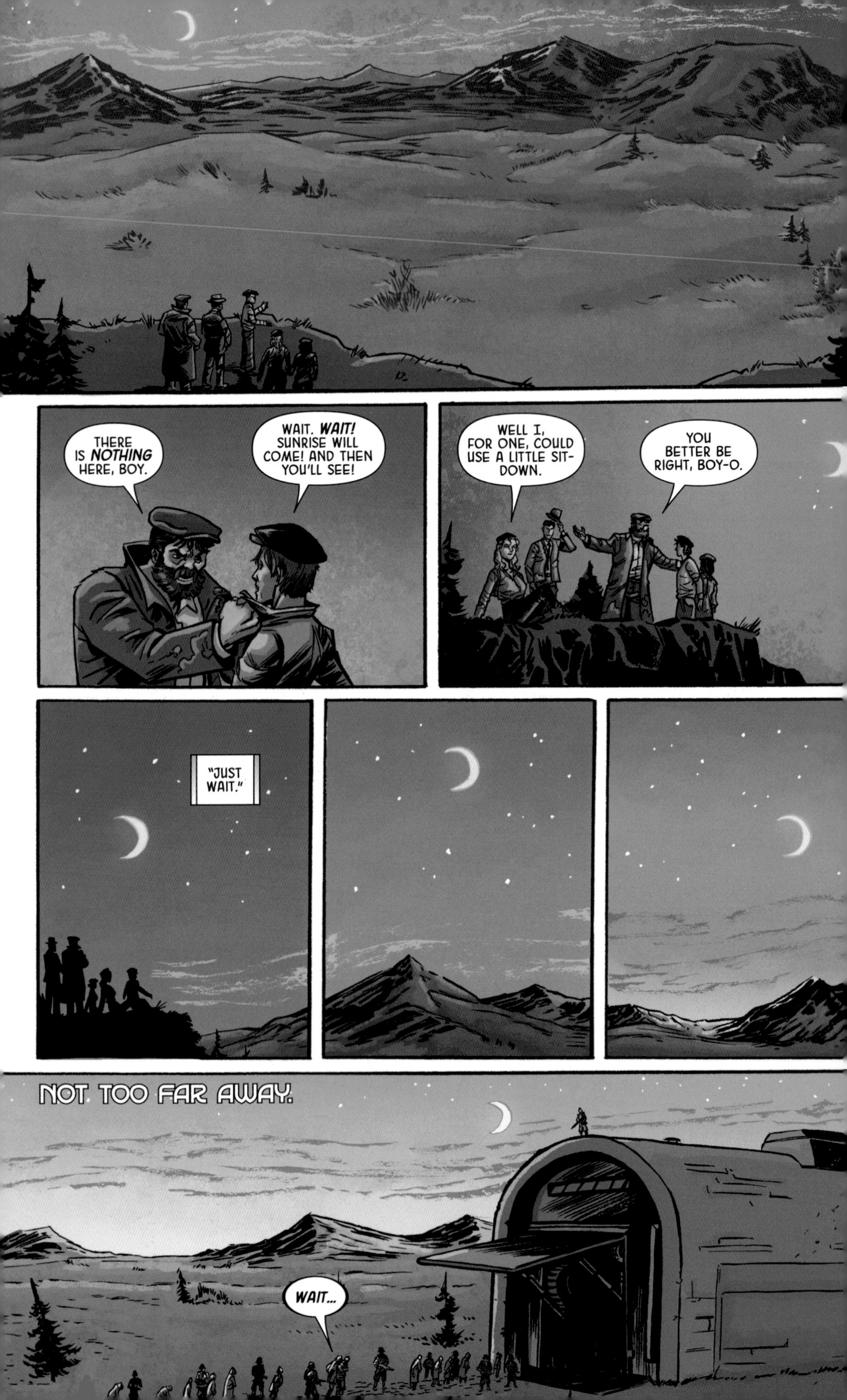
THERE IS NOTHING HERE, BOY.
WAIT. WAIT! SUNRISE WILL COME! AND THEN YOU'LL SEE!
WELL I, FOR ONE, COULD USE A LITTLE SIT-DOWN.
YOU BETTER BE RIGHT, BOY-O.
"JUST WAIT."
NOT TOO FAR AWAY.
WAIT...

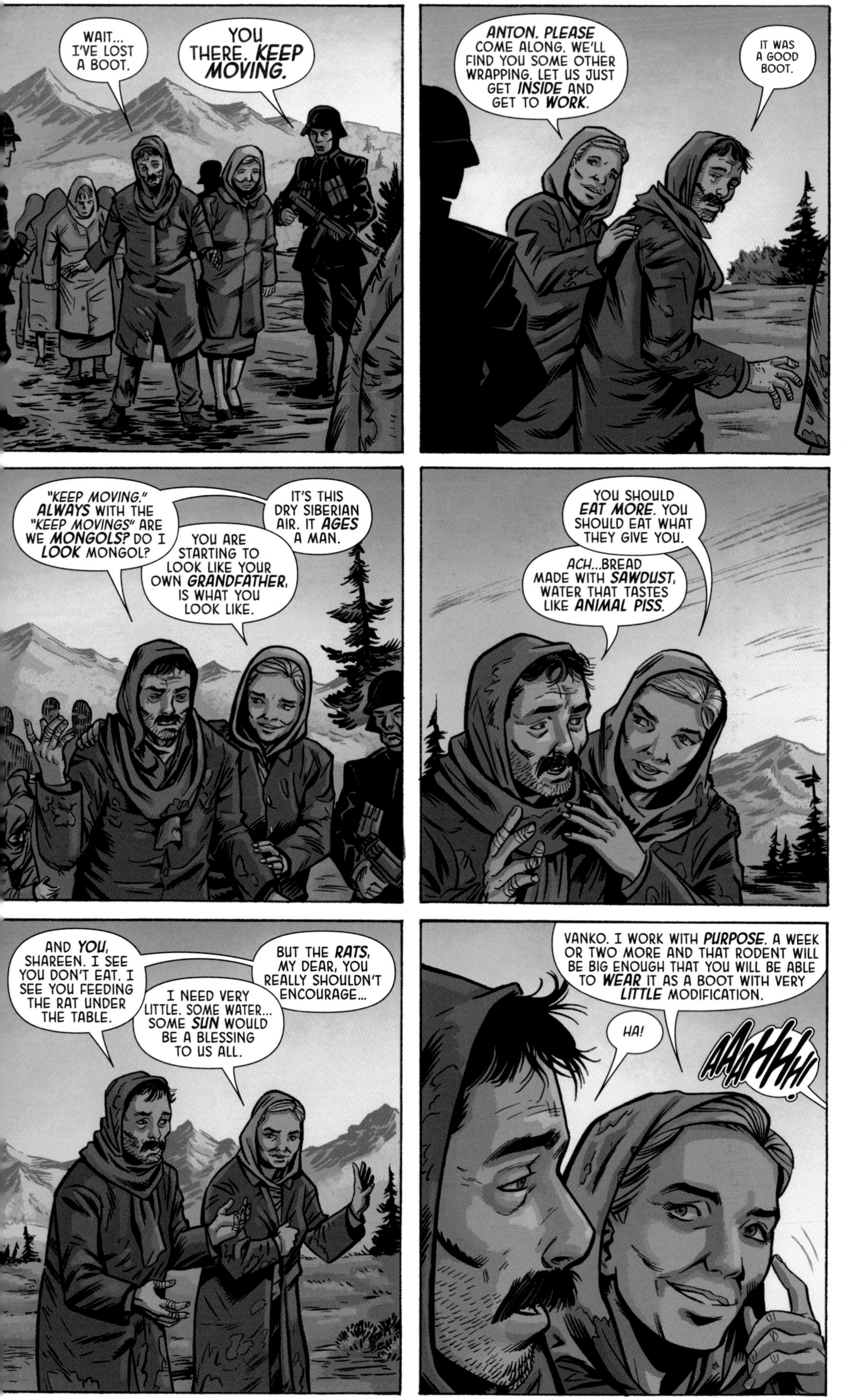
WAIT... I'VE LOST A BOOT.
YOU THERE. KEEP MOVING.
ANTON. PLEASE COME ALONG. WE'LL FIND YOU SOME OTHER WRAPPING. LET US JUST GET INSIDE AND GET TO WORK.
IT WAS A GOOD BOOT.
"KEEP MOVING." ALWAYS WITH THE "KEEP MOVINGS" ARE WE MONGOLS? DO I LOOK MONGOL?
YOU ARE STARTING TO LOOK LIKE YOUR OWN GRANDFATHER, IS WHAT YOU LOOK LIKE.
IT'S THIS DRY SIBERIAN AIR. IT AGES A MAN.
YOU SHOULD EAT MORE. YOU SHOULD EAT WHAT THEY GIVE YOU.
ACH...BREAD MADE WITH SAWDUST, WATER THAT TASTES LIKE ANIMAL PISS.
AND YOU, SHAREEN. I SEE YOU DON'T EAT. I SEE YOU FEEDING THE RAT UNDER THE TABLE.
I NEED VERY LITTLE. SOME WATER... SOME SUN WOULD BE A BLESSING TO US ALL.
BUT THE RATS, MY DEAR, YOU REALLY SHOULDN'T ENCOURAGE...
VANKO. I WORK WITH PURPOSE. A WEEK OR TWO MORE AND THAT RODENT WILL BE BIG ENOUGH THAT YOU WILL BE ABLE TO WEAR IT AS A BOOT WITH VERY LITTLE MODIFICATION.
HA!
AAAHHH!

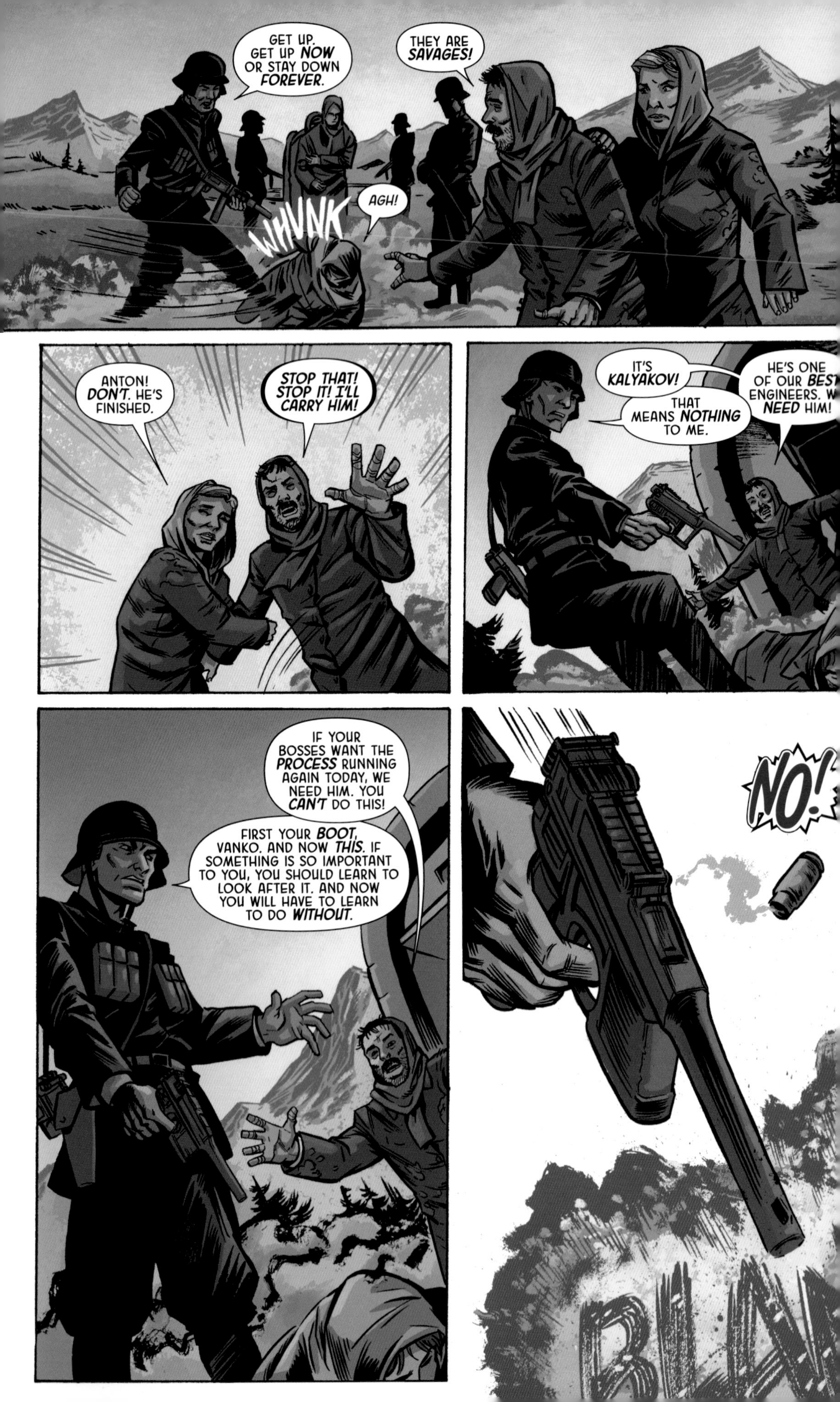
GET UP. GET UP NOW OR STAY DOWN FOREVER.
THEY ARE SAVAGES!
WHVNK
AGH!
ANTON! DON'T. HE'S FINISHED.
STOP THAT! STOP IT! I'LL CARRY HIM!
IT'S KALYAKOV!
HE'S ONE OF OUR BEST ENGINEERS. WE NEED HIM!
THAT MEANS NOTHING TO ME.
IF YOUR BOSSES WANT THE PROCESS RUNNING AGAIN TODAY, WE NEED HIM. YOU CAN'T DO THIS!
FIRST YOUR BOOT, VANKO. AND NOW THIS. IF SOMETHING IS SO IMPORTANT TO YOU, YOU SHOULD LEARN TO LOOK AFTER IT. AND NOW YOU WILL HAVE TO LEARN TO DO WITHOUT.
NO!

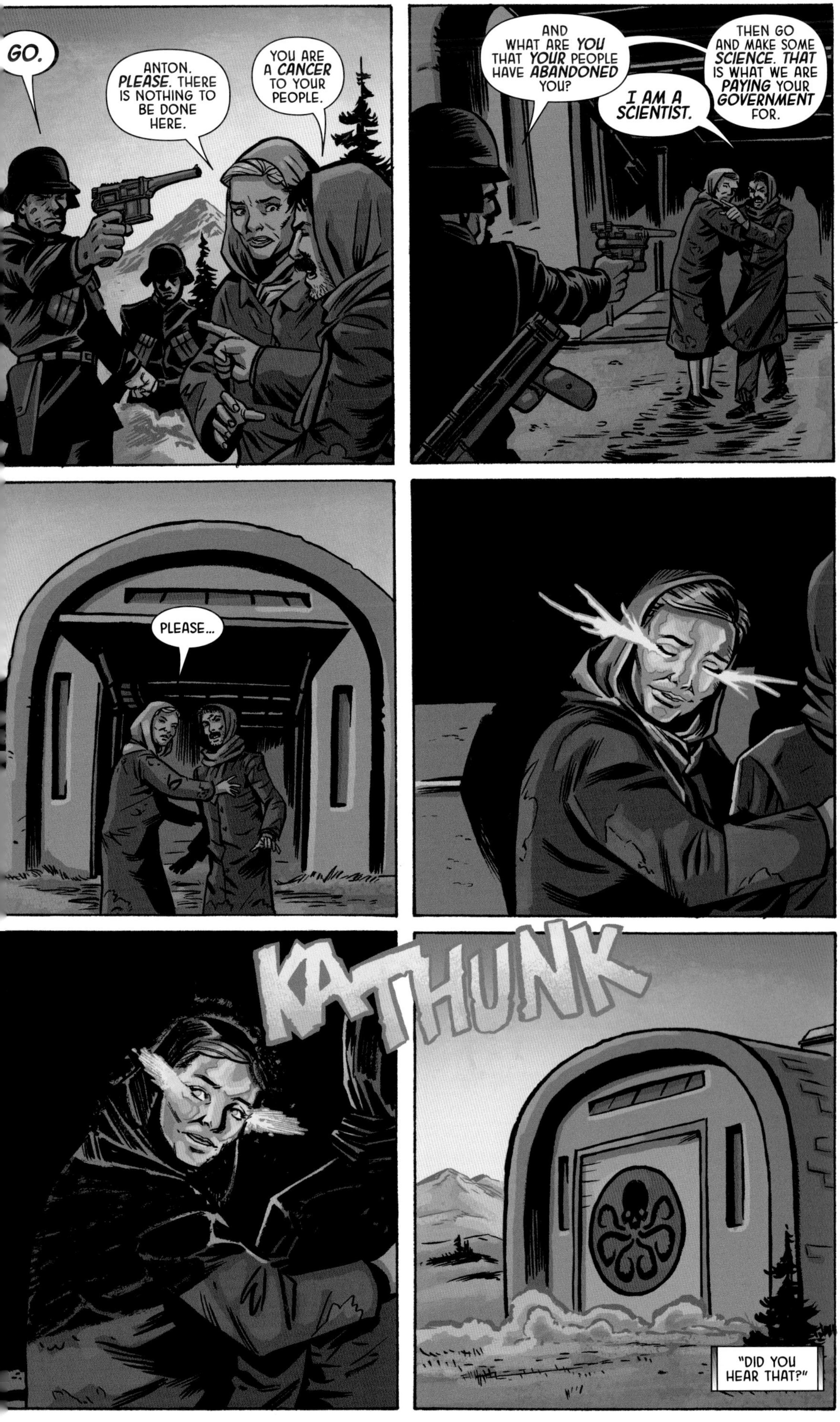
GO.
ANTON. PLEASE. THERE IS NOTHING TO BE DONE HERE.
YOU ARE A CANCER TO YOUR PEOPLE.
AND WHAT ARE YOU THAT YOUR PEOPLE HAVE ABANDONED YOU?
I AM A SCIENTIST.
THEN GO AND MAKE SOME SCIENCE. THAT IS WHAT WE ARE PAYING YOUR GOVERNMENT FOR.
PLEASE...
KATHUNK
"DID YOU HEAR THAT?"

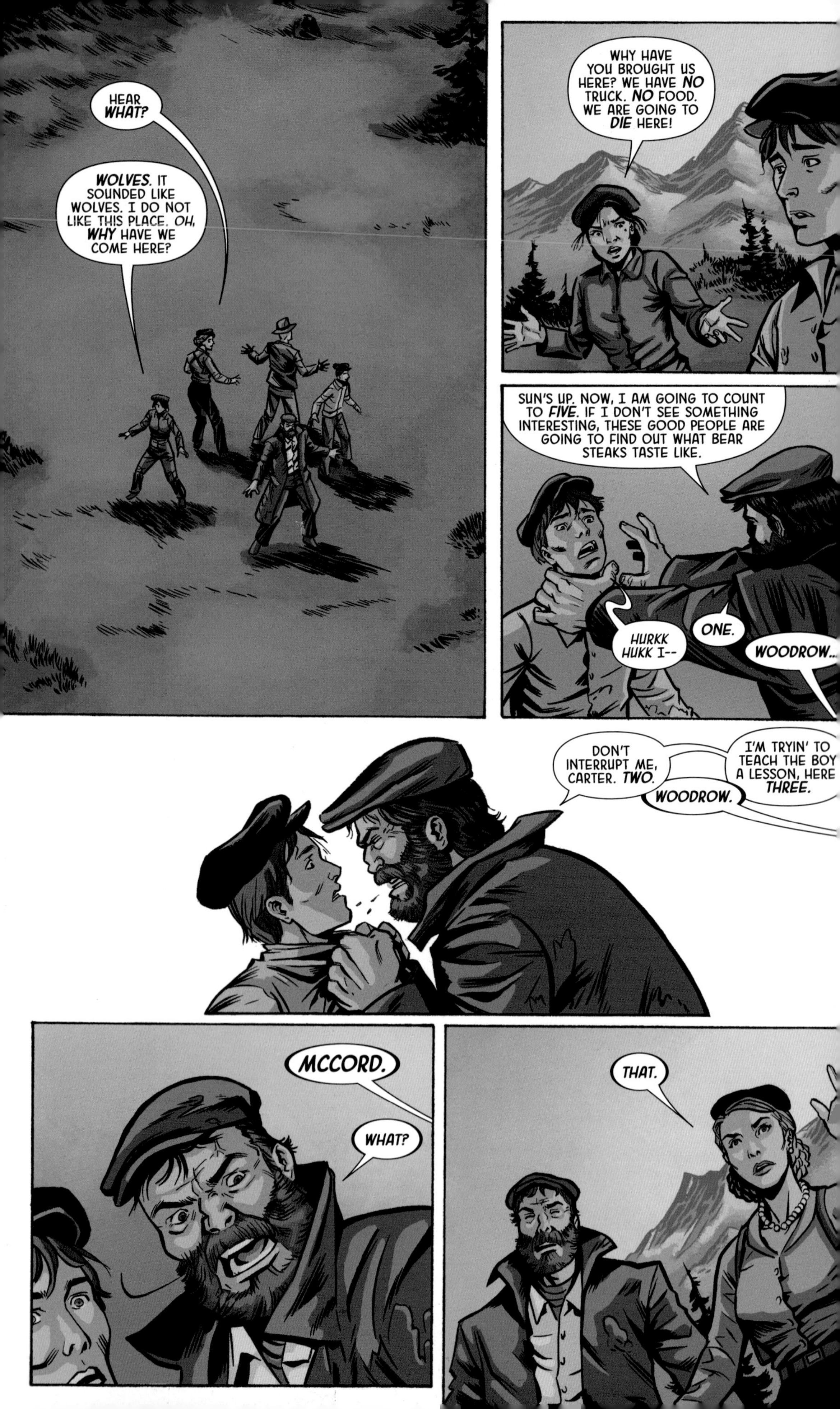
HEAR WHAT?
WOLVES. IT SOUNDED LIKE WOLVES. I DO NOT LIKE THIS PLACE. OH, WHY HAVE WE COME HERE?
WHY HAVE YOU BROUGHT US HERE? WE HAVE NO TRUCK. NO FOOD. WE ARE GOING TO DIE HERE!
SUN'S UP. NOW, I AM GOING TO COUNT TO FIVE. IF I DON'T SEE SOMETHING INTERESTING, THESE GOOD PEOPLE ARE GOING TO FIND OUT WHAT BEAR STEAKS TASTE LIKE.
HURKK HUKK I--
ONE.
WOODROW...
DON'T INTERRUPT ME, CARTER. TWO.
WOODROW.
I'M TRYIN' TO TEACH THE BOY A LESSON, HERE. THREE.
MCCORD.
WHAT?
THAT.

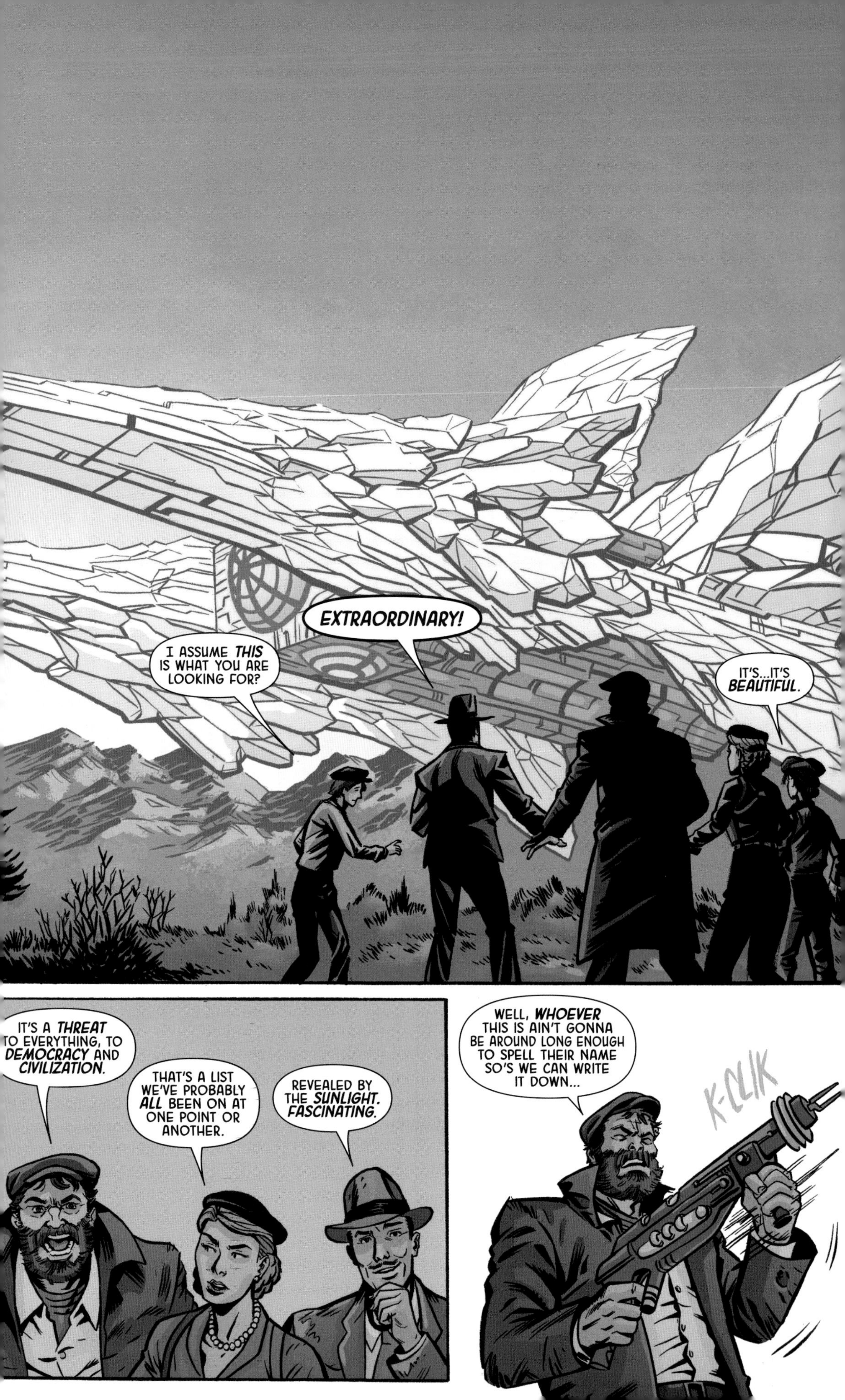
I ASSUME THIS IS WHAT YOU ARE LOOKING FOR?
EXTRAORDINARY!
IT'S...IT'S BEAUTIFUL.
IT'S A THREAT TO EVERYTHING, TO DEMOCRACY AND CIVILIZATION.
THAT'S A LIST WE'VE PROBABLY ALL BEEN ON AT ONE POINT OR ANOTHER.
REVEALED BY THE SUNLIGHT. FASCINATING.
WELL, WHOEVER THIS IS AIN'T GONNA BE AROUND LONG ENOUGH TO SPELL THEIR NAME SO'S WE CAN WRITE IT DOWN...
K-CLIK

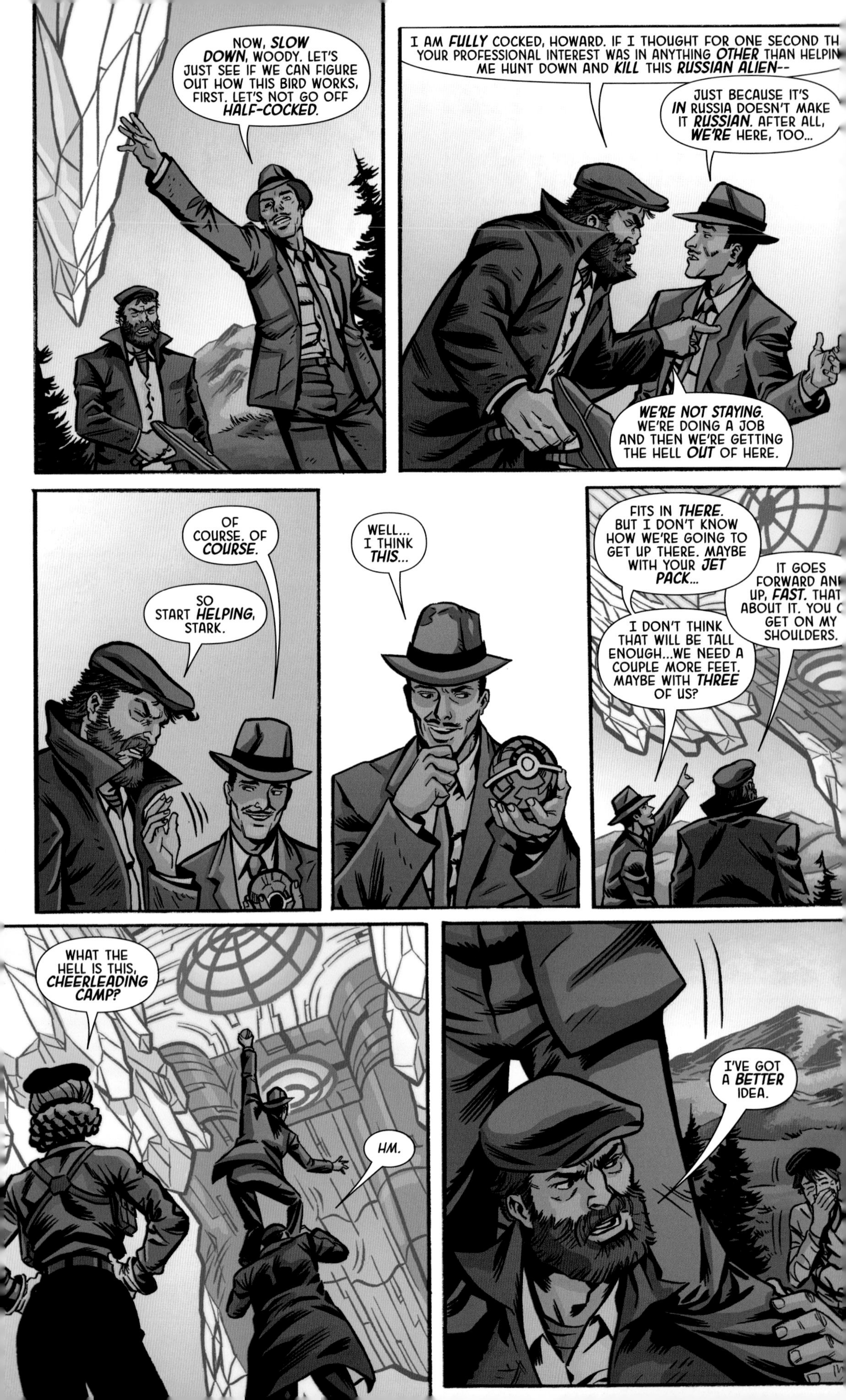
NOW, SLOW DOWN, WOODY. LET'S JUST SEE IF WE CAN FIGURE OUT HOW THIS BIRD WORKS, FIRST. LET'S NOT GO OFF HALF-COCKED.
I AM FULLY COCKED, HOWARD. IF I THOUGHT FOR ONE SECOND TH YOUR PROFESSIONAL INTEREST WAS IN ANYTHING OTHER THAN HELPIN ME HUNT DOWN AND KILL THIS RUSSIAN ALIEN--
JUST BECAUSE IT'S IN RUSSIA DOESN'T MAKE IT RUSSIAN. AFTER ALL, WE'RE HERE, TOO...
WE'RE NOT STAYING. WE'RE DOING A JOB AND THEN WE'RE GETTING THE HELL OUT OF HERE.
OF COURSE. OF COURSE.
SO START HELPING, STARK.
WELL... I THINK THIS...
FITS IN THERE. BUT I DON'T KNOW HOW WE'RE GOING TO GET UP THERE. MAYBE WITH YOUR JET PACK...
IT GOES FORWARD AN UP, FAST. THAT ABOUT IT. YOU C GET ON MY SHOULDERS.
I DON'T THINK THAT WILL BE TALL ENOUGH...WE NEED A COUPLE MORE FEET. MAYBE WITH THREE OF US?
WHAT THE HELL IS THIS, CHEERLEADING CAMP?
HM.
I'VE GOT A BETTER IDEA.

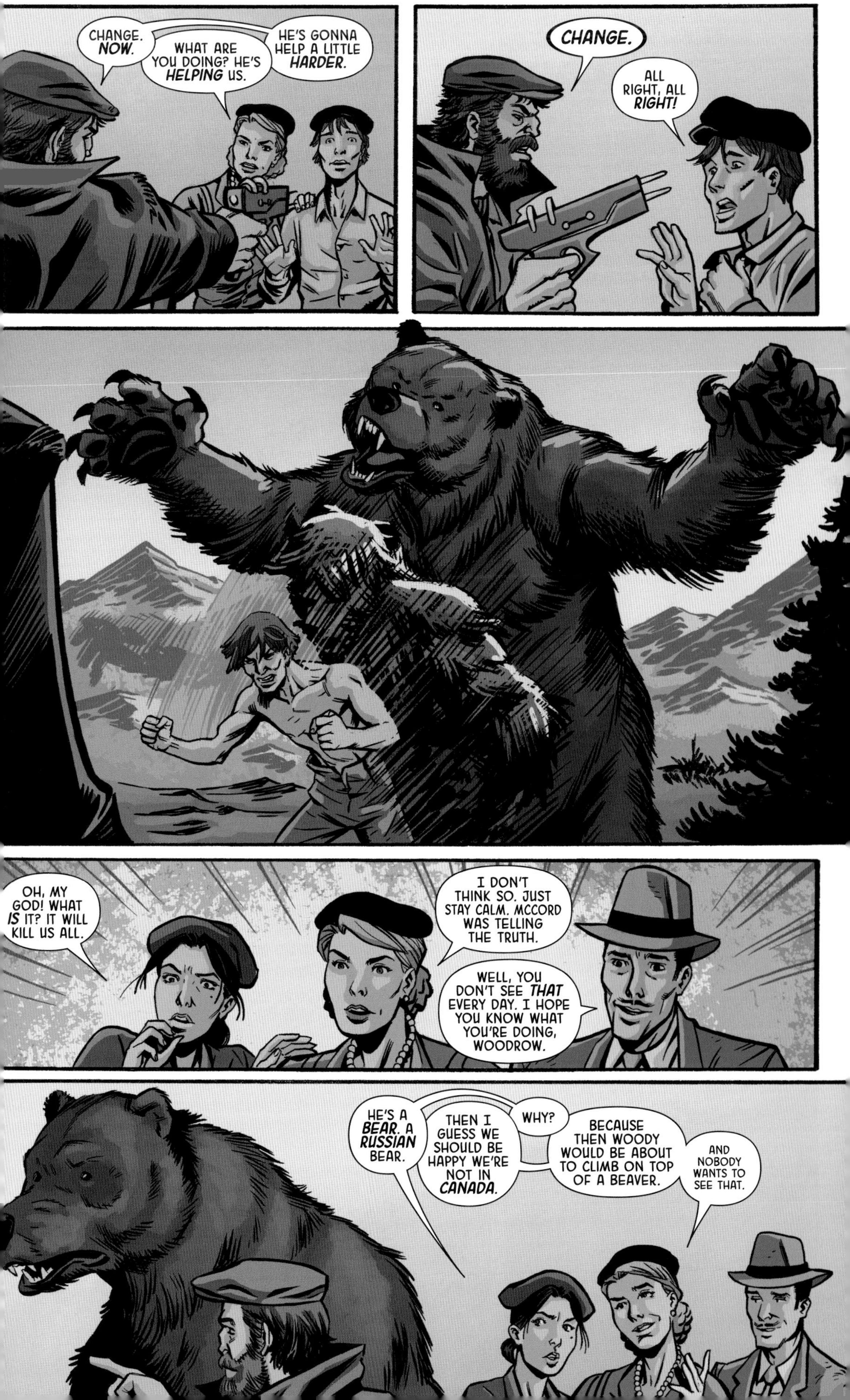
CHANGE. NOW.
WHAT ARE YOU DOING? HE'S HELPING US.
HE'S GONNA HELP A LITTLE HARDER.
CHANGE.
ALL RIGHT, ALL RIGHT!
OH, MY GOD! WHAT IS IT? IT WILL KILL US ALL.
I DON'T THINK SO. JUST STAY CALM. MCCORD WAS TELLING THE TRUTH.
WELL, YOU DON'T SEE THAT EVERY DAY. I HOPE YOU KNOW WHAT YOU'RE DOING, WOODROW.
HE'S A BEAR. A RUSSIAN BEAR.
THEN I GUESS WE SHOULD BE HAPPY WE'RE NOT IN CANADA.
WHY?
BECAUSE THEN WOODY WOULD BE ABOUT TO CLIMB ON TOP OF A BEAVER.
AND NOBODY WANTS TO SEE THAT.

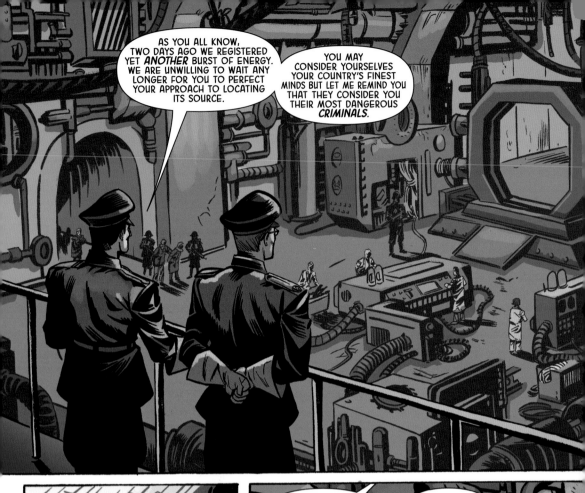

AS YOU ALL KNOW, TWO DAYS AGO WE REGISTERED YET *ANOTHER* BURST OF ENERGY. WE ARE UNWILLING TO WAIT ANY LONGER FOR YOU TO PERFECT YOUR APPROACH TO LOCATING ITS SOURCE.

YOU MAY CONSIDER YOURSELVES YOUR COUNTRY'S FINEST MINDS BUT LET ME REMIND YOU THAT THEY CONSIDER YOU THEIR MOST DANGEROUS *CRIMINALS.*

"AND WHEREAS YOUR SO-CALLED *GOVERNMENT* LEFT YOU TO ROT, *HYDRA* HAS GIVEN YOU PURPOSE AGAIN."

BUT THERE HAVE BEEN *DELAYS.* COSTLY, *UNEXPLAINED* DELAYS FOR WHICH WE ARE TIRED OF ACCOUNTING. HYDRA IS PAYING HANDSOMELY FOR YOUR SERVICES.

FUNNY. I HAVEN'T SEEN A RUBLE. PERHAPS IT IS BEING INVESTED FOR US.

SHHHH...

CHINK

"TODAY THE PROCESS *WILL* BE ACTIVATED. NO MORE *EXCUSES!*"

OH, NO.

HAIL HYDRA!

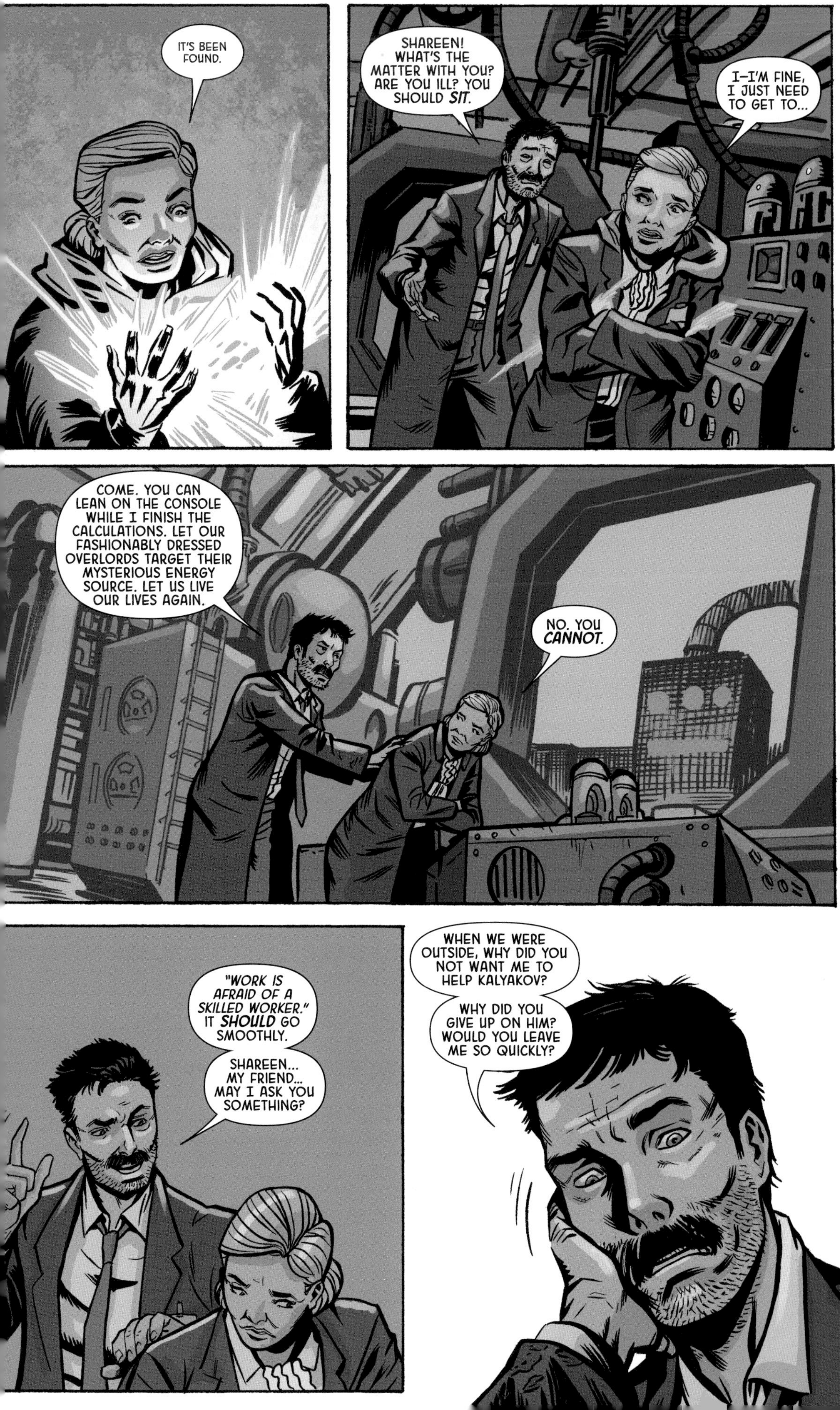
IT'S BEEN FOUND.
SHAREEN! WHAT'S THE MATTER WITH YOU? ARE YOU ILL? YOU SHOULD *SIT*.
I—I'M FINE, I JUST NEED TO GET TO...
COME. YOU CAN LEAN ON THE CONSOLE WHILE I FINISH THE CALCULATIONS. LET OUR FASHIONABLY DRESSED OVERLORDS TARGET THEIR MYSTERIOUS ENERGY SOURCE. LET US LIVE OUR LIVES AGAIN.
NO. YOU *CANNOT*.
"WORK IS AFRAID OF A SKILLED WORKER." IT *SHOULD* GO SMOOTHLY.
SHAREEN... MY FRIEND... MAY I ASK YOU SOMETHING?
WHEN WE WERE OUTSIDE, WHY DID YOU NOT WANT ME TO HELP KALYAKOV?
WHY DID YOU GIVE UP ON HIM? WOULD YOU LEAVE ME SO QUICKLY?

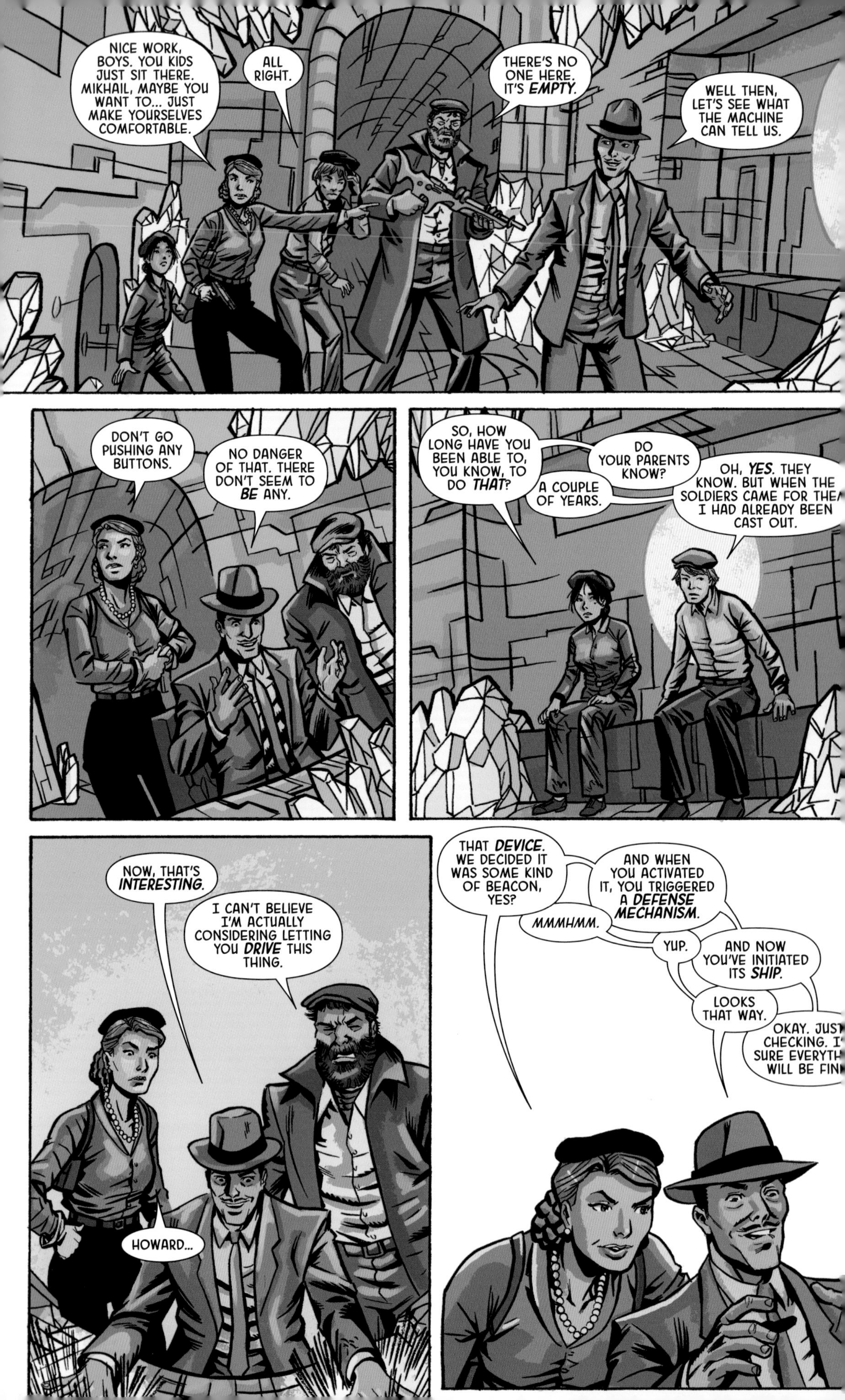
NICE WORK, BOYS. YOU KIDS JUST SIT THERE. MIKHAIL, MAYBE YOU WANT TO... JUST MAKE YOURSELVES COMFORTABLE.
ALL RIGHT.
THERE'S NO ONE HERE. IT'S *EMPTY*.
WELL THEN, LET'S SEE WHAT THE MACHINE CAN TELL US.
DON'T GO PUSHING ANY BUTTONS.
NO DANGER OF THAT. THERE DON'T SEEM TO *BE* ANY.
SO, HOW LONG HAVE YOU BEEN ABLE TO, YOU KNOW, TO DO *THAT*?
A COUPLE OF YEARS.
DO YOUR PARENTS KNOW?
OH, *YES*. THEY KNOW. BUT WHEN THE SOLDIERS CAME FOR THE
I HAD ALREADY BEEN CAST OUT.
NOW, THAT'S *INTERESTING*.
I CAN'T BELIEVE I'M ACTUALLY CONSIDERING LETTING YOU *DRIVE* THIS THING.
HOWARD...
THAT *DEVICE*. WE DECIDED IT WAS SOME KIND OF BEACON, YES?
MMMHMM.
AND WHEN YOU ACTIVATED IT, YOU TRIGGERED A *DEFENSE MECHANISM*.
YUP.
AND NOW YOU'VE INITIATED ITS *SHIP*.
LOOKS THAT WAY.
OKAY. JUST CHECKING.

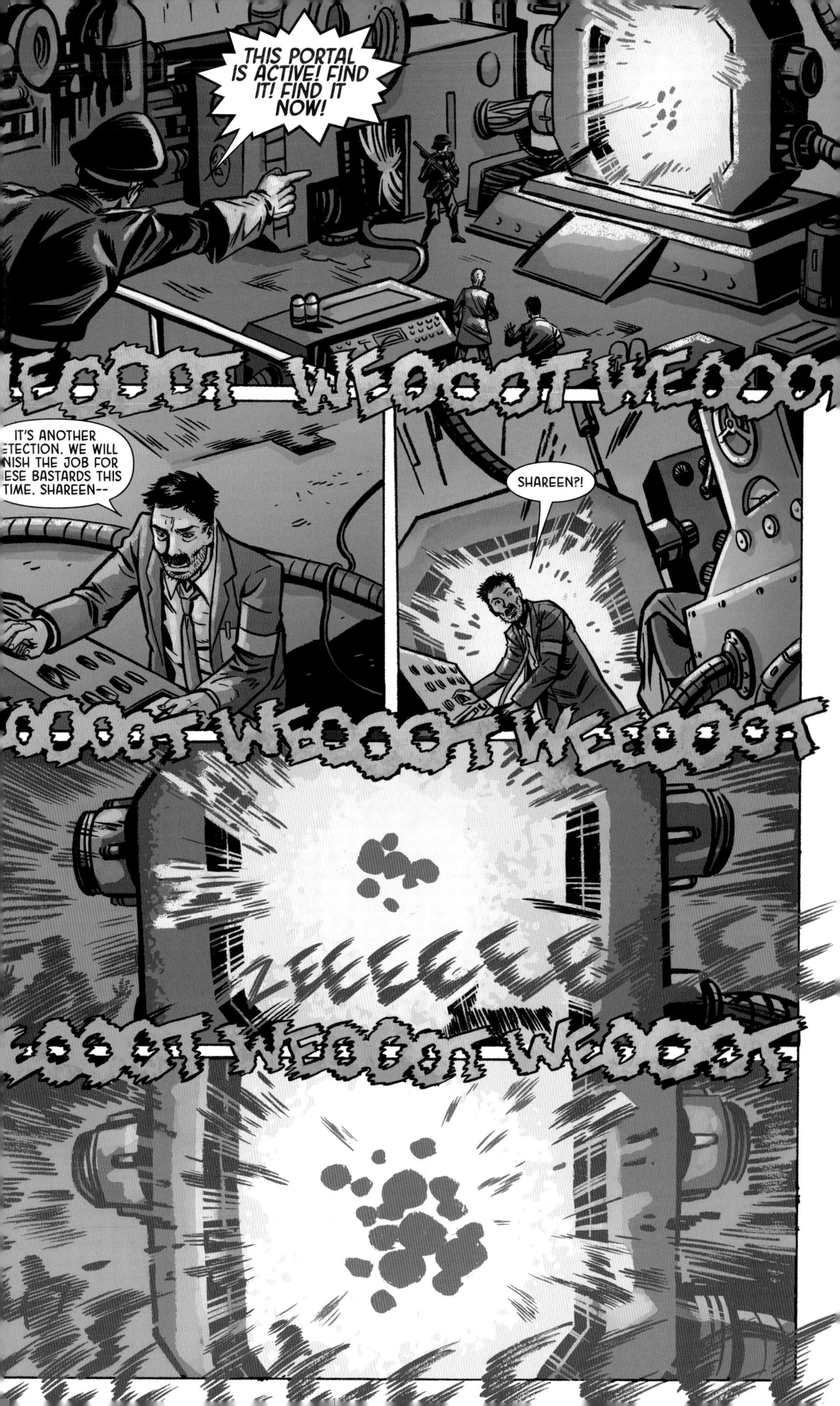
THIS PORTAL IS ACTIVE! FIND IT! FIND IT NOW!
IT'S ANOTHER ETECTION. WE WILL NISH THE JOB FOR ESE BASTARDS THIS TIME. SHAREEN--
SHAREEN?!

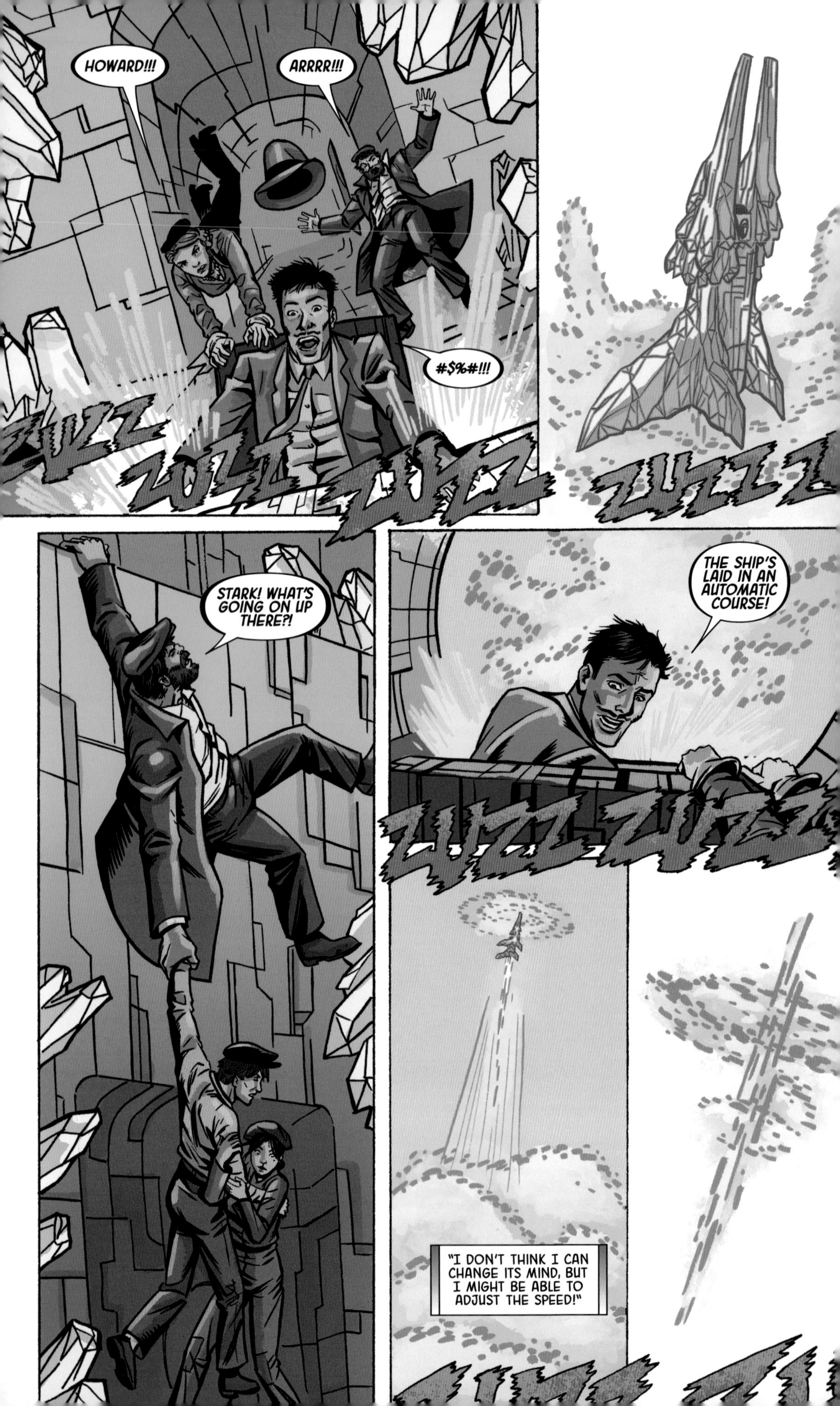
HOWARD!!!
ARRRR!!!
#$%#!!!
ZUZZ ZUZZ ZUZZ ZUZZZ
STARK! WHAT'S GOING ON UP THERE?!
THE SHIP'S LAID IN AN AUTOMATIC COURSE!
"I DON'T THINK I CAN CHANGE ITS MIND, BUT I MIGHT BE ABLE TO ADJUST THE SPEED!"

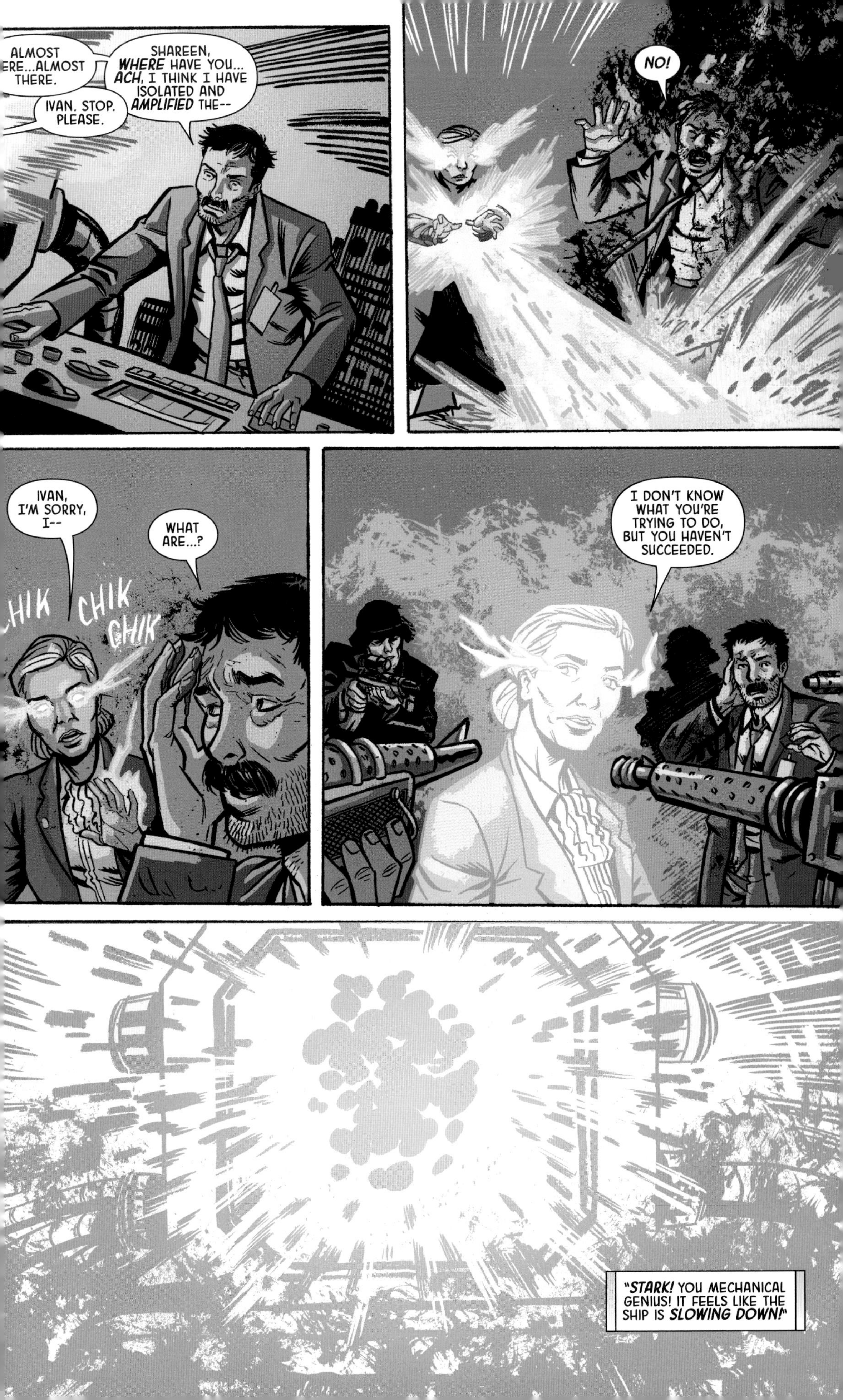
ALMOST ...ERE...ALMOST THERE.
SHAREEN, WHERE HAVE YOU... ACH, I THINK I HAVE ISOLATED AND AMPLIFIED THE--
IVAN. STOP. PLEASE.
NO!
IVAN, I'M SORRY, I--
WHAT ARE...?
CHIK CHIK CHIK
I DON'T KNOW WHAT YOU'RE TRYING TO DO, BUT YOU HAVEN'T SUCCEEDED.
"STARK! YOU MECHANICAL GENIUS! IT FEELS LIKE THE SHIP IS SLOWING DOWN!"

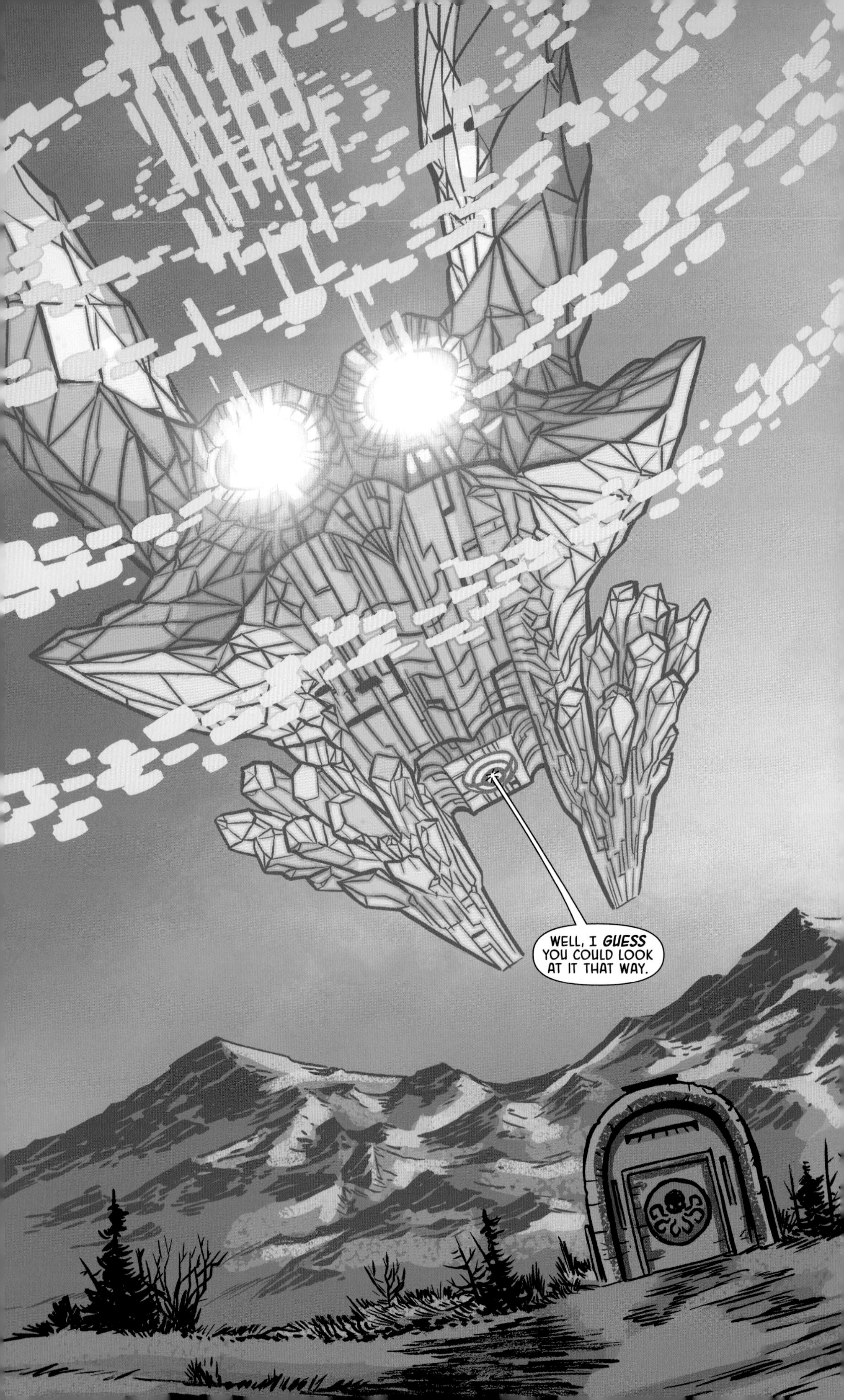
WELL, I *GUESS* YOU COULD LOOK AT IT THAT WAY.

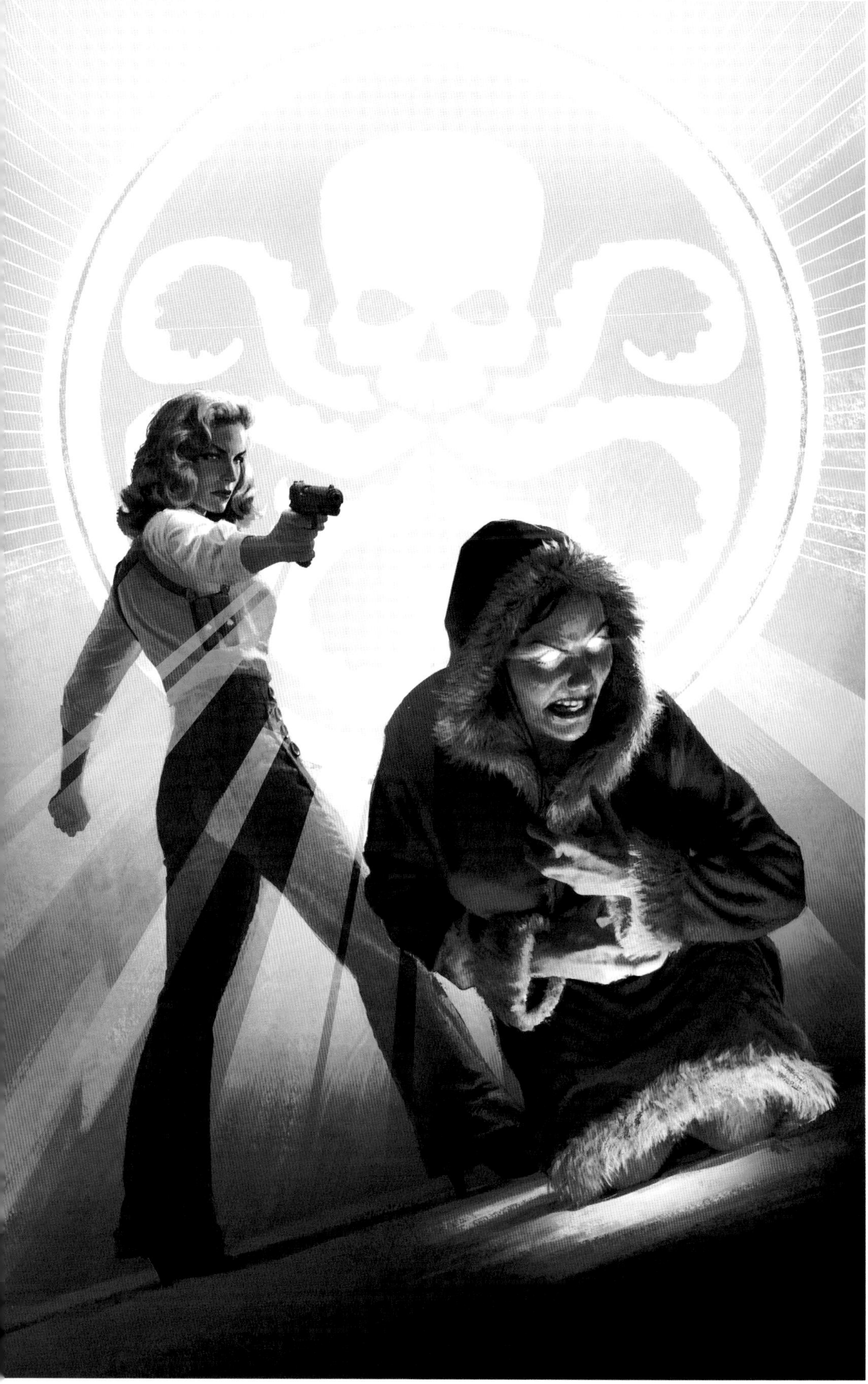

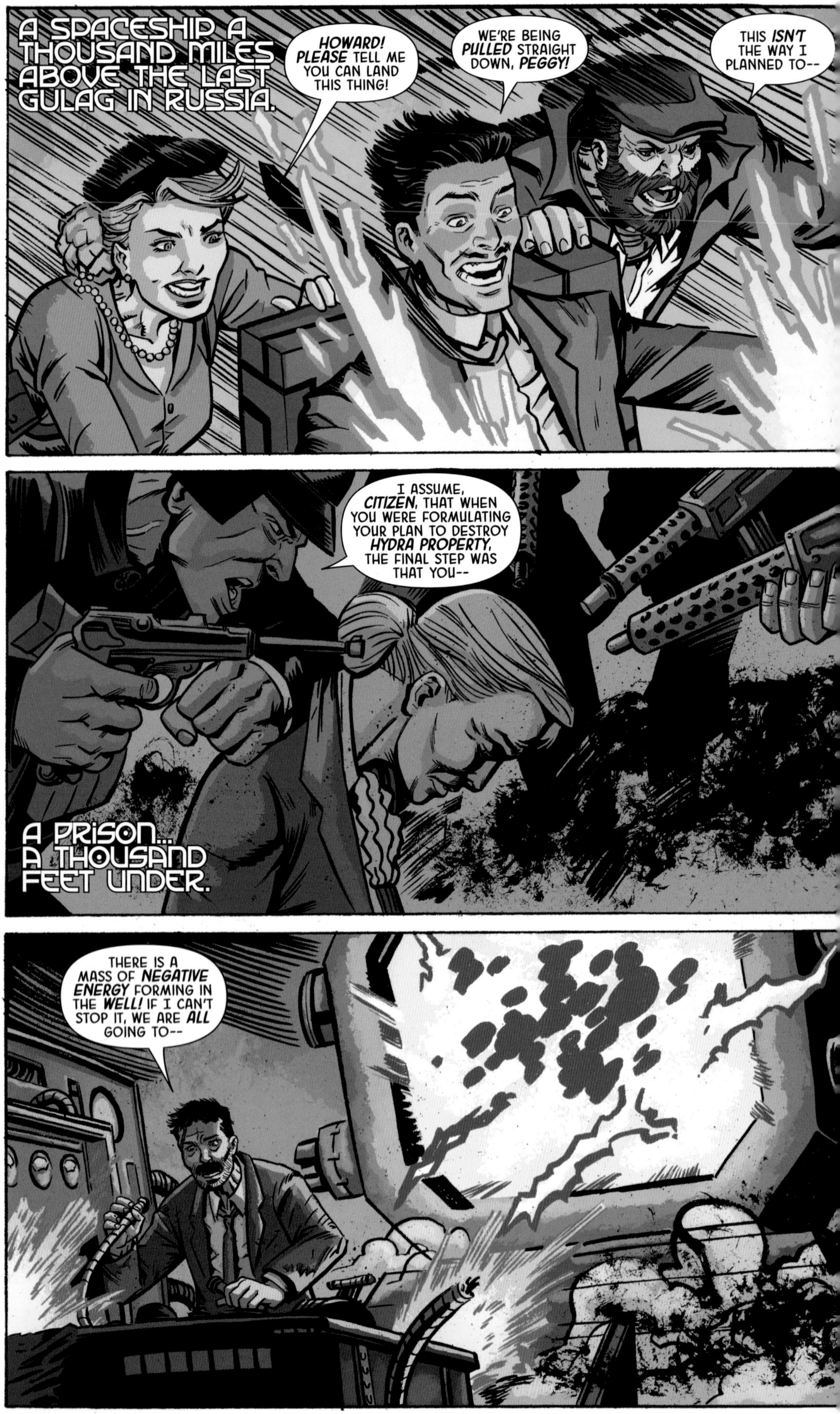
A SPACESHIP A THOUSAND MILES ABOVE THE LAST GULAG IN RUSSIA.
HOWARD! PLEASE TELL ME YOU CAN LAND THIS THING!
WE'RE BEING PULLED STRAIGHT DOWN, PEGGY!
THIS ISN'T THE WAY I PLANNED TO--
I ASSUME, CITIZEN, THAT WHEN YOU WERE FORMULATING YOUR PLAN TO DESTROY HYDRA PROPERTY, THE FINAL STEP WAS THAT YOU--
A PRISON... A THOUSAND FEET UNDER.
THERE IS A MASS OF NEGATIVE ENERGY FORMING IN THE WELL! IF I CAN'T STOP IT, WE ARE ALL GOING TO--

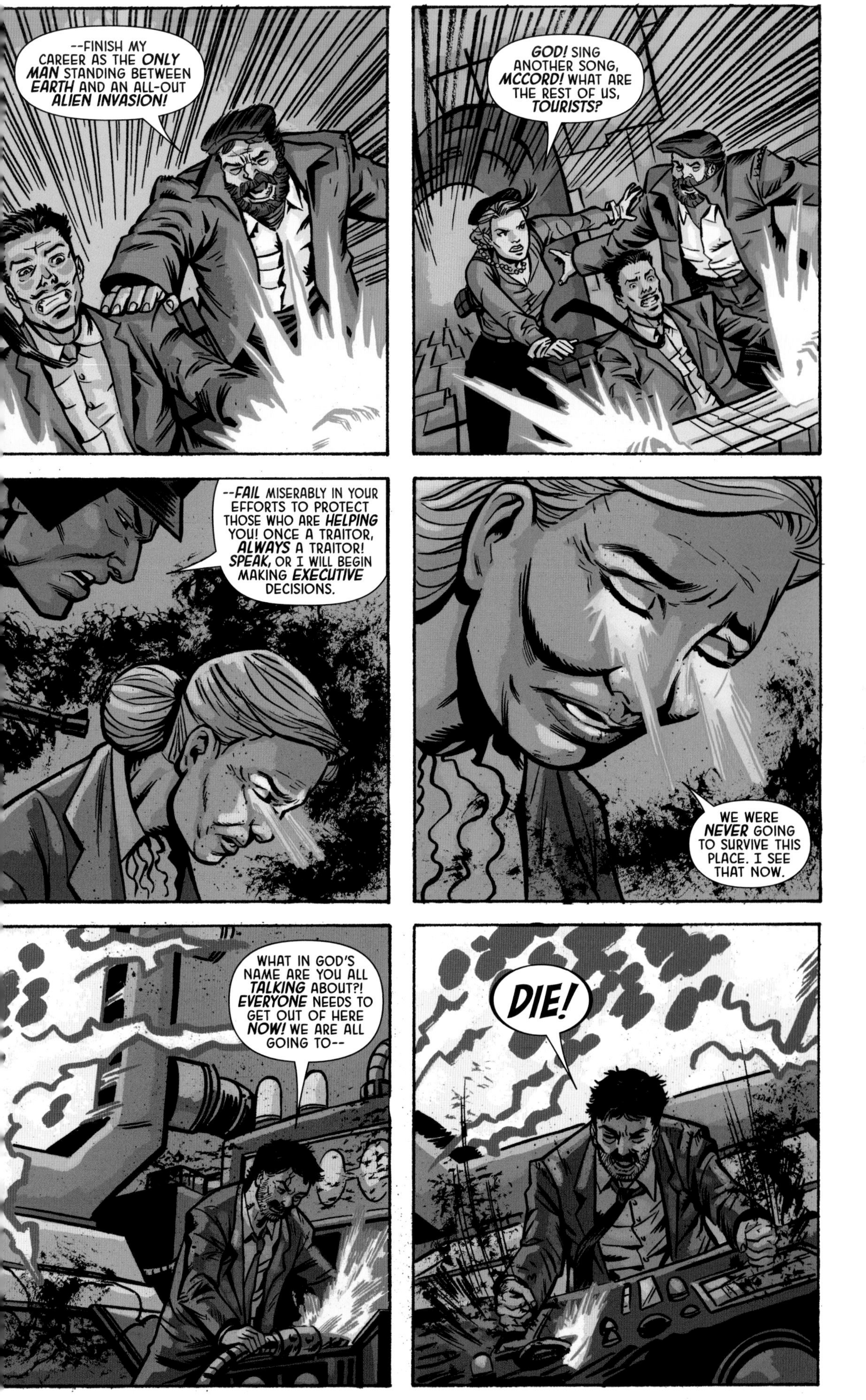
--FINISH MY CAREER AS THE ONLY MAN STANDING BETWEEN EARTH AND AN ALL-OUT ALIEN INVASION!
GOD! SING ANOTHER SONG, MCCORD! WHAT ARE THE REST OF US, TOURISTS?
--FAIL MISERABLY IN YOUR EFFORTS TO PROTECT THOSE WHO ARE HELPING YOU! ONCE A TRAITOR, ALWAYS A TRAITOR! SPEAK, OR I WILL BEGIN MAKING EXECUTIVE DECISIONS.
WE WERE NEVER GOING TO SURVIVE THIS PLACE. I SEE THAT NOW.
WHAT IN GOD'S NAME ARE YOU ALL TALKING ABOUT?! EVERYONE NEEDS TO GET OUT OF HERE NOW! WE ARE ALL GOING TO--
DIE!

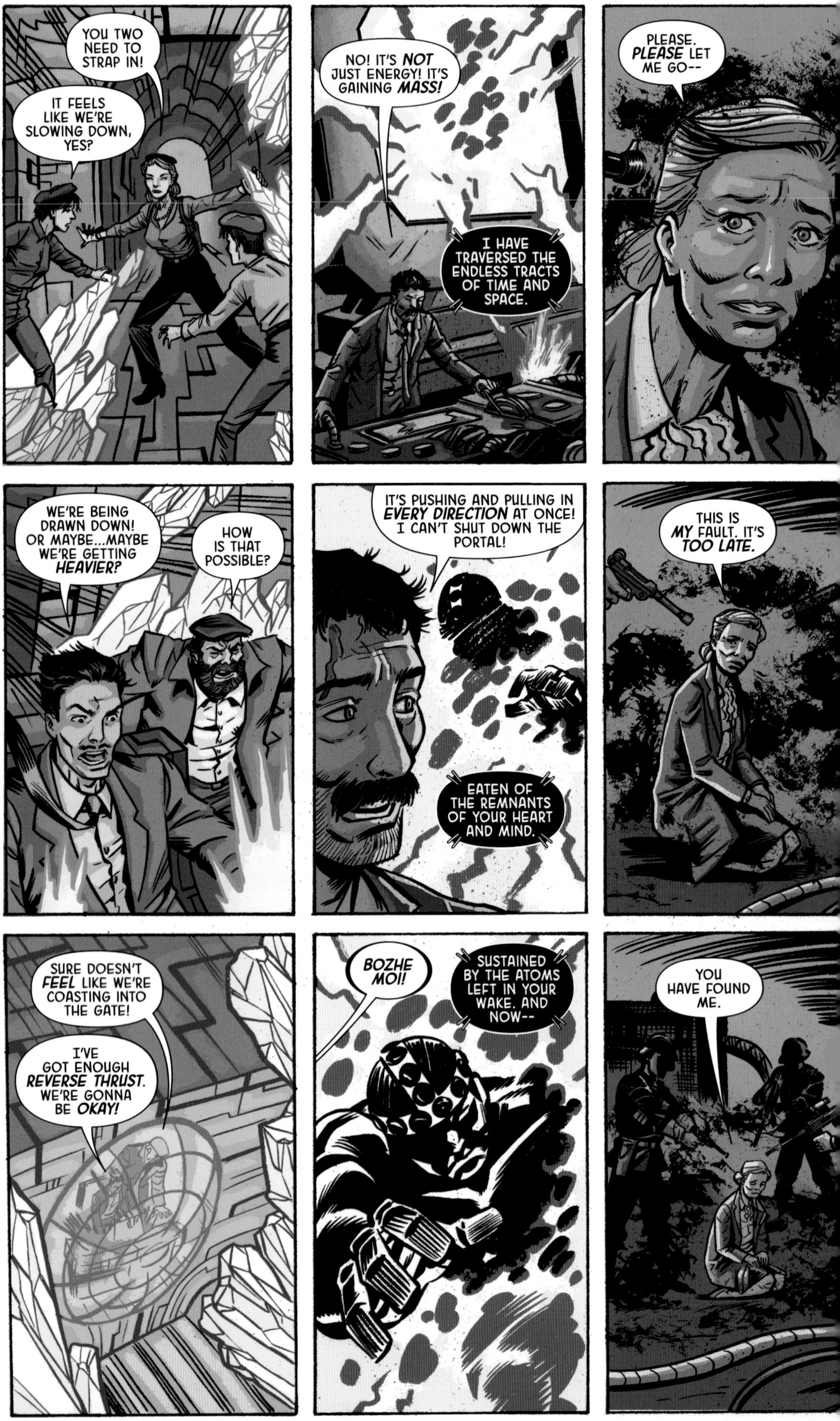
YOU TWO NEED TO STRAP IN!
IT FEELS LIKE WE'RE SLOWING DOWN, YES?
NO! IT'S NOT JUST ENERGY! IT'S GAINING MASS!
I HAVE TRAVERSED THE ENDLESS TRACTS OF TIME AND SPACE.
PLEASE. PLEASE LET ME GO--
WE'RE BEING DRAWN DOWN! OR MAYBE...MAYBE WE'RE GETTING HEAVIER?
HOW IS THAT POSSIBLE?
IT'S PUSHING AND PULLING IN EVERY DIRECTION AT ONCE! I CAN'T SHUT DOWN THE PORTAL!
EATEN OF THE REMNANTS OF YOUR HEART AND MIND.
THIS IS MY FAULT. IT'S TOO LATE.
SURE DOESN'T FEEL LIKE WE'RE COASTING INTO THE GATE!
I'VE GOT ENOUGH REVERSE THRUST. WE'RE GONNA BE OKAY!
BOZHE MOI!
SUSTAINED BY THE ATOMS LEFT IN YOUR WAKE. AND NOW--
YOU HAVE FOUND ME.

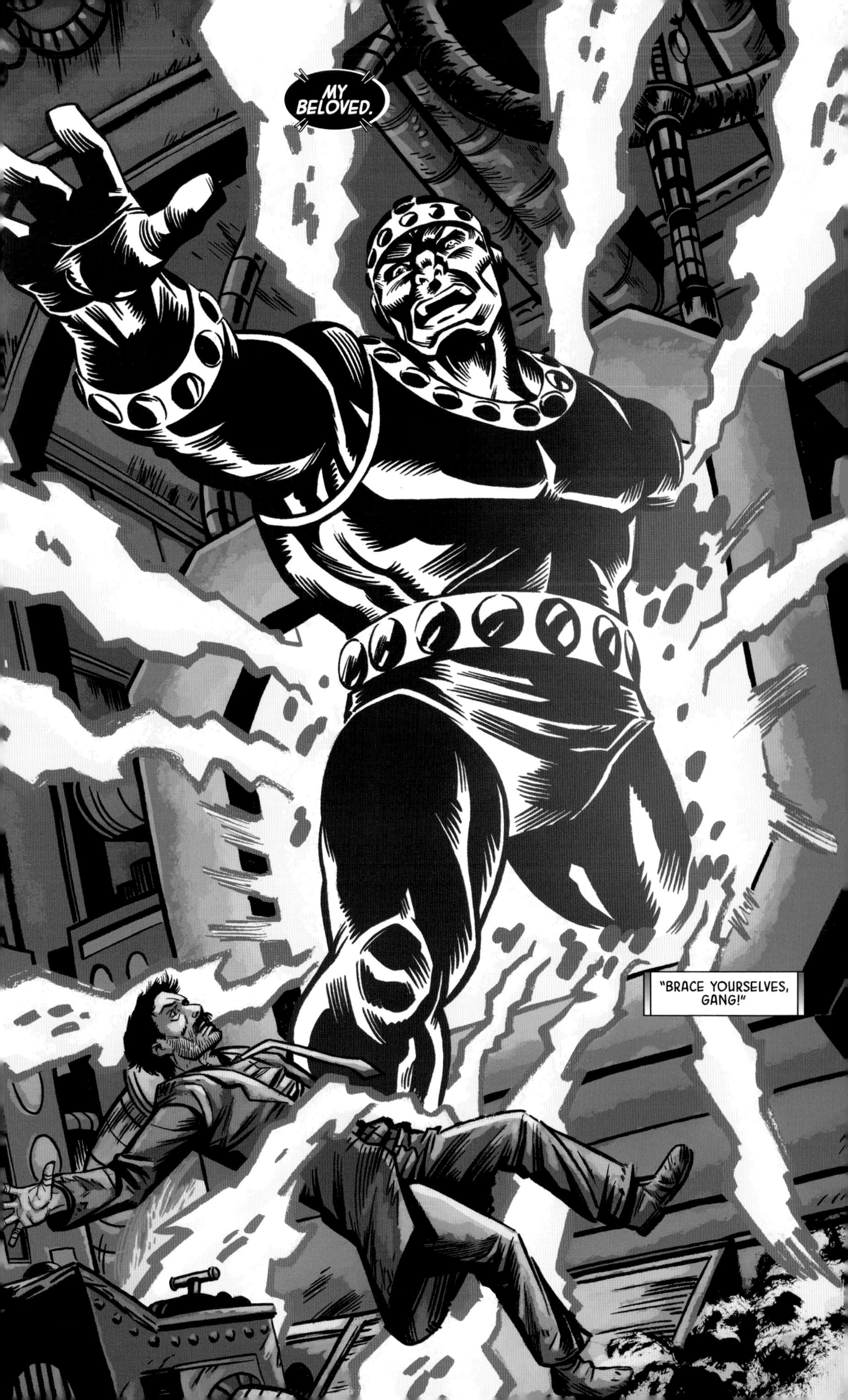
MY BELOVED.
"BRACE YOURSELVES, GANG!"

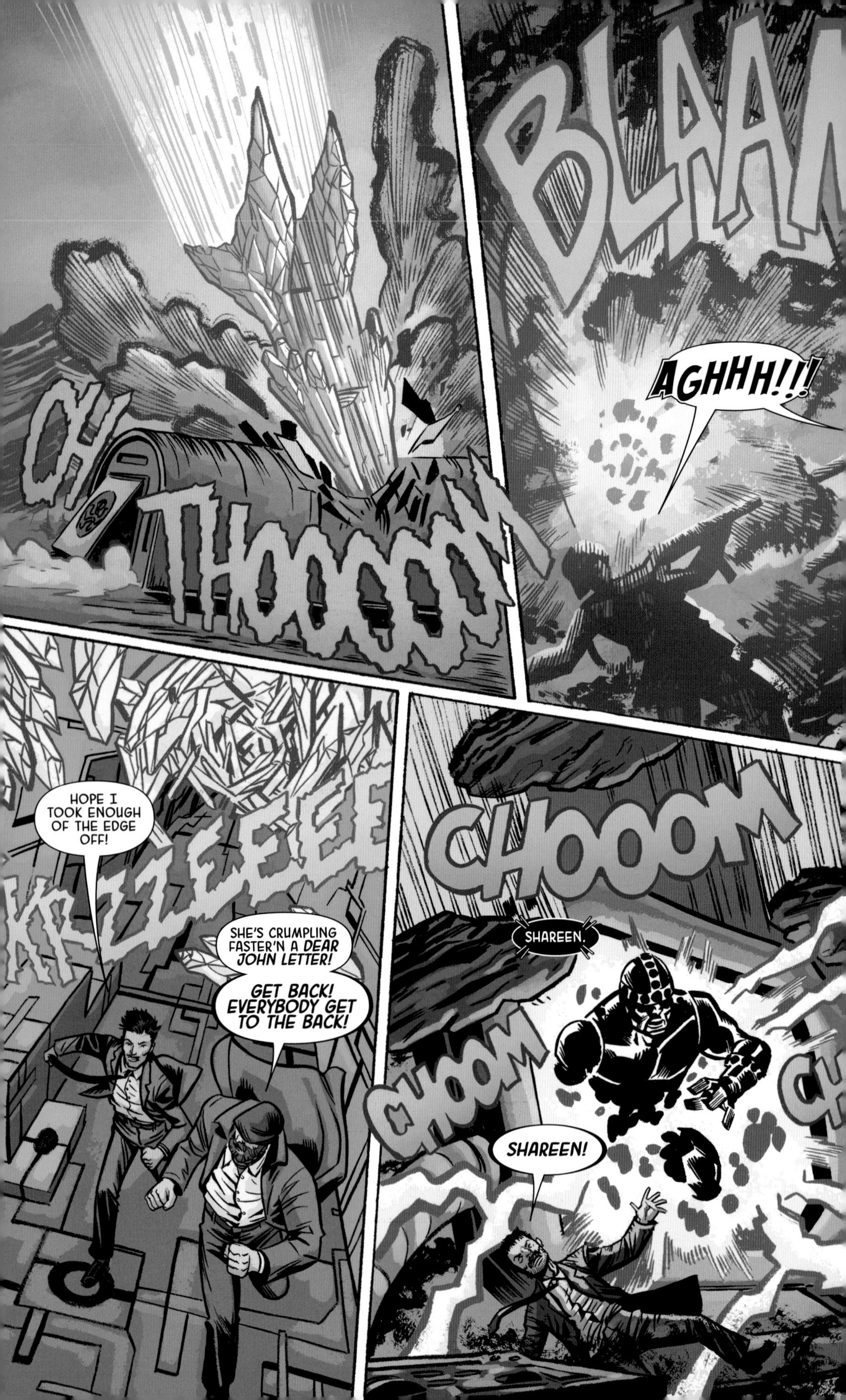
CH
THOOOOM
BLAAM
AGHHH!!!
KRZZEEE
HOPE I TOOK ENOUGH OF THE EDGE OFF!
SHE'S CRUMPLING FASTER'N A *DEAR JOHN LETTER!*
GET BACK! EVERYBODY GET TO THE BACK!
CHOOOM
SHAREEN.
CHOOM
SHAREEN!

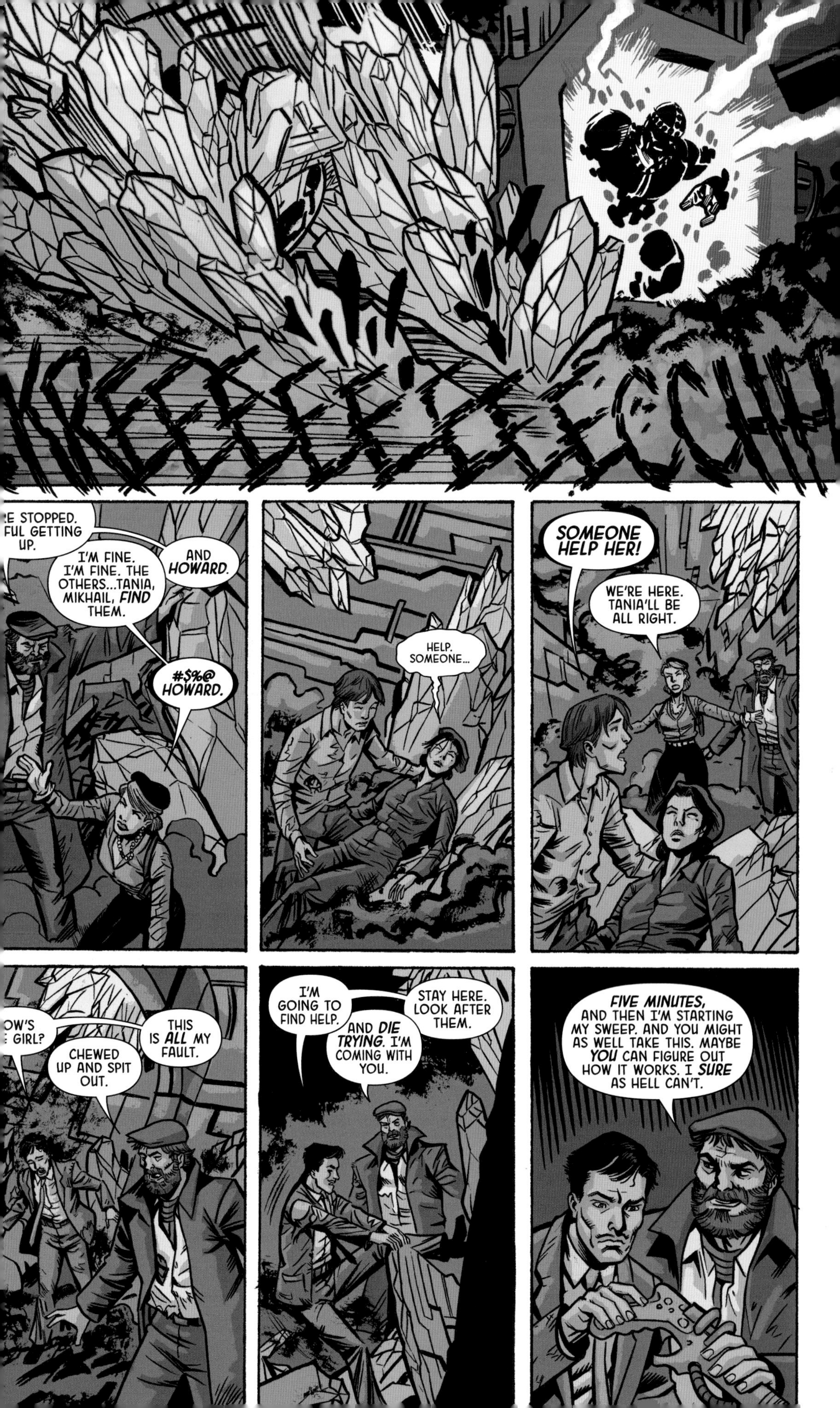
KREEEEEEEECCHH
…E STOPPED. …FUL GETTING UP.
I'M FINE. I'M FINE. THE OTHERS...TANIA, MIKHAIL, FIND THEM.
AND HOWARD.
#$%@ HOWARD.
HELP. SOMEONE...
SOMEONE HELP HER!
WE'RE HERE. TANIA'LL BE ALL RIGHT.
…OW'S …E GIRL?
CHEWED UP AND SPIT OUT.
THIS IS ALL MY FAULT.
I'M GOING TO FIND HELP.
STAY HERE. LOOK AFTER THEM.
AND DIE TRYING. I'M COMING WITH YOU.
FIVE MINUTES, AND THEN I'M STARTING MY SWEEP. AND YOU MIGHT AS WELL TAKE THIS. MAYBE YOU CAN FIGURE OUT HOW IT WORKS. I SURE AS HELL CAN'T.

OH, GOD.

UNGHH!

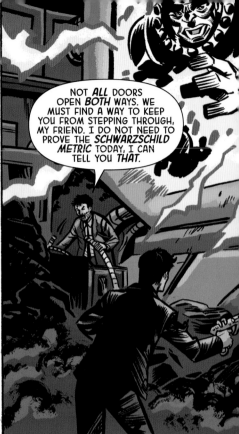

NOT **ALL** DOORS OPEN **BOTH** WAYS. WE MUST FIND A WAY TO KEEP YOU FROM STEPPING THROUGH, MY FRIEND. I DO NOT NEED TO PROVE THE **SCHWARZSCHILD METRIC** TODAY, I CAN TELL YOU **THAT**.

WHAT ON EARTH ARE YOU **DOING** HERE?

SCHTOH?!

SCHWARZSCHILD. YOU SAID **SCHWARZSCHILD**. IS THAT...IS THAT A **DARK STAR?** MY GOD. WHAT ARE YOU **RUSSIANS** TRYING TO **DO?**

ANTON VANKO. SCIENTIST. AND I AM **TRYING** TO FIND A STABLE SOLUTION. IF YOU CAN HELP ME, **DO SO**. IF YOU CAN'T, THEN I ADVISE YOU TO HELP **YOURSELF**.

HOWARD STAR AMERICAN. HA YOU CALCULAT THE RADIUS?

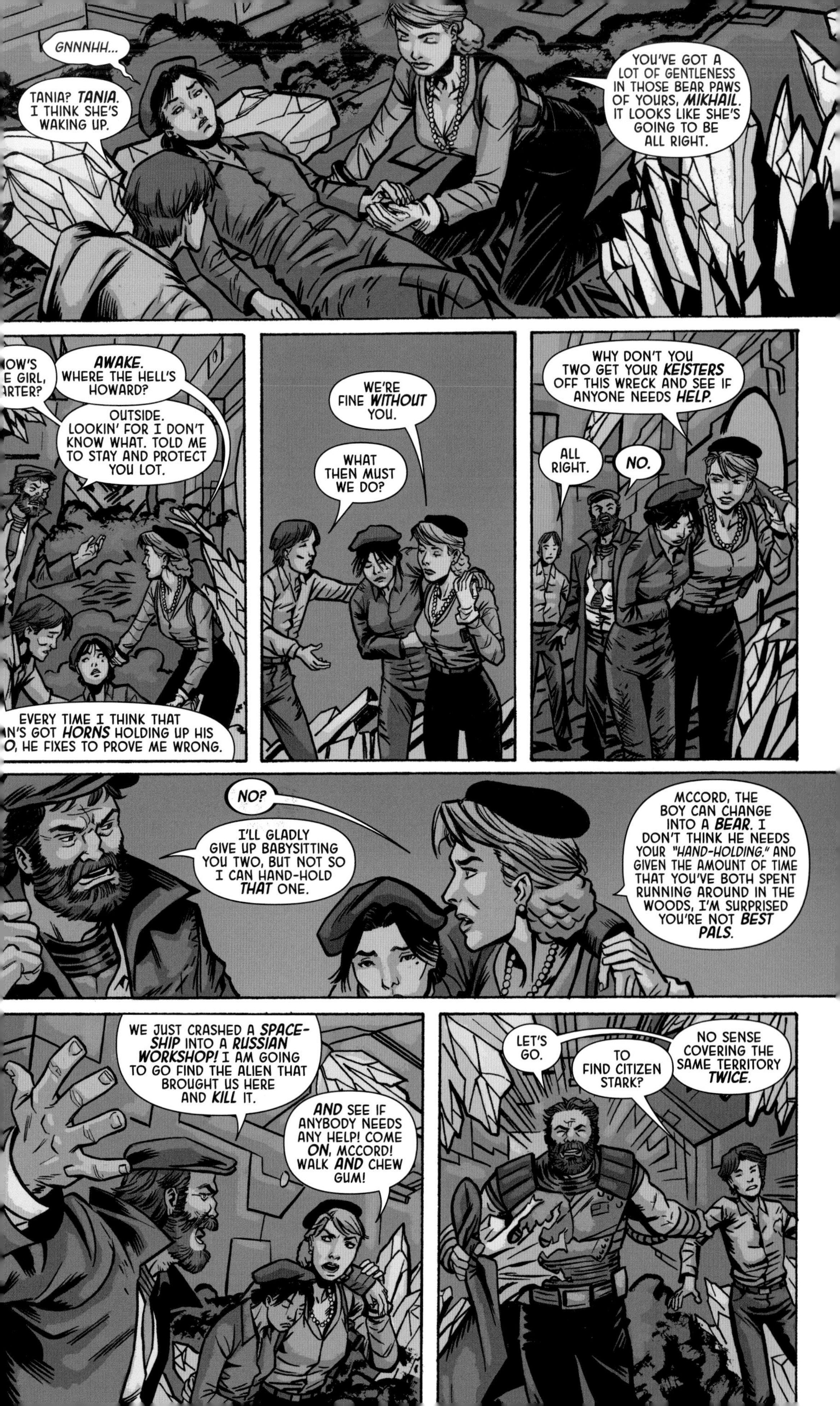

GNNNHH...
TANIA? TANIA. I THINK SHE'S WAKING UP.
YOU'VE GOT A LOT OF GENTLENESS IN THOSE BEAR PAWS OF YOURS, MIKHAIL. IT LOOKS LIKE SHE'S GOING TO BE ALL RIGHT.
OW'S E GIRL, RTER?
AWAKE. WHERE THE HELL'S HOWARD?
OUTSIDE. LOOKIN' FOR I DON'T KNOW WHAT. TOLD ME TO STAY AND PROTECT YOU LOT.
EVERY TIME I THINK THAT N'S GOT HORNS HOLDING UP HIS O, HE FIXES TO PROVE ME WRONG.
WHAT THEN MUST WE DO?
WE'RE FINE WITHOUT YOU.
WHY DON'T YOU TWO GET YOUR KEISTERS OFF THIS WRECK AND SEE IF ANYONE NEEDS HELP.
ALL RIGHT.
NO.
NO?
I'LL GLADLY GIVE UP BABYSITTING YOU TWO, BUT NOT SO I CAN HAND-HOLD THAT ONE.
MCCORD, THE BOY CAN CHANGE INTO A BEAR. I DON'T THINK HE NEEDS YOUR "HAND-HOLDING," AND GIVEN THE AMOUNT OF TIME THAT YOU'VE BOTH SPENT RUNNING AROUND IN THE WOODS, I'M SURPRISED YOU'RE NOT BEST PALS.
WE JUST CRASHED A SPACE-SHIP INTO A RUSSIAN WORKSHOP! I AM GOING TO GO FIND THE ALIEN THAT BROUGHT US HERE AND KILL IT.
AND SEE IF ANYBODY NEEDS ANY HELP! COME ON, MCCORD! WALK AND CHEW GUM!
LET'S GO.
TO FIND CITIZEN STARK?
NO SENSE COVERING THE SAME TERRITORY TWICE.

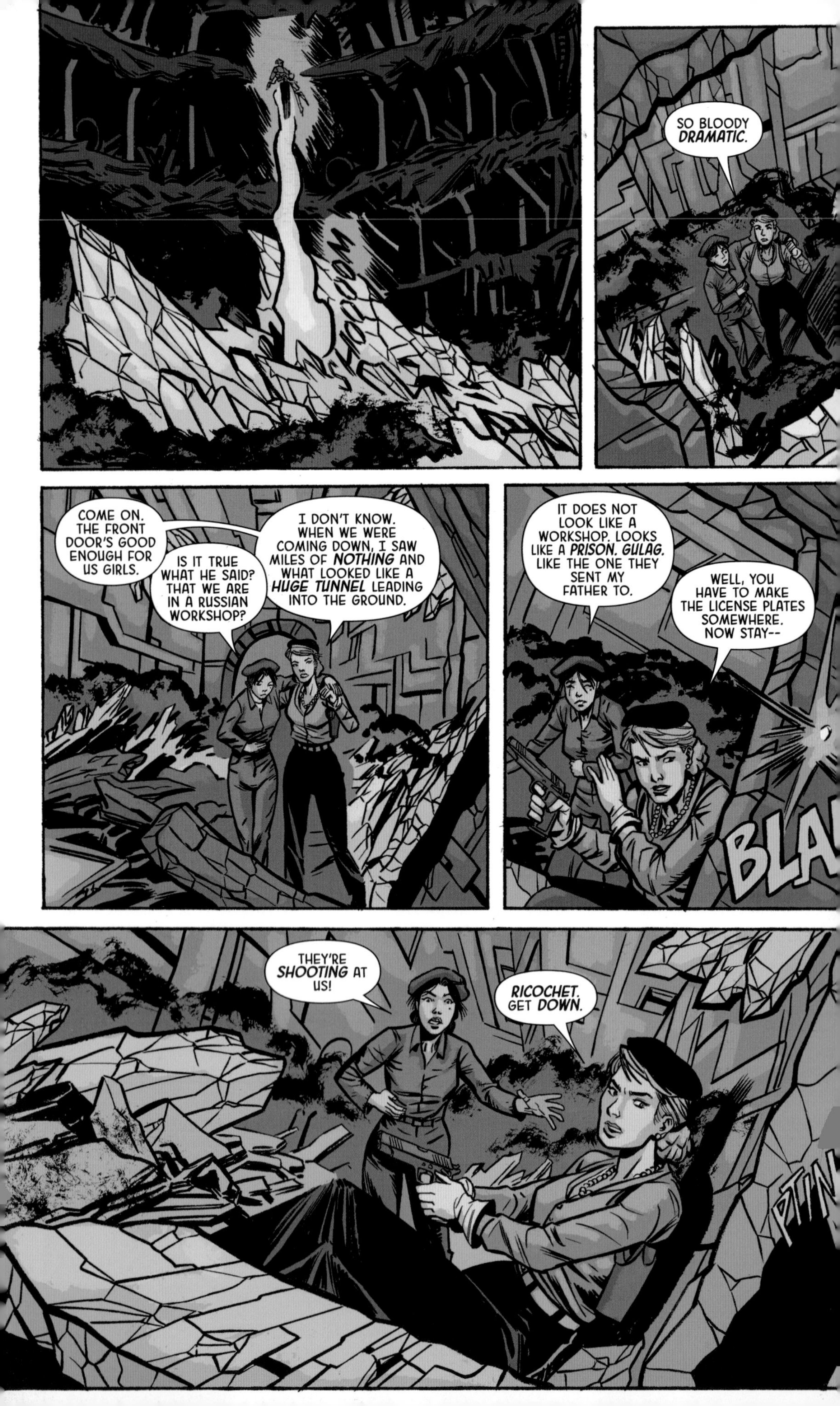
SO BLOODY *DRAMATIC*.
COME ON. THE FRONT DOOR'S GOOD ENOUGH FOR US GIRLS.
IS IT TRUE WHAT HE SAID? THAT WE ARE IN A RUSSIAN WORKSHOP?
I DON'T KNOW. WHEN WE WERE COMING DOWN, I SAW MILES OF *NOTHING* AND WHAT LOOKED LIKE A *HUGE TUNNEL* LEADING INTO THE GROUND.
IT DOES NOT LOOK LIKE A WORKSHOP. LOOKS LIKE A *PRISON. GULAG.* LIKE THE ONE THEY SENT MY FATHER TO.
WELL, YOU HAVE TO MAKE THE LICENSE PLATES SOMEWHERE. NOW STAY--
BLA
THEY'RE *SHOOTING* AT US!
RICOCHET. GET *DOWN*.
PTN

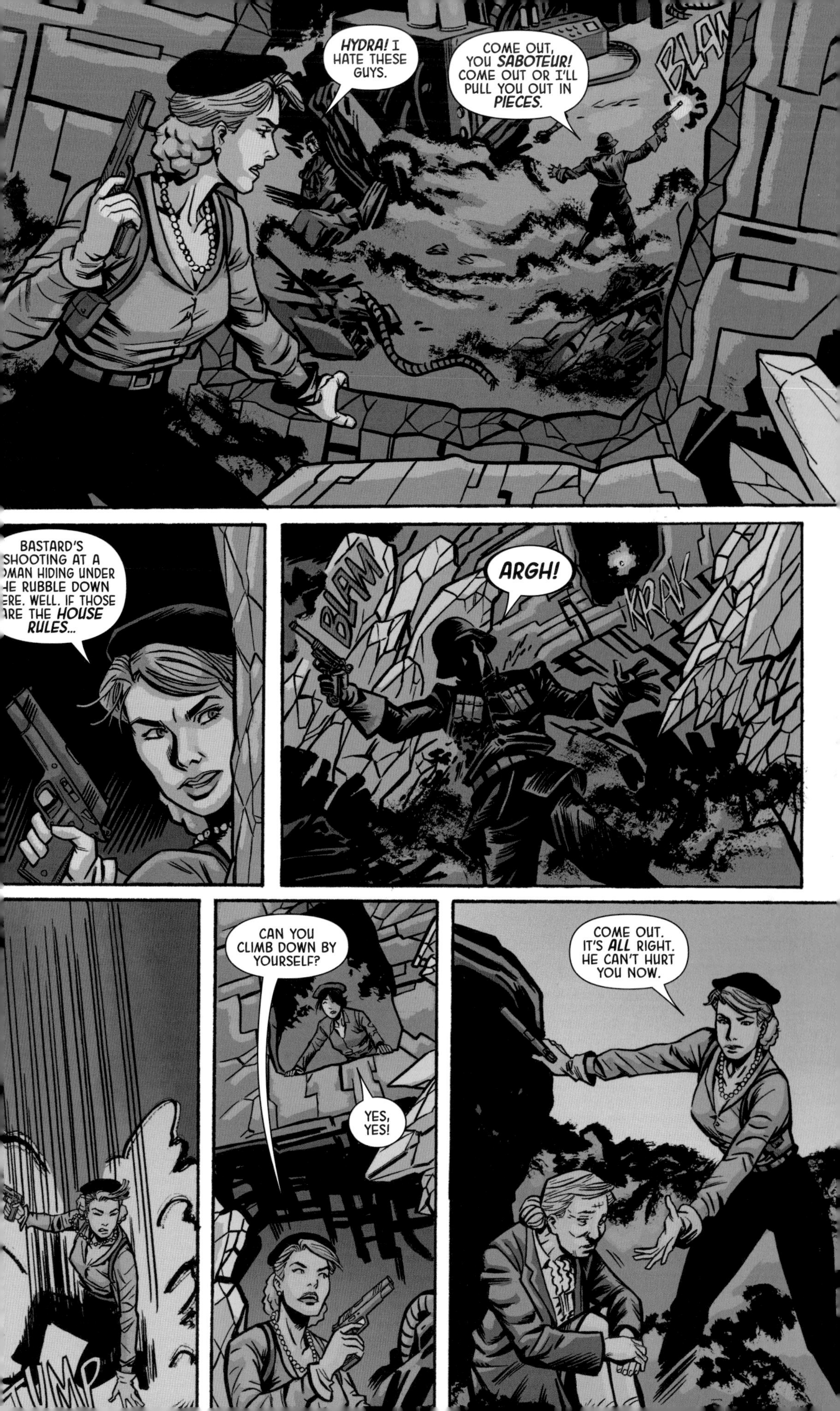
HYDRA! I HATE THESE GUYS.
COME OUT, YOU SABOTEUR! COME OUT OR I'LL PULL YOU OUT IN PIECES.
BLA
BASTARD'S SHOOTING AT A
OMAN HIDING UNDER
HE RUBBLE DOWN
ERE. WELL. IF THOSE
ARE THE HOUSE RULES...
BLAM
ARGH!
KRAK
THUMP
CAN YOU CLIMB DOWN BY YOURSELF?
YES, YES!
COME OUT. IT'S ALL RIGHT. HE CAN'T HURT YOU NOW.

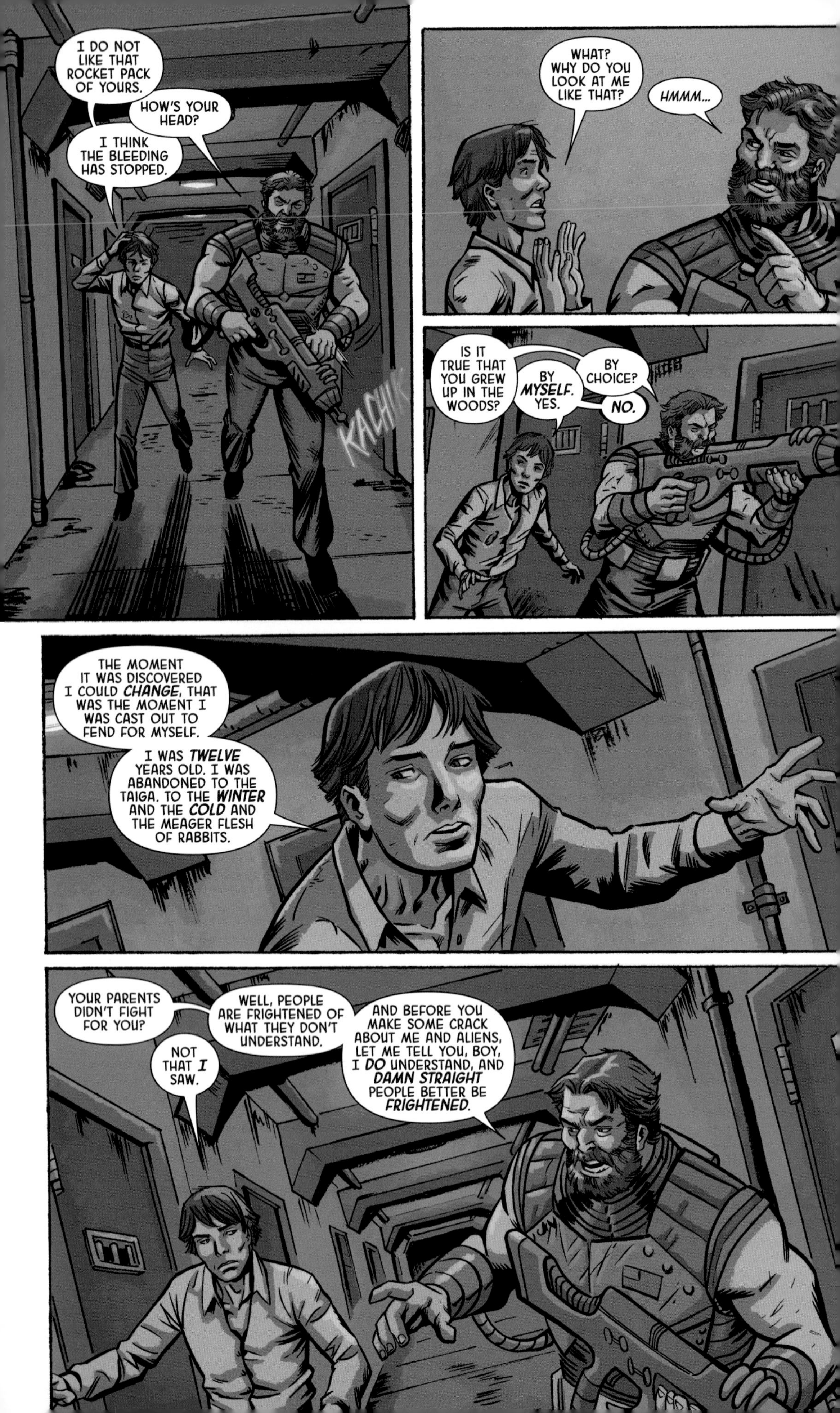
I DO NOT LIKE THAT ROCKET PACK OF YOURS.
HOW'S YOUR HEAD?
I THINK THE BLEEDING HAS STOPPED.
KACHIK
WHAT? WHY DO YOU LOOK AT ME LIKE THAT?
HMMM...
IS IT TRUE THAT YOU GREW UP IN THE WOODS?
BY MYSELF. YES.
BY CHOICE?
NO.
THE MOMENT IT WAS DISCOVERED I COULD CHANGE, THAT WAS THE MOMENT I WAS CAST OUT TO FEND FOR MYSELF.
I WAS TWELVE YEARS OLD. I WAS ABANDONED TO THE TAIGA. TO THE WINTER AND THE COLD AND THE MEAGER FLESH OF RABBITS.
YOUR PARENTS DIDN'T FIGHT FOR YOU?
NOT THAT I SAW.
WELL, PEOPLE ARE FRIGHTENED OF WHAT THEY DON'T UNDERSTAND.
AND BEFORE YOU MAKE SOME CRACK ABOUT ME AND ALIENS, LET ME TELL YOU, BOY, I DO UNDERSTAND, AND DAMN STRAIGHT PEOPLE BETTER BE FRIGHTENED.

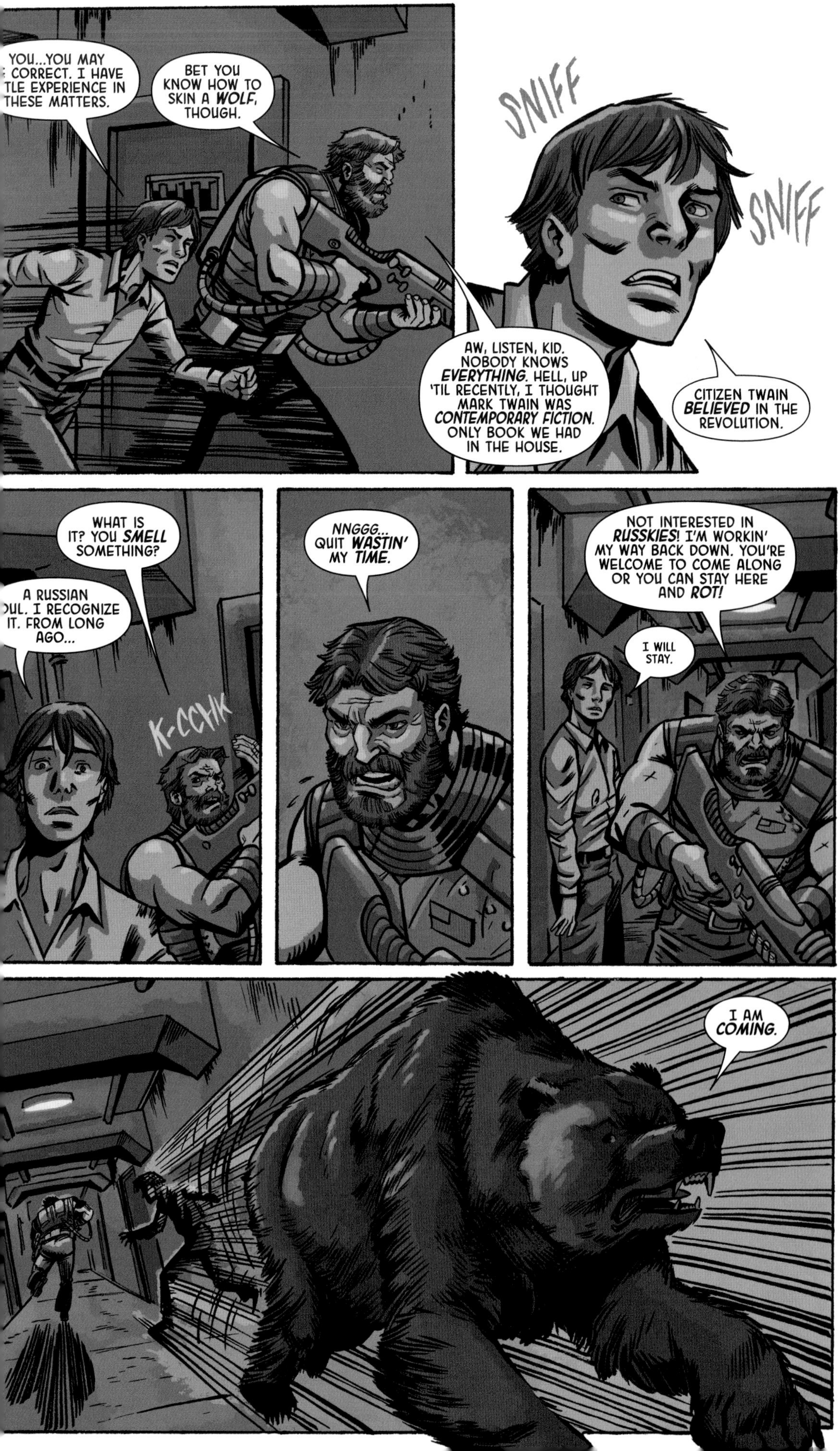

YOU...YOU MAY
CORRECT. I HAVE
TLE EXPERIENCE IN
THESE MATTERS.
BET YOU KNOW HOW TO SKIN A *WOLF*, THOUGH.
SNIFF
SNIFF
AW, LISTEN, KID. NOBODY KNOWS *EVERYTHING*. HELL, UP 'TIL RECENTLY, I THOUGHT MARK TWAIN WAS *CONTEMPORARY FICTION*. ONLY BOOK WE HAD IN THE HOUSE.
CITIZEN TWAIN *BELIEVED* IN THE REVOLUTION.
WHAT IS IT? YOU *SMELL* SOMETHING?
A RUSSIAN
OUL. I RECOGNIZE
IT. FROM LONG
AGO...
K-CCHK
NNGGG... QUIT *WASTIN'* MY *TIME*.
NOT INTERESTED IN *RUSSKIES*! I'M WORKIN' MY WAY BACK DOWN. YOU'RE WELCOME TO COME ALONG OR YOU CAN STAY HERE AND *ROT*!
I WILL STAY.
I AM *COMING*.

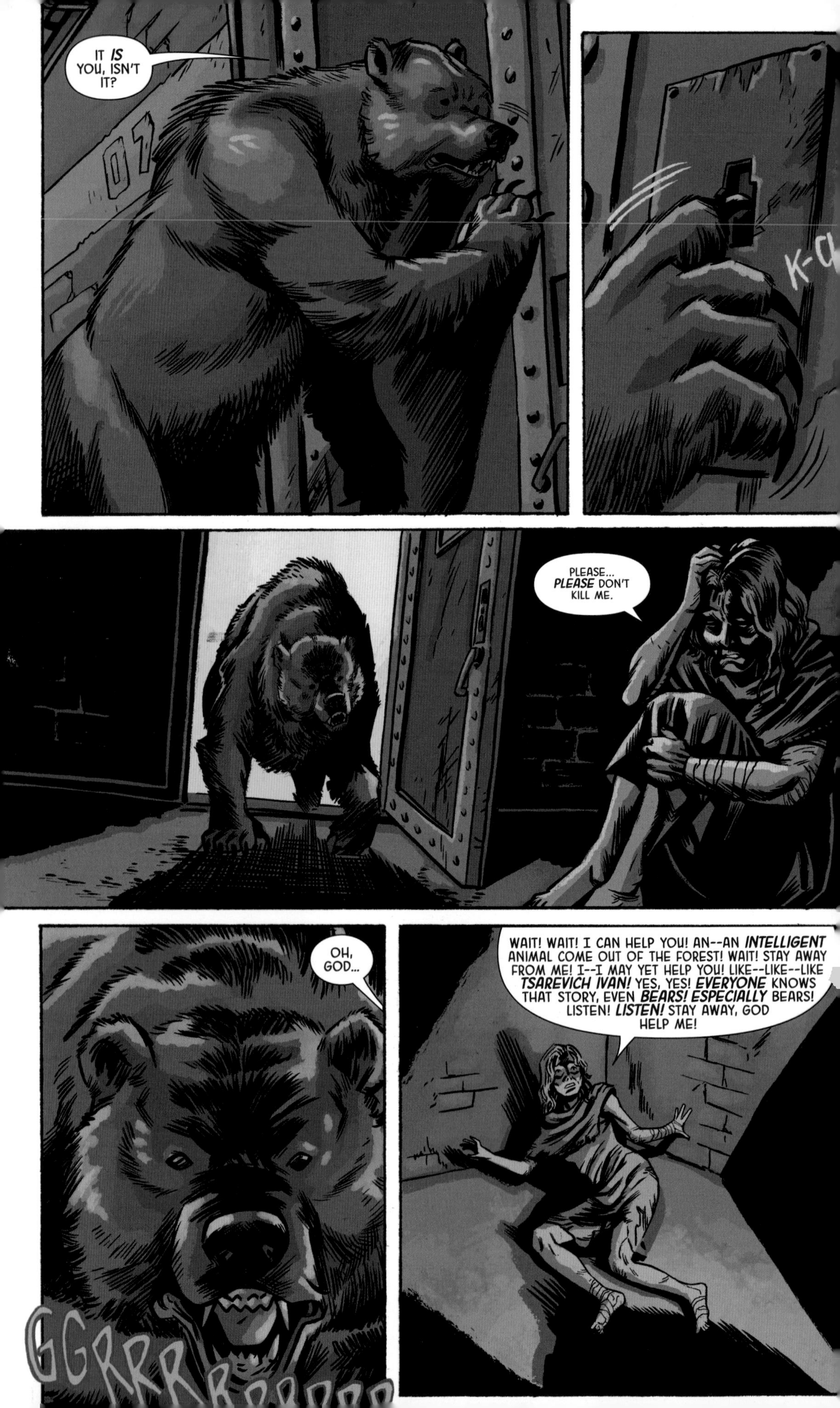

IT IS YOU, ISN'T IT?
K-C
PLEASE... PLEASE DON'T KILL ME.
OH, GOD...
GGRRRRRRRRR
WAIT! WAIT! I CAN HELP YOU! AN--AN INTELLIGENT ANIMAL COME OUT OF THE FOREST! WAIT! STAY AWAY FROM ME! I--I MAY YET HELP YOU! LIKE--LIKE--LIKE TSAREVICH IVAN! YES, YES! EVERYONE KNOWS THAT STORY, EVEN BEARS! ESPECIALLY BEARS! LISTEN! LISTEN! STAY AWAY, GOD HELP ME!

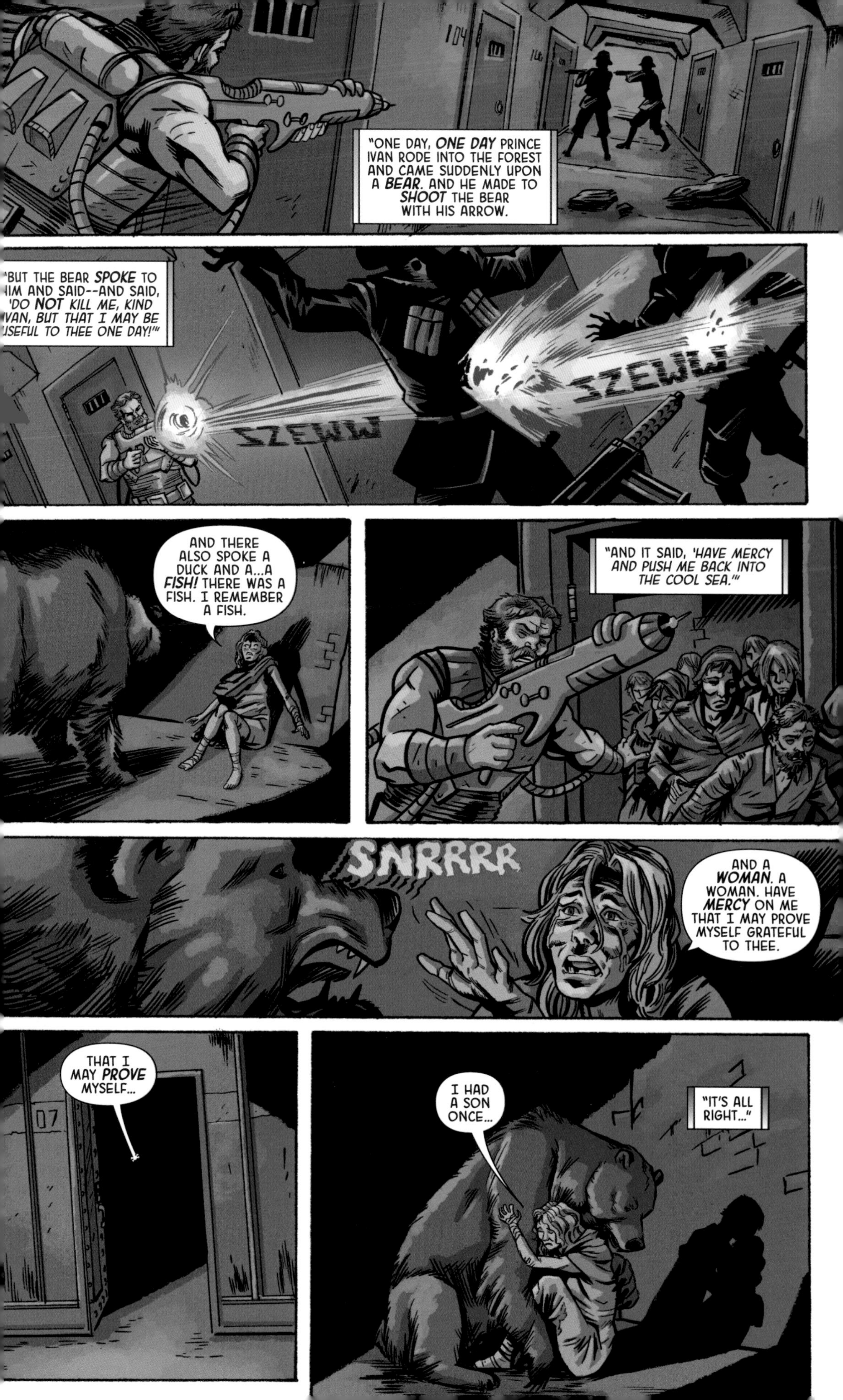
"ONE DAY, ONE DAY PRINCE IVAN RODE INTO THE FOREST AND CAME SUDDENLY UPON A BEAR. AND HE MADE TO SHOOT THE BEAR WITH HIS ARROW.
'BUT THE BEAR SPOKE TO HIM AND SAID--AND SAID, 'DO NOT KILL ME, KIND IVAN, BUT THAT I MAY BE USEFUL TO THEE ONE DAY!'"
SZEWW
SZEWW
AND THERE ALSO SPOKE A DUCK AND A...A FISH! THERE WAS A FISH. I REMEMBER A FISH.
"AND IT SAID, 'HAVE MERCY AND PUSH ME BACK INTO THE COOL SEA.'"
SNRRRR
AND A WOMAN. A WOMAN. HAVE MERCY ON ME THAT I MAY PROVE MYSELF GRATEFUL TO THEE.
THAT I MAY PROVE MYSELF...
I HAD A SON ONCE...
"IT'S ALL RIGHT..."

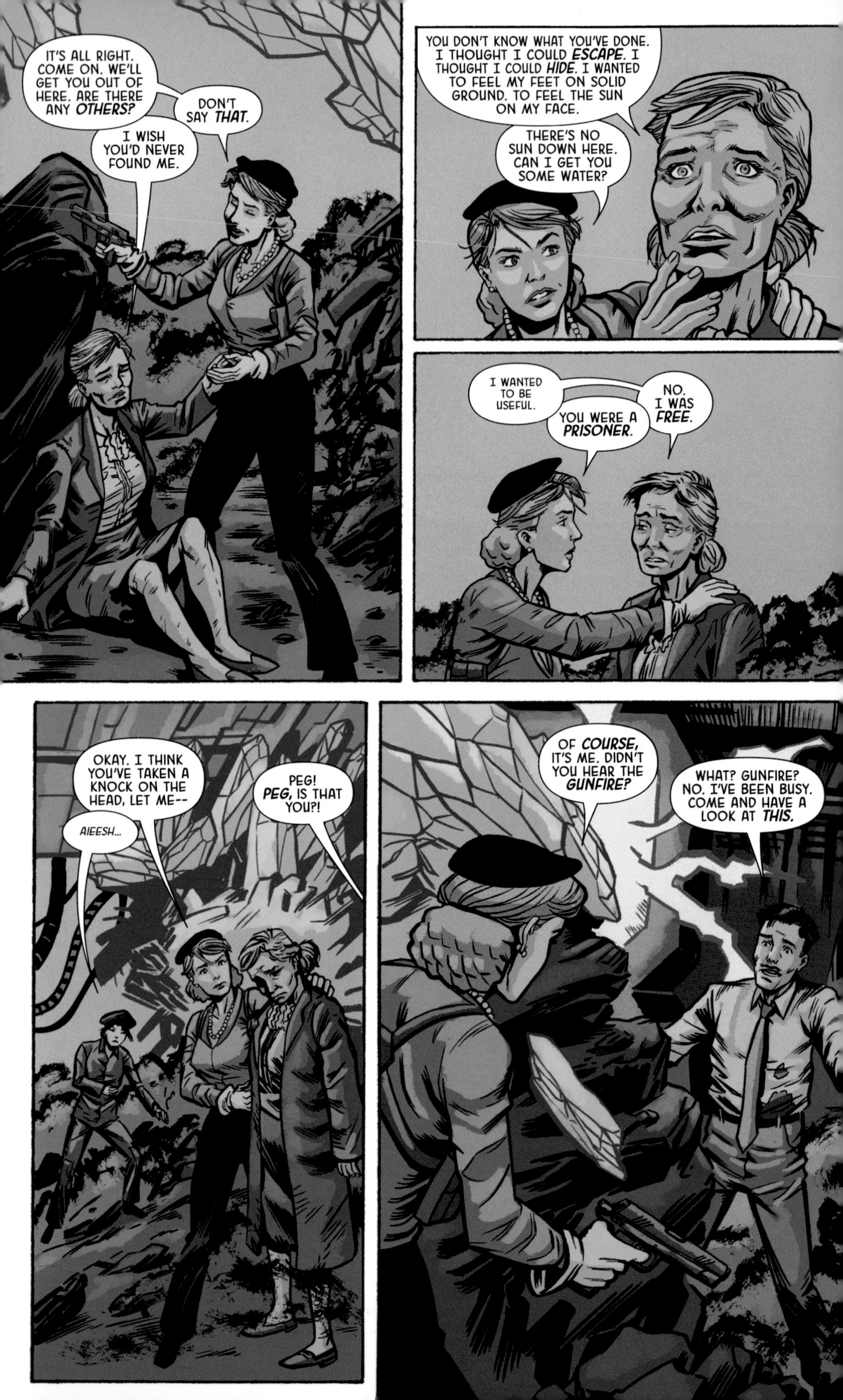
IT'S ALL RIGHT. COME ON. WE'LL GET YOU OUT OF HERE. ARE THERE ANY OTHERS?
DON'T SAY THAT.
I WISH YOU'D NEVER FOUND ME.
YOU DON'T KNOW WHAT YOU'VE DONE. I THOUGHT I COULD ESCAPE. I THOUGHT I COULD HIDE. I WANTED TO FEEL MY FEET ON SOLID GROUND. TO FEEL THE SUN ON MY FACE.
THERE'S NO SUN DOWN HERE. CAN I GET YOU SOME WATER?
I WANTED TO BE USEFUL.
YOU WERE A PRISONER.
NO. I WAS FREE.
OKAY. I THINK YOU'VE TAKEN A KNOCK ON THE HEAD, LET ME--
AIEESH...
PEG! PEG, IS THAT YOU?!
OF COURSE, IT'S ME. DIDN'T YOU HEAR THE GUNFIRE?
WHAT? GUNFIRE? NO. I'VE BEEN BUSY. COME AND HAVE A LOOK AT THIS.

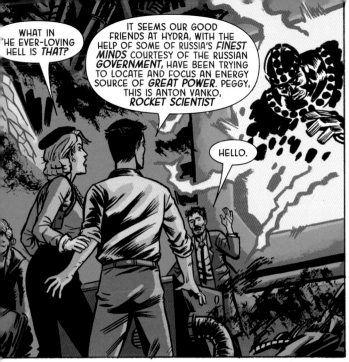

WHAT IN THE EVER-LOVING HELL IS *THAT?*

IT SEEMS OUR GOOD FRIENDS AT HYDRA, WITH THE HELP OF SOME OF RUSSIA'S *FINEST MINDS* COURTESY OF THE RUSSIAN *GOVERNMENT*, HAVE BEEN TRYING TO LOCATE AND FOCUS AN ENERGY SOURCE OF *GREAT POWER.* PEGGY, THIS IS ANTON VANKO, *ROCKET SCIENTIST*

HELLO.

I HAVE COME FOR YOU.

LOOKS LIKE THEY'VE DONE MORE THAN *TRY.*

YOU WERE A PARTY TO THIS? SURELY YOU KNOW WHAT HYDRA'S *CAPABLE* OF. DID YOU THINK YOU WERE DEVELOPING A BETTER METHOD FOR *PEELING BEETS?*

YOU DO *NOT* JUDGE US. WE WERE TRYING TO CONTINUE OUR WORK, *ANY* WORK, IN THE FACE OF *STARVATION* AND *DEATH.*

I FEEL LIKE WE'RE FACING AT LEAST *ONE* OF THOSE THINGS.

DON'T SAY THAT.

WHO IS SHE TALKING TO?

I WAS WRONG TO THINK I COULD PREVENT THIS.

STOP.

MY LOVE.

YOU ARE WRONG.

OH. *TERRIFIC.*

WHO **ARE** YOU?

IT DOESN'T MATTER. NOT WHO I WAS.

IT MATTERS TO ME. WHAT IS THAT...THAT THING TO YOU?

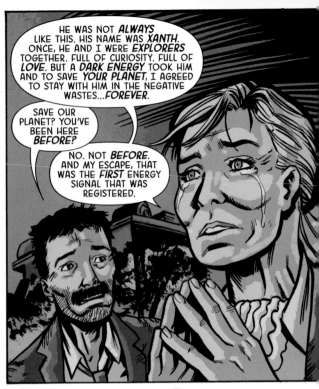

HE WAS NOT **ALWAYS** LIKE THIS. HIS NAME WAS **XANTH**. ONCE, HE AND I WERE **EXPLORERS** TOGETHER. FULL OF CURIOSITY. FULL OF **LOVE**. BUT A **DARK ENERGY** TOOK HIM AND TO SAVE **YOUR PLANET**, I AGREED TO STAY WITH HIM IN THE NEGATIVE WASTES...**FOREVER**.

SAVE OUR PLANET? YOU'VE BEEN HERE **BEFORE**?

NO. NOT **BEFORE**. AND MY ESCAPE, THAT WAS THE **FIRST** ENERGY SIGNAL THAT WAS REGISTERED.

BUT YOU WERE HELPING US! YOU WERE HELPING **ME**.

JUST **ENOUGH** TO BE ABLE TO ST' HERE. WITH YOU. EN TO KEEP YOU CLOS' THE SOLUTION B NEVER **QUITE** GET THERE.

MY APOLOGIES BUT I MAY HAVE **UNDERESTIMATED** YOUR **INTELLIGENCE**.

SO, IS THAT **THING** COMING THROUGH OR WHAT?

THE ENERGY OUTPUT IS **IMMENSE** BUT **STABLE**. IT'S MORE LIKE HE'S TRAPPED IN A REVOLVING DOOR. NOT SURE **WHICH WAY** IT'S GOING TO TURN, THOUGH.

WHEN YOU FOUND AND **ACTIVATED** / SHIP, THAT WAS THE MOMENT XANT FOUND ME. I THOUGHT IT WAS A **WASTELAND**. I NEVER EXPECTED TO FIND THESE PEOPLE.

THIS WILL ONLY STOP WHEN I RETURN TO HIM. I NEVER MEANT FOR ANY OF THIS TO HAPPEN. I JUST WANTED--

YEAH, YEAH. SUN ON YOUR FACE. FEET ON TH' GROUND. BLOODY **SCIENTISTS** AND YOUR **TUNNEL VISION**.

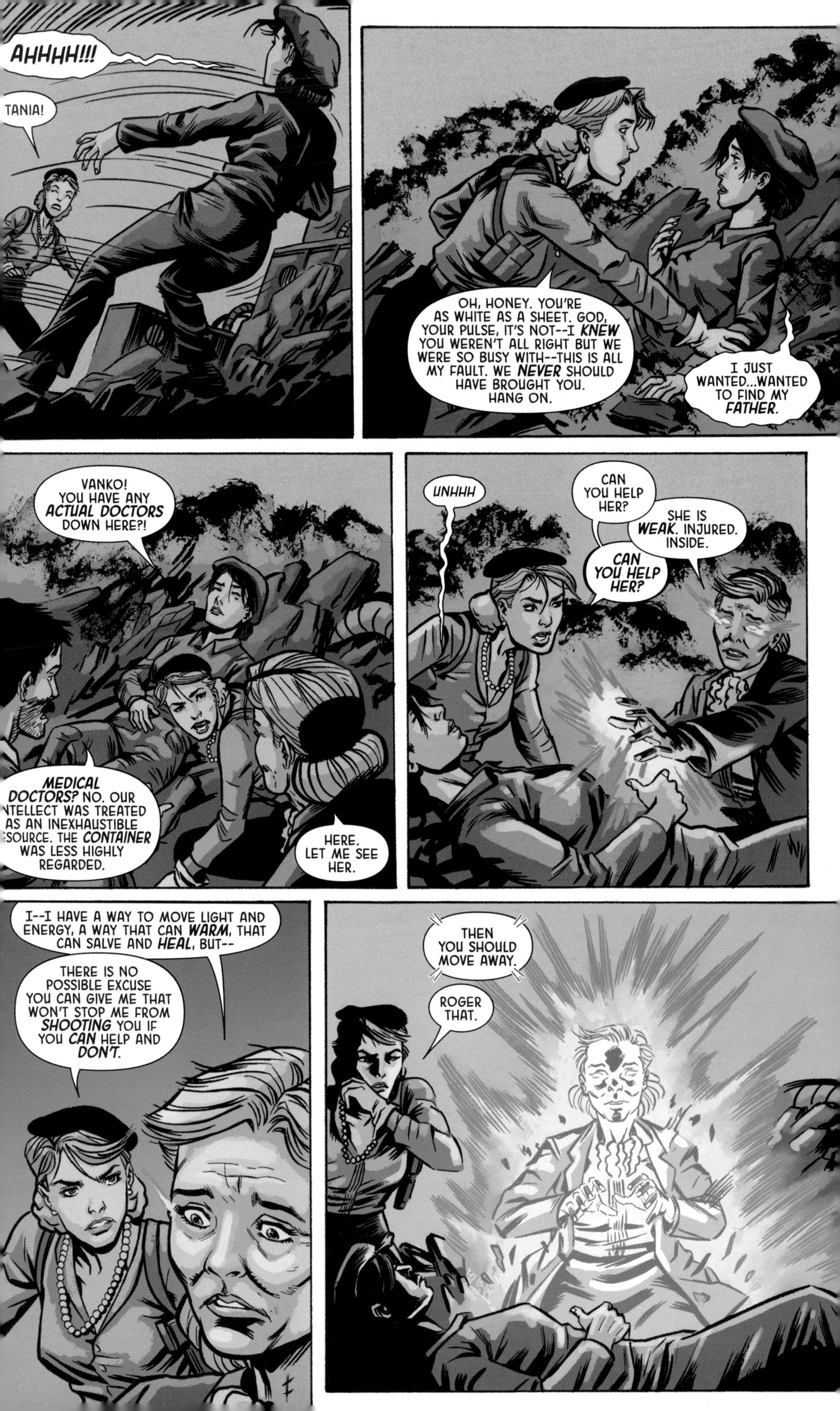
AHHHH!!!
TANIA!
OH, HONEY. YOU'RE AS WHITE AS A SHEET. GOD, YOUR PULSE, IT'S NOT--I KNEW YOU WEREN'T ALL RIGHT BUT WE WERE SO BUSY WITH--THIS IS ALL MY FAULT. WE NEVER SHOULD HAVE BROUGHT YOU. HANG ON.
I JUST WANTED...WANTED TO FIND MY FATHER.
VANKO! YOU HAVE ANY ACTUAL DOCTORS DOWN HERE?!
MEDICAL DOCTORS? NO. OUR NTELLECT WAS TREATED AS AN INEXHAUSTIBLE ESOURCE. THE CONTAINER WAS LESS HIGHLY REGARDED.
HERE. LET ME SEE HER.
UNHHH
CAN YOU HELP HER?
SHE IS WEAK. INJURED. INSIDE.
CAN YOU HELP HER?
I--I HAVE A WAY TO MOVE LIGHT AND ENERGY, A WAY THAT CAN WARM, THAT CAN SALVE AND HEAL, BUT--
THERE IS NO POSSIBLE EXCUSE YOU CAN GIVE ME THAT WON'T STOP ME FROM SHOOTING YOU IF YOU CAN HELP AND DON'T.
THEN YOU SHOULD MOVE AWAY.
ROGER THAT.

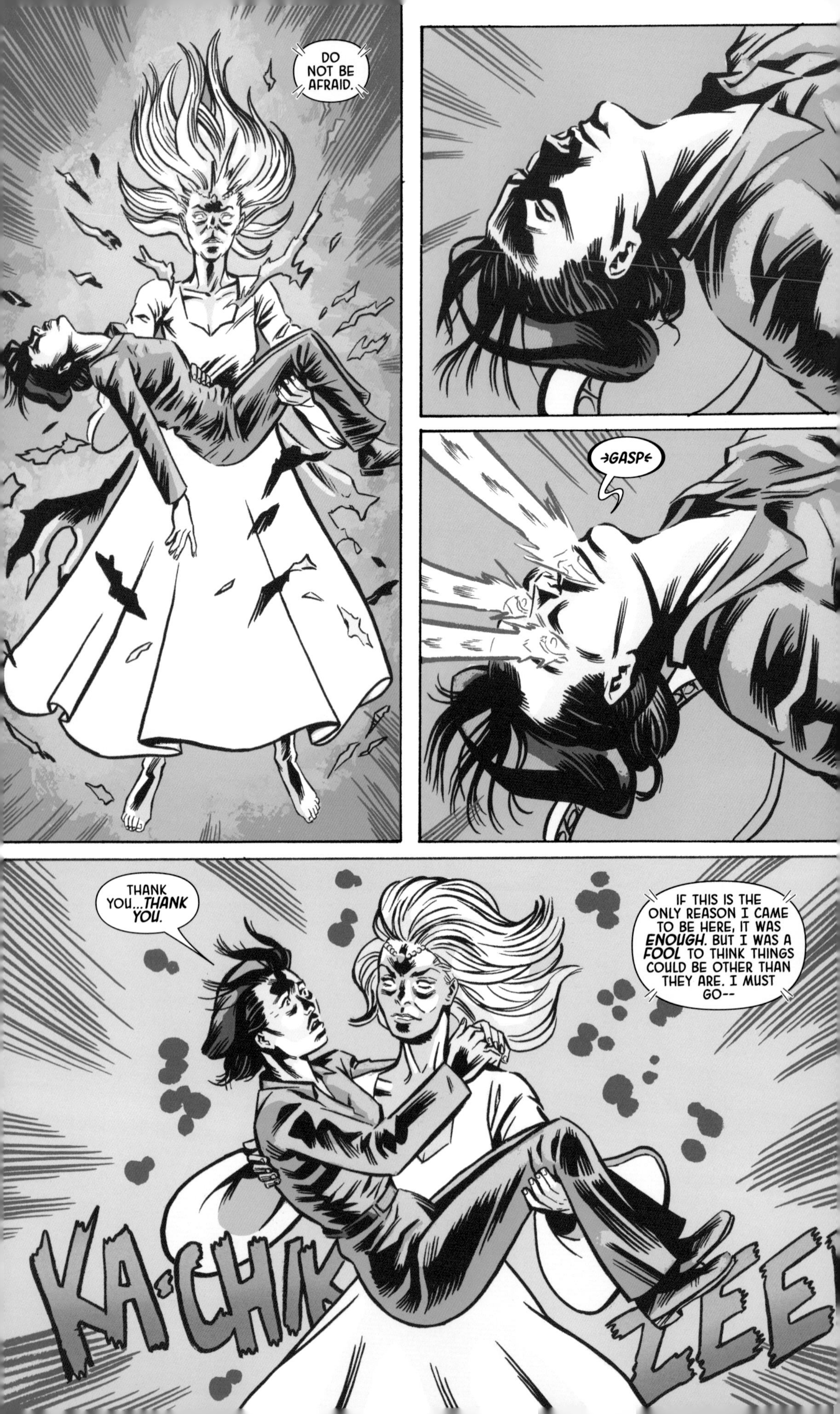
DO NOT BE AFRAID.
GASP
THANK YOU...THANK YOU.
IF THIS IS THE ONLY REASON I CAME TO BE HERE, IT WAS ENOUGH. BUT I WAS A FOOL TO THINK THINGS COULD BE OTHER THAN THEY ARE. I MUST GO--
KA-CHK
ZEE

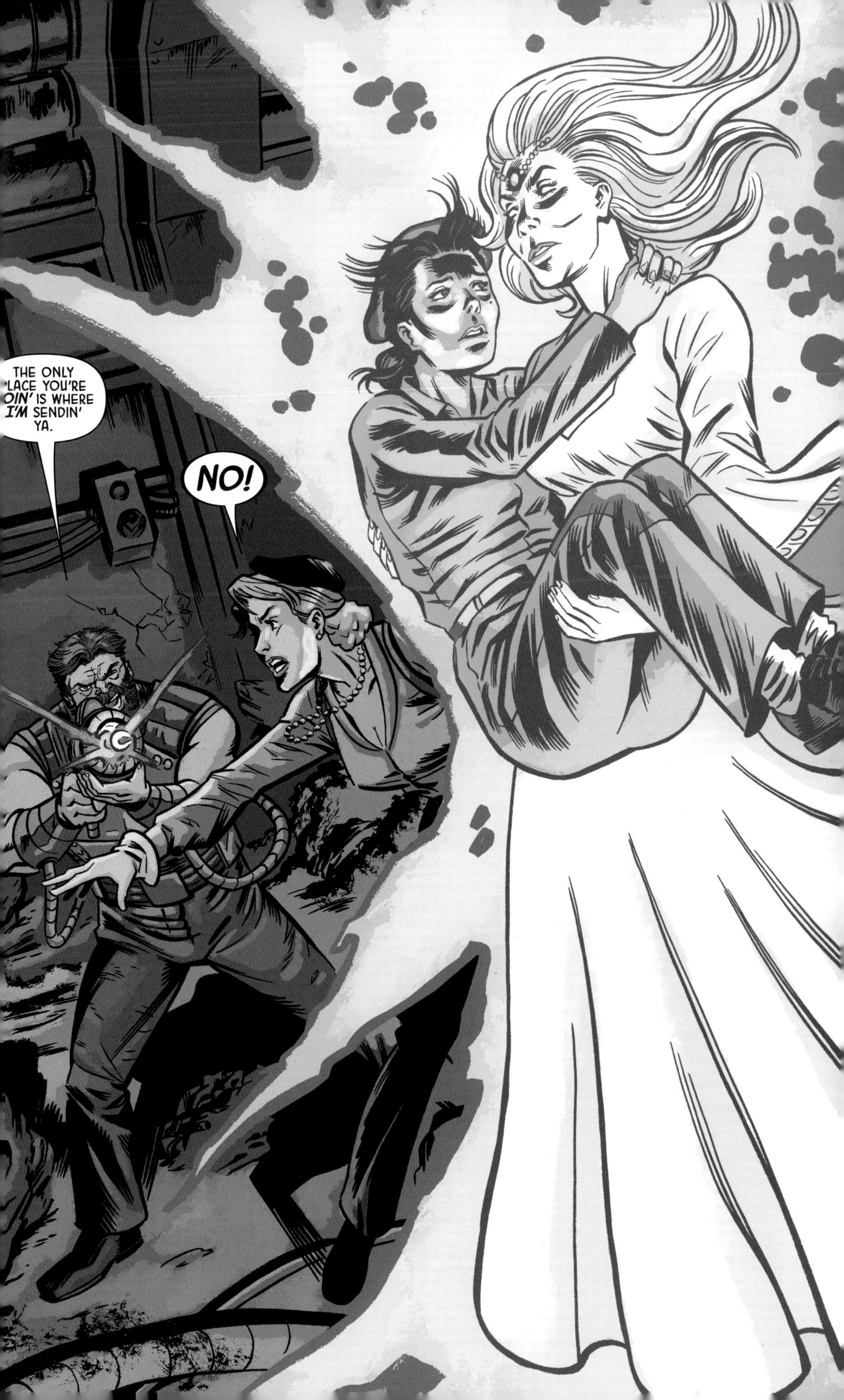
THE ONLY 'LACE YOU'RE OIN' IS WHERE I'M SENDIN' YA.
NO!

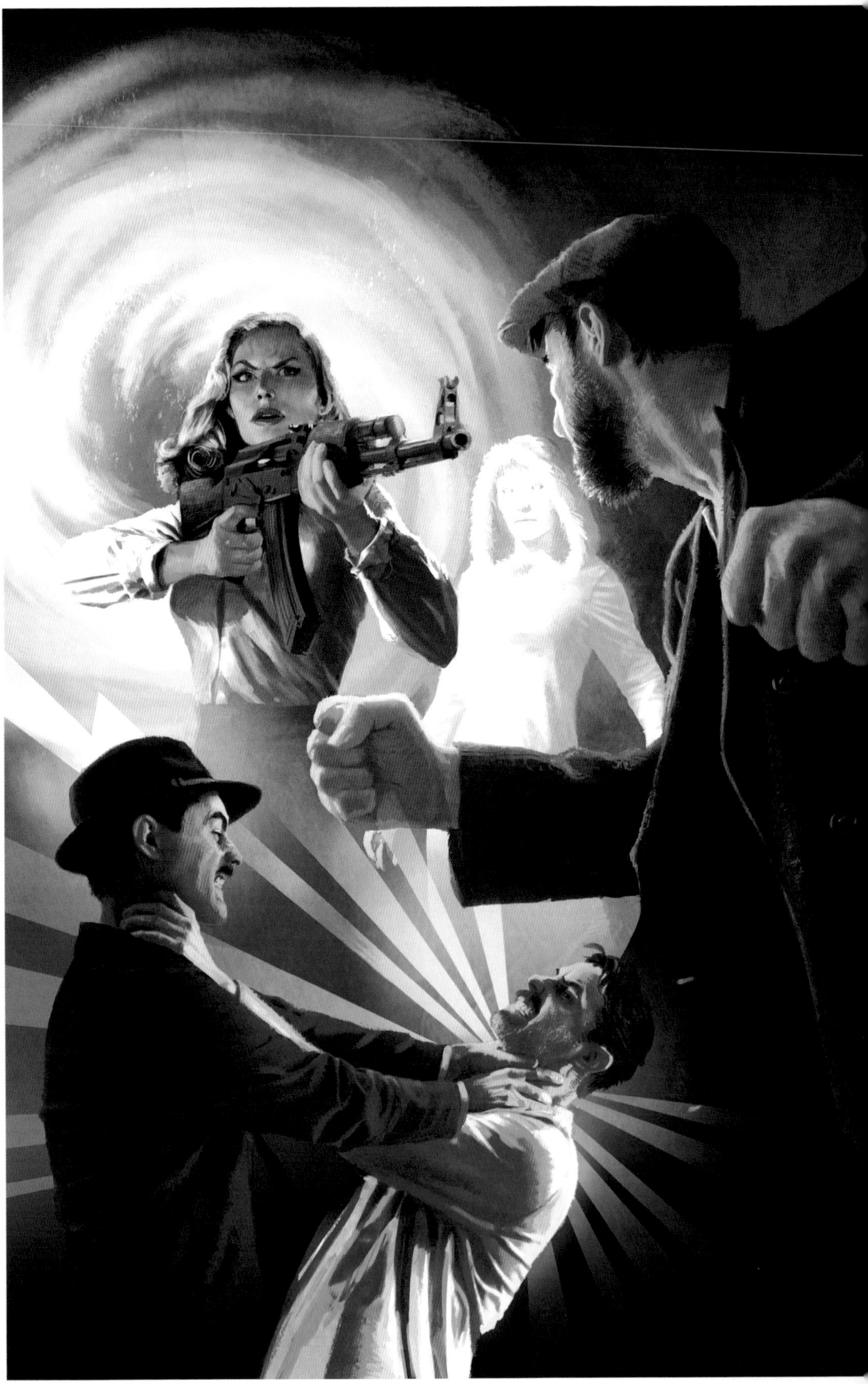

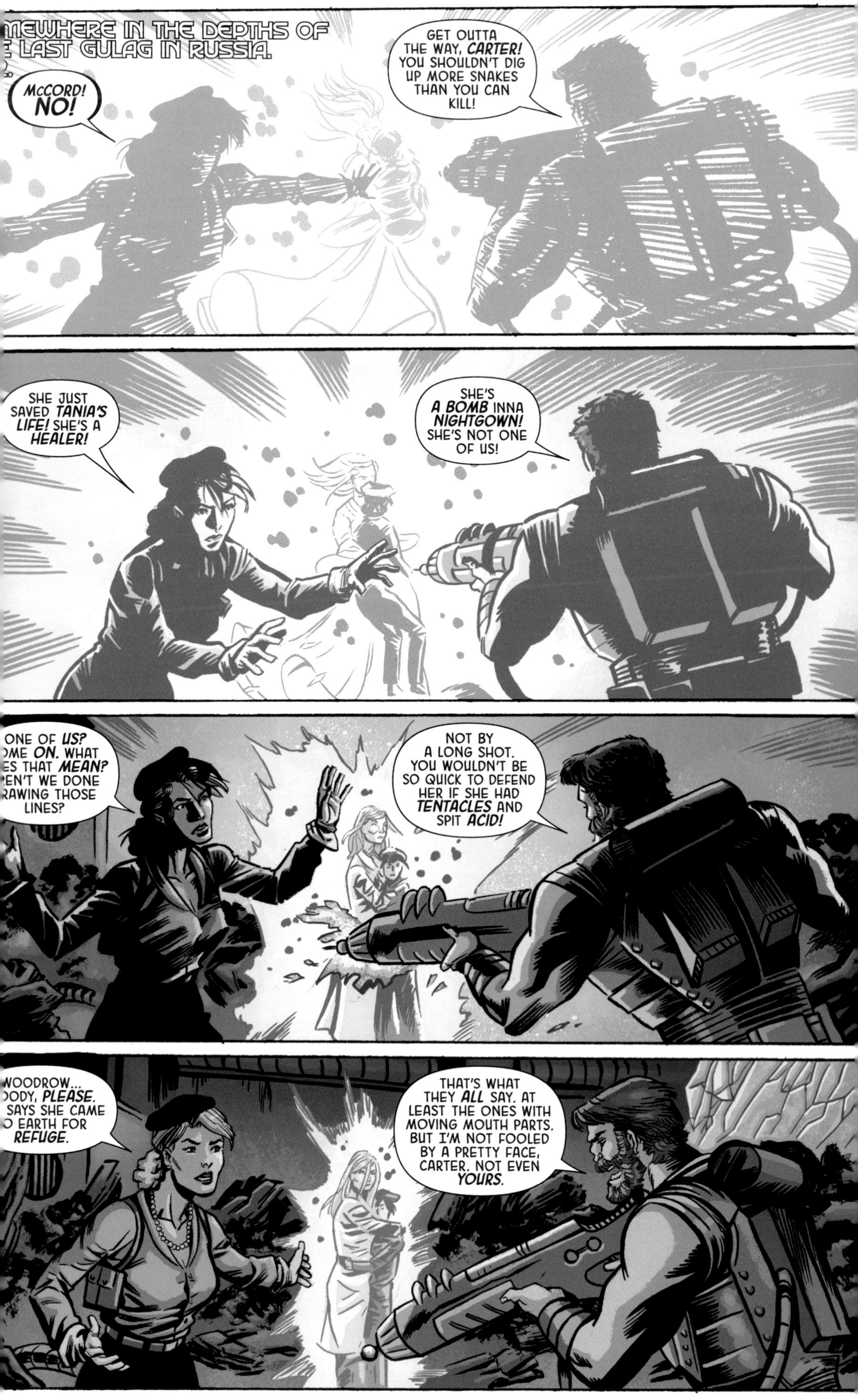
MEWHERE IN THE DEPTHS OF
E LAST GULAG IN RUSSIA.
McCORD! NO!
GET OUTTA THE WAY, CARTER! YOU SHOULDN'T DIG UP MORE SNAKES THAN YOU CAN KILL!
SHE JUST SAVED TANIA'S LIFE! SHE'S A HEALER!
SHE'S A BOMB INNA NIGHTGOWN! SHE'S NOT ONE OF US!
ONE OF US? OME ON. WHAT ES THAT MEAN? REN'T WE DONE RAWING THOSE LINES?
NOT BY A LONG SHOT. YOU WOULDN'T BE SO QUICK TO DEFEND HER IF SHE HAD TENTACLES AND SPIT ACID!
WOODROW... ODY, PLEASE. SAYS SHE CAME O EARTH FOR REFUGE.
THAT'S WHAT THEY ALL SAY. AT LEAST THE ONES WITH MOVING MOUTH PARTS. BUT I'M NOT FOOLED BY A PRETTY FACE, CARTER. NOT EVEN YOURS.

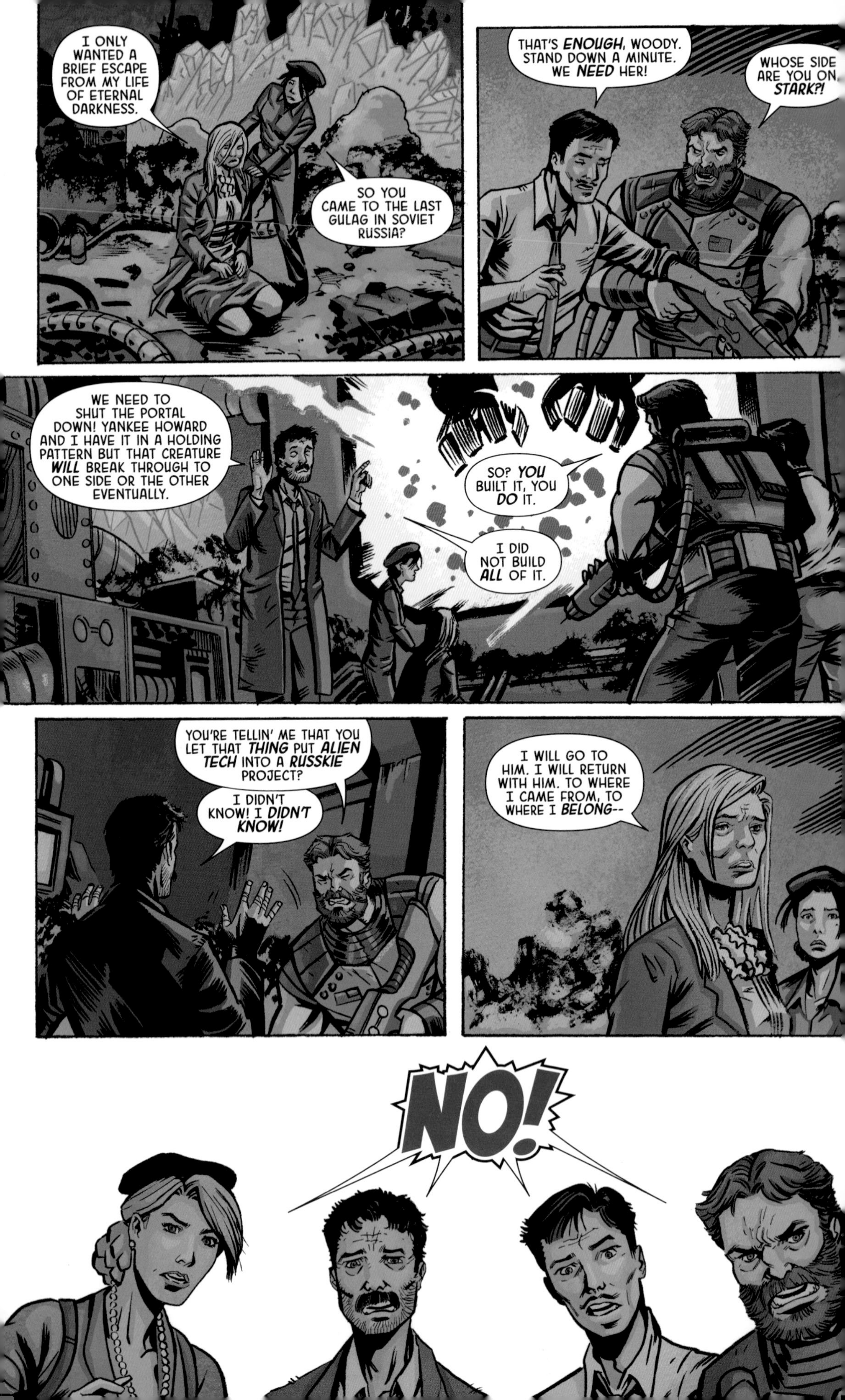
I ONLY WANTED A BRIEF ESCAPE FROM MY LIFE OF ETERNAL DARKNESS.
SO YOU CAME TO THE LAST GULAG IN SOVIET RUSSIA?
THAT'S ENOUGH, WOODY. STAND DOWN A MINUTE. WE NEED HER!
WHOSE SIDE ARE YOU ON, STARK?!
WE NEED TO SHUT THE PORTAL DOWN! YANKEE HOWARD AND I HAVE IT IN A HOLDING PATTERN BUT THAT CREATURE WILL BREAK THROUGH TO ONE SIDE OR THE OTHER EVENTUALLY.
SO? YOU BUILT IT, YOU DO IT.
I DID NOT BUILD ALL OF IT.
YOU'RE TELLIN' ME THAT YOU LET THAT THING PUT ALIEN TECH INTO A RUSSKIE PROJECT?
I DIDN'T KNOW! I DIDN'T KNOW!
I WILL GO TO HIM. I WILL RETURN WITH HIM. TO WHERE I CAME FROM, TO WHERE I BELONG--
NO!

SHE MAY BE THE ONLY ONE WHO CAN HELP HERE. SO *GET. IN. LINE.*

SHAREEN, *PLEASE.*

HE WAS MY ONE TRUE LOVE AND I ABANDONED HIM.

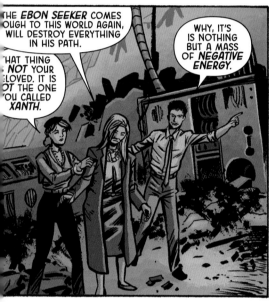

HE *EBON SEEKER* COMES OUGH TO THIS WORLD AGAIN, WILL DESTROY EVERYTHING IN HIS PATH.

HAT THING S *NOT* YOUR LOVED. IT IS OT THE ONE OU CALLED *XANTH.*

WHY, IT'S IS NOTHING BUT A MASS OF *NEGATIVE ENERGY.*

WELL, WE'VE *ALL* HAD RELATIONSHIPS LIKE THAT.

HE IS A *LIVING BLACK HOLE!* ARE YOU JESTING?

IT'S ALL RIGHT. WE'RE HUMAN. IT'S A CRISIS. IT'S WHAT WE SEEM TO DO WHEN WE'RE NOT SHOOTING EACH OTHER.

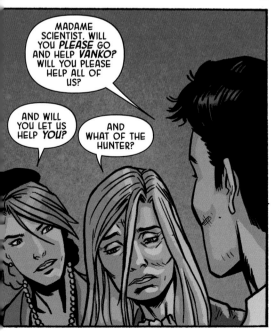

MADAME SCIENTIST. WILL YOU *PLEASE* GO AND HELP *VANKO?* WILL YOU PLEASE HELP ALL OF US?

AND WILL YOU LET US HELP *YOU?*

AND WHAT OF THE HUNTER?

ONE THING AT A TIME.

GRIND

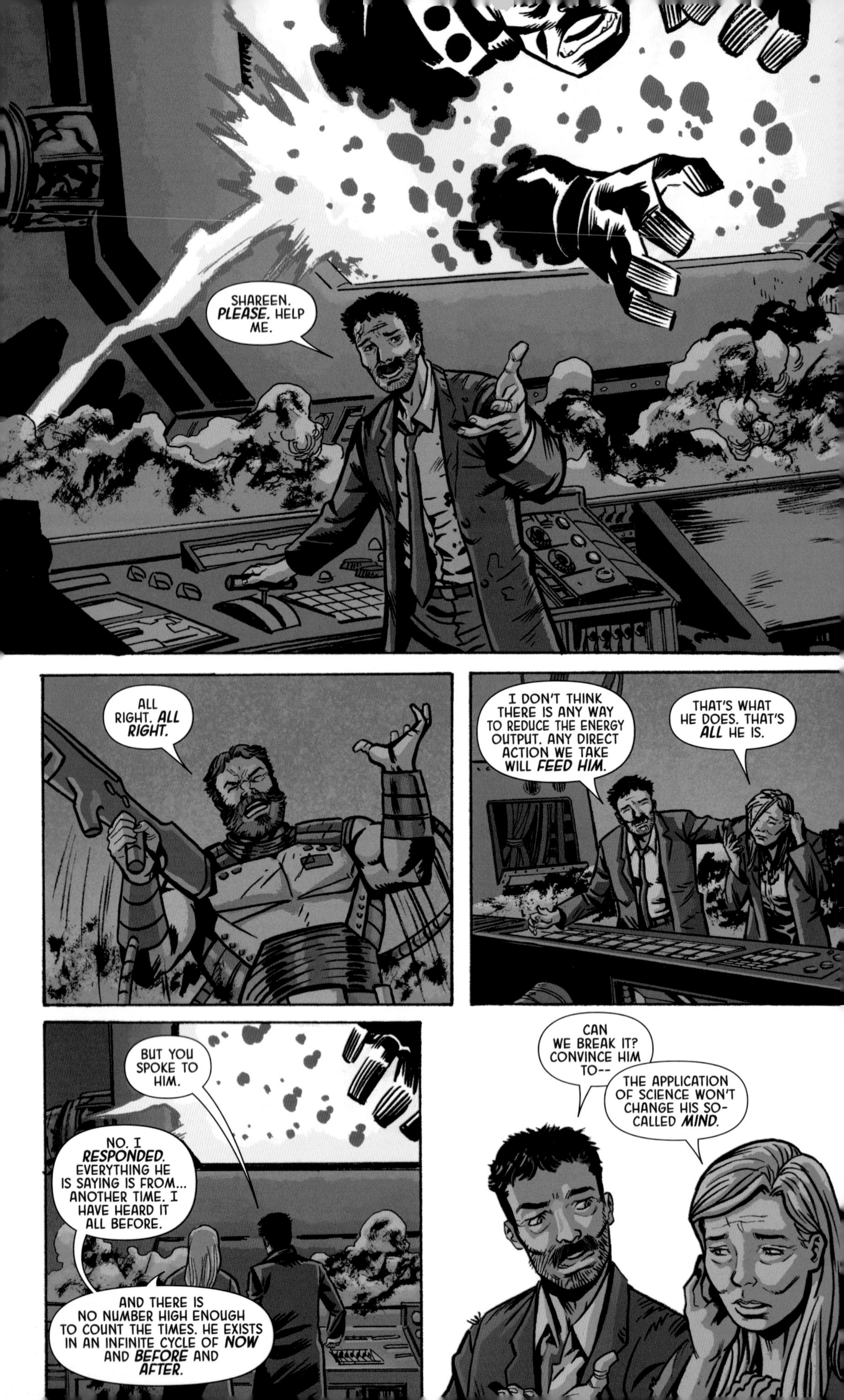
SHAREEN. PLEASE. HELP ME.
ALL RIGHT. ALL RIGHT.
I DON'T THINK THERE IS ANY WAY TO REDUCE THE ENERGY OUTPUT. ANY DIRECT ACTION WE TAKE WILL FEED HIM.
THAT'S WHAT HE DOES. THAT'S ALL HE IS.
BUT YOU SPOKE TO HIM.
NO. I RESPONDED. EVERYTHING HE IS SAYING IS FROM... ANOTHER TIME. I HAVE HEARD IT ALL BEFORE.
AND THERE IS NO NUMBER HIGH ENOUGH TO COUNT THE TIMES. HE EXISTS IN AN INFINITE CYCLE OF NOW AND BEFORE AND AFTER.
CAN WE BREAK IT? CONVINCE HIM TO--
THE APPLICATION OF SCIENCE WON'T CHANGE HIS SO-CALLED MIND.

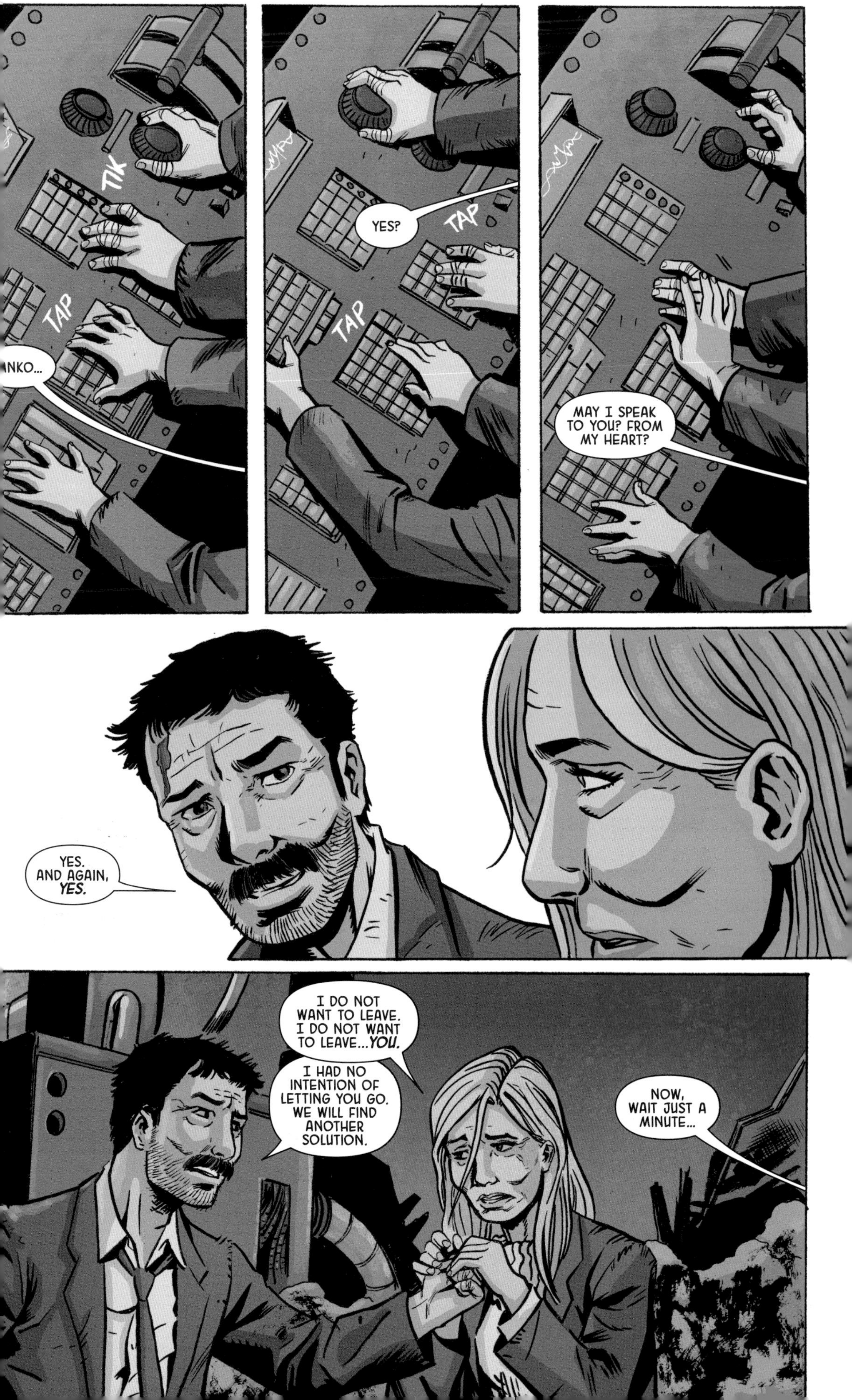
TIK
TAP
NKO...
YES?
TAP
TAP
MAY I SPEAK TO YOU? FROM MY HEART?
YES. AND AGAIN, *YES.*
I DO NOT WANT TO LEAVE. I DO NOT WANT TO LEAVE...*YOU.*
I HAD NO INTENTION OF LETTING YOU GO. WE WILL FIND ANOTHER SOLUTION.
NOW, WAIT JUST A MINUTE...

THIS IS NONE OF YOUR BUSINESS, STARK.

THE *HELL* IT ISN'T. YOU THINK I DON'T SEE WHAT CAN HAPPEN HERE?

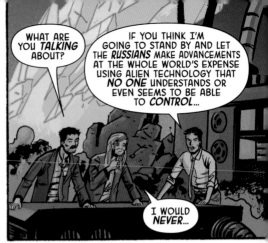

WHAT ARE YOU *TALKING* ABOUT?

IF YOU THINK I'M GOING TO STAND BY AND LET THE *RUSSIANS* MAKE ADVANCEMENTS AT THE WHOLE WORLD'S EXPENSE USING ALIEN TECHNOLOGY THAT *NO ONE* UNDERSTANDS OR EVEN SEEMS TO BE ABLE TO *CONTROL*...

I WOULD *NEVER*...

YOU'RE NOT WORRIED ABOUT THE *WORLD*. YOU'RE WORRIED ABOUT *AMERICA'S* PLACE *IN IT.*

THIS IS *IRRESPONSIBLE!*

THAT'S NOT IT. YOU THINK IT'S AN *ADVANTAGE*, THAT IT'S *UNFAIR.*

LET ME TELL YOU WHAT IS *UNFAIR.* BEING CRIPPLED BY A SYSTEM THAT ONLY EVER LETS YOU HAVE *LESS* THAN YOU NEED BUT TELLS YOU IT'S *ENOUGH.*

YOU DID IT TO *YOURSELVES.*

IT WAS *NOT MY* DOING!

AND KEEPING *HER* AS A *RESOURCE* WON' FIX IT. YOU CAN'T DO THIS. I NOT *RIGHT.* IT'S IRRESPONSIBL YOU'RE *NOT READY.*

WE'RE NOT READY? *WE'RE* NOT READY? SHOULD WE WAIT FOR THE GREAT DEMOCRACY OF WEALTH FROM THE *WEST* TO SHOW US THE WAY?

SAYS THE MAN WHO PAYS ATTENTION IN *HARD CURRENCY.*

IT'S NOT ABOUT *POLITICS* AND IT'S NOT ABOUT *MONEY*, VANKO.

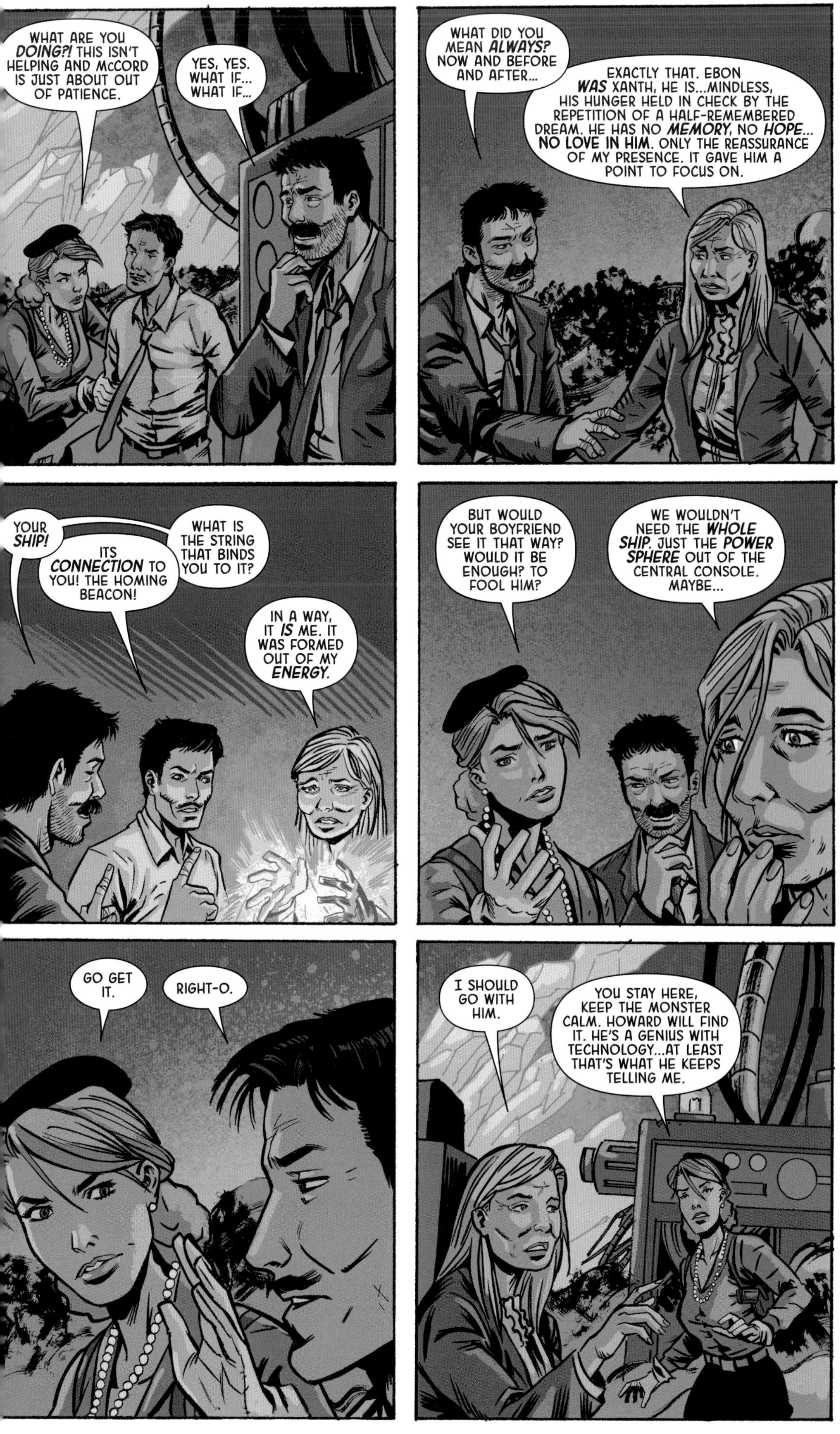
WHAT ARE YOU DOING?! THIS ISN'T HELPING AND McCORD IS JUST ABOUT OUT OF PATIENCE.
YES, YES. WHAT IF... WHAT IF...
WHAT DID YOU MEAN ALWAYS? NOW AND BEFORE AND AFTER...
EXACTLY THAT. EBON WAS XANTH, HE IS...MINDLESS, HIS HUNGER HELD IN CHECK BY THE REPETITION OF A HALF-REMEMBERED DREAM. HE HAS NO MEMORY, NO HOPE... NO LOVE IN HIM. ONLY THE REASSURANCE OF MY PRESENCE. IT GAVE HIM A POINT TO FOCUS ON.
YOUR SHIP!
WHAT IS THE STRING THAT BINDS YOU TO IT?
ITS CONNECTION TO YOU! THE HOMING BEACON!
IN A WAY, IT IS ME. IT WAS FORMED OUT OF MY ENERGY.
BUT WOULD YOUR BOYFRIEND SEE IT THAT WAY? WOULD IT BE ENOUGH? TO FOOL HIM?
WE WOULDN'T NEED THE WHOLE SHIP. JUST THE POWER SPHERE OUT OF THE CENTRAL CONSOLE. MAYBE...
GO GET IT.
RIGHT-O.
I SHOULD GO WITH HIM.
YOU STAY HERE, KEEP THE MONSTER CALM. HOWARD WILL FIND IT. HE'S A GENIUS WITH TECHNOLOGY...AT LEAST THAT'S WHAT HE KEEPS TELLING ME.

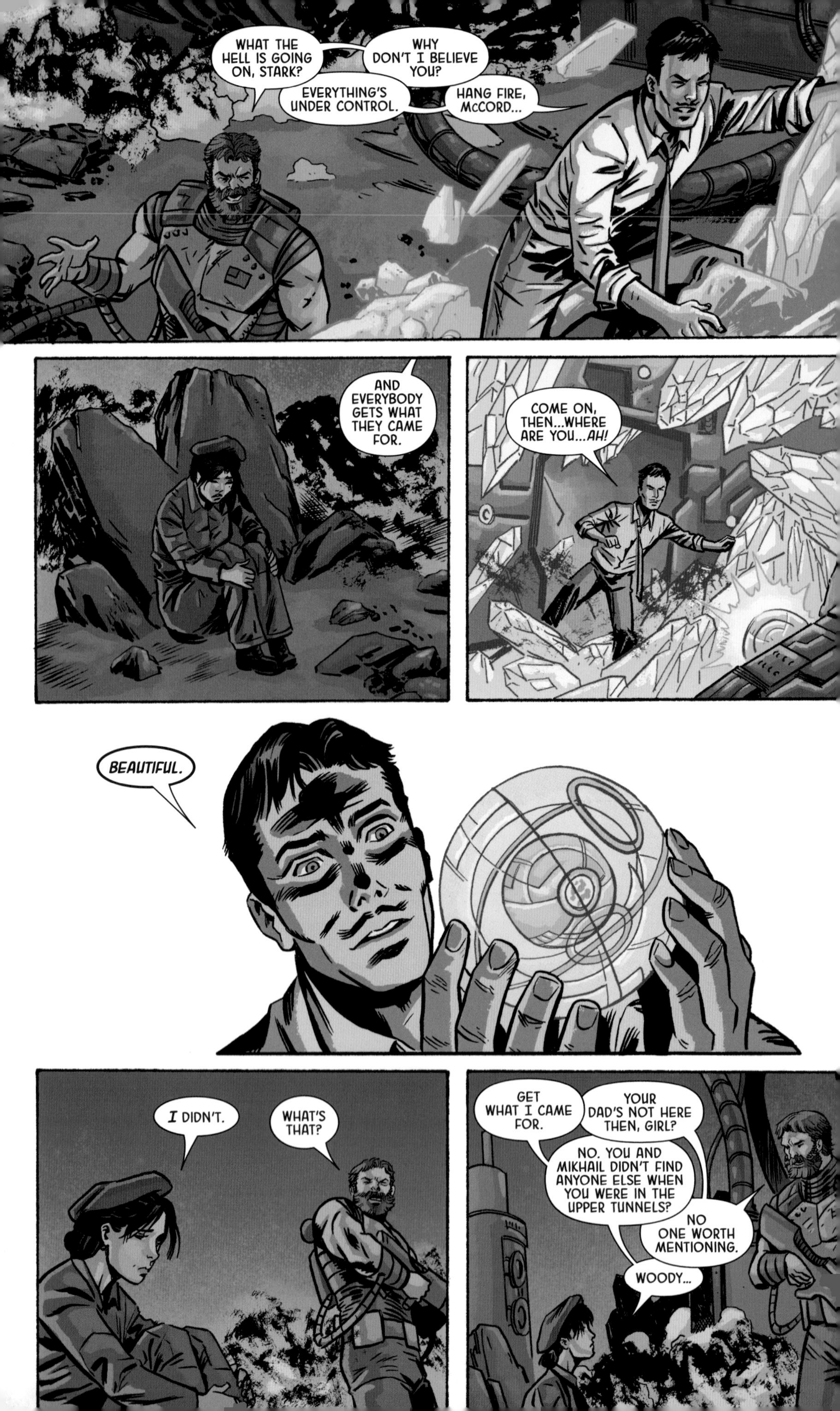
WHAT THE HELL IS GOING ON, STARK?
WHY DON'T I BELIEVE YOU?
EVERYTHING'S UNDER CONTROL.
HANG FIRE, McCORD...
AND EVERYBODY GETS WHAT THEY CAME FOR.
COME ON, THEN...WHERE ARE YOU...AH!
BEAUTIFUL.
I DIDN'T.
WHAT'S THAT?
GET WHAT I CAME FOR.
YOUR DAD'S NOT HERE THEN, GIRL?
NO. YOU AND MIKHAIL DIDN'T FIND ANYONE ELSE WHEN YOU WERE IN THE UPPER TUNNELS?
NO ONE WORTH MENTIONING.
WOODY...

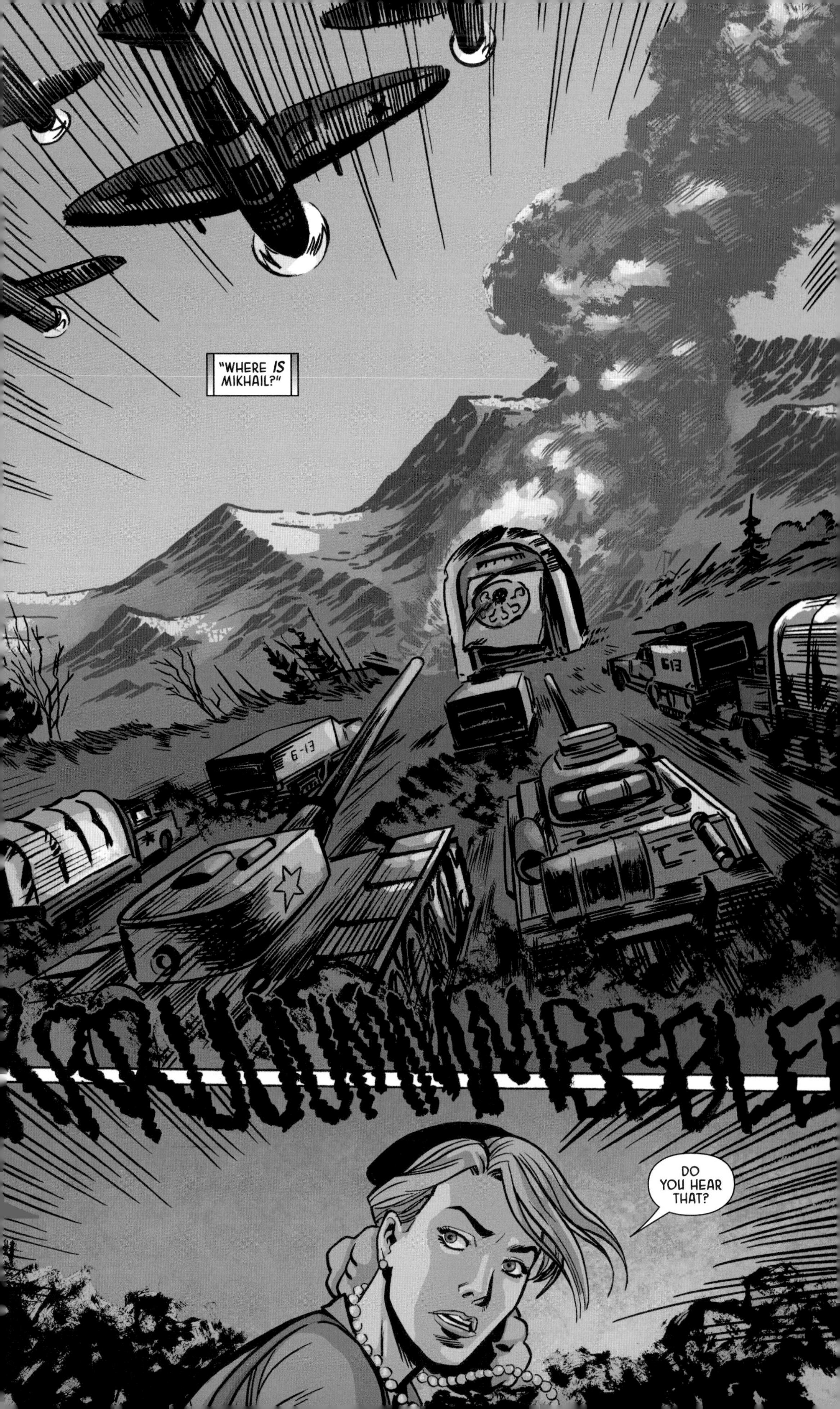
"WHERE IS MIKHAIL?"
RRRUUMMMBBBLE
DO YOU HEAR THAT?

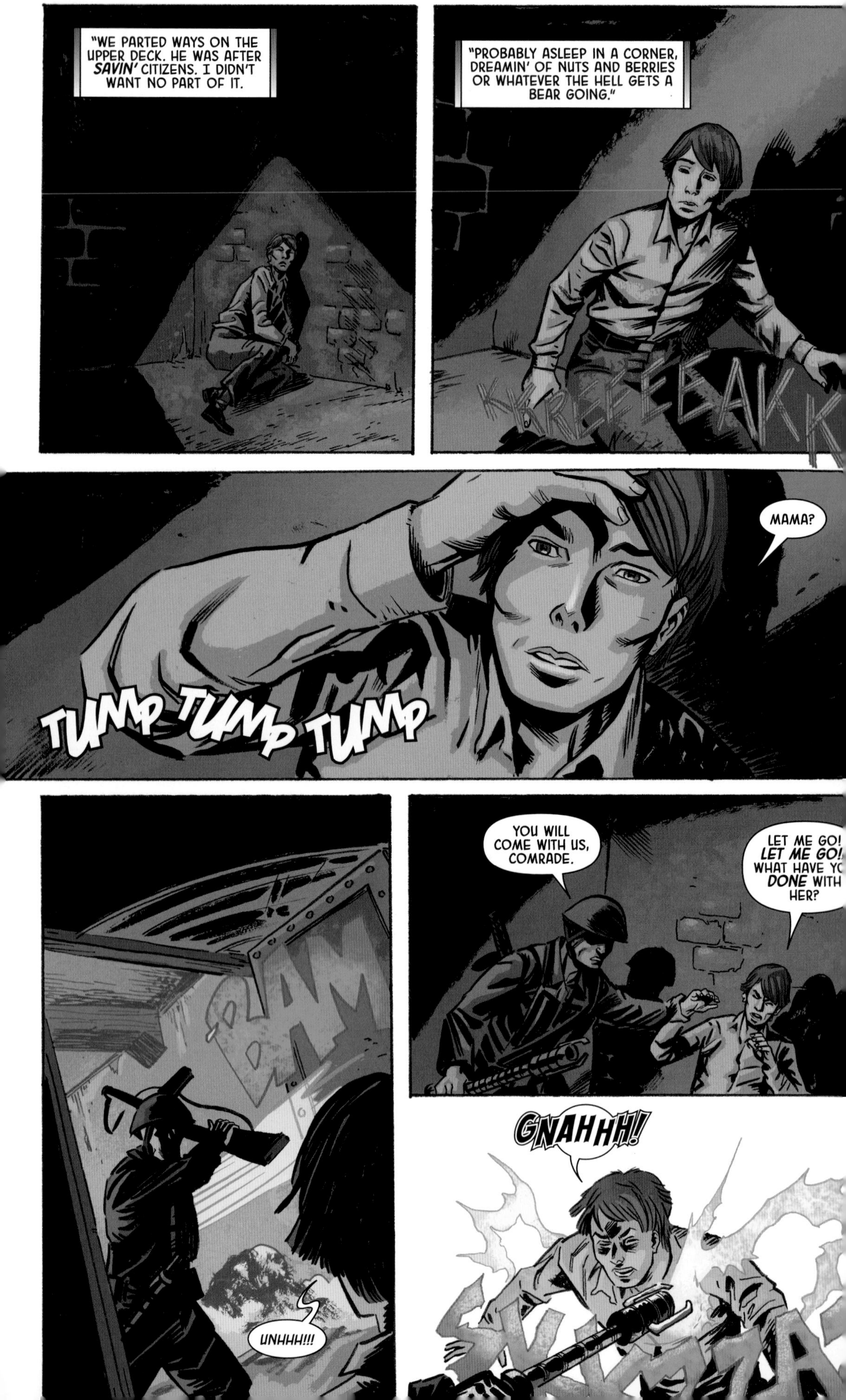
"WE PARTED WAYS ON THE UPPER DECK. HE WAS AFTER *SAVIN'* CITIZENS. I DIDN'T WANT NO PART OF IT.
"PROBABLY ASLEEP IN A CORNER, DREAMIN' OF NUTS AND BERRIES OR WHATEVER THE HELL GETS A BEAR GOING."
KKREEEEAKK
MAMA?
TUMP TUMP TUMP
YOU WILL COME WITH US, COMRADE.
LET ME GO! *LET ME GO!* WHAT HAVE YO *DONE* WITH HER?
UNHHH!!!
GNAHHH!

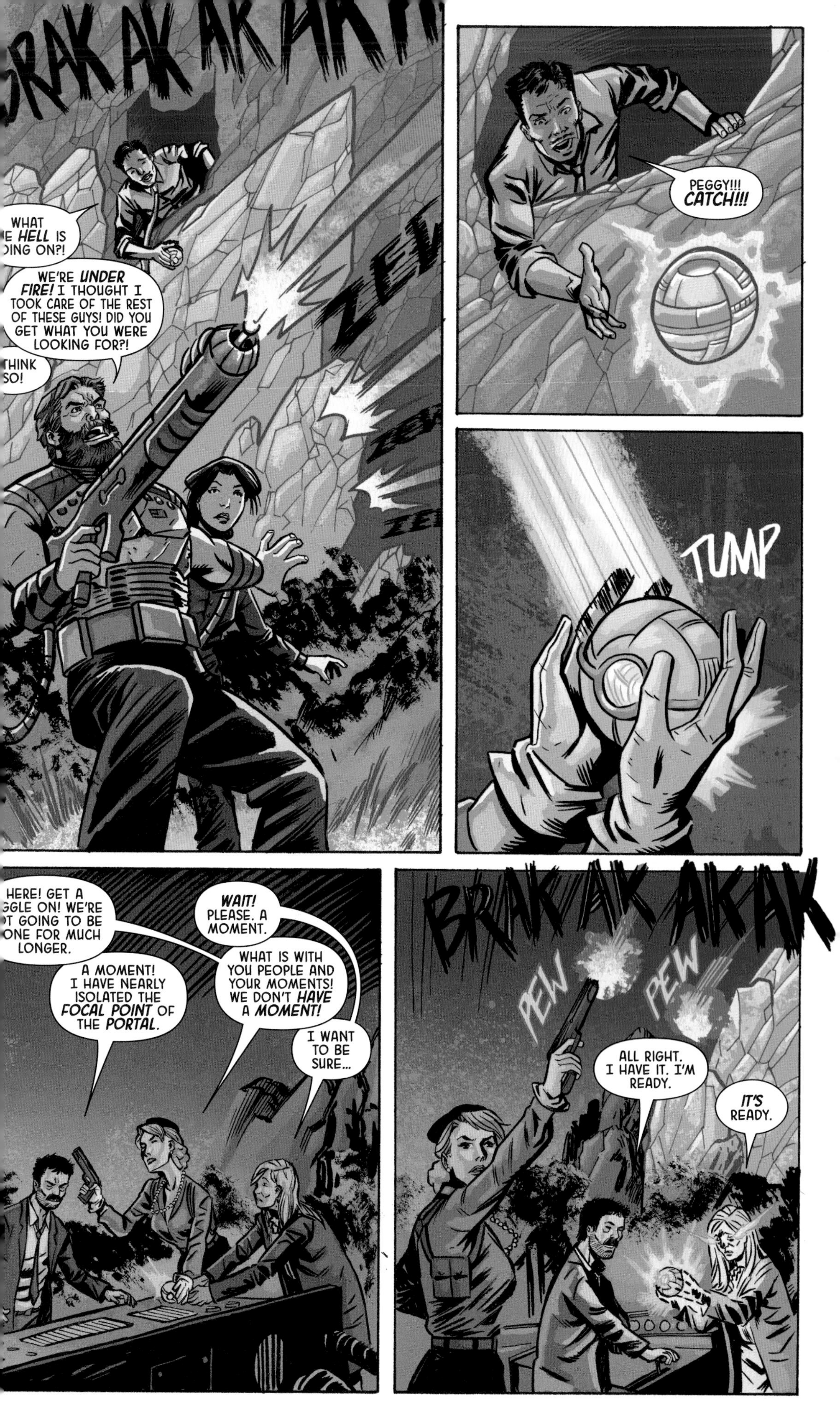
BRAKAKAKAK!!
WHAT E HELL IS OING ON?!
WE'RE UNDER FIRE! I THOUGHT I TOOK CARE OF THE REST OF THESE GUYS! DID YOU GET WHAT YOU WERE LOOKING FOR?!
THINK SO!
ZEW
PEGGY!!! CATCH!!!
TUMP
HERE! GET A GGLE ON! WE'RE T GOING TO BE ONE FOR MUCH LONGER.
WAIT! PLEASE. A MOMENT.
A MOMENT! I HAVE NEARLY ISOLATED THE FOCAL POINT OF THE PORTAL.
WHAT IS WITH YOU PEOPLE AND YOUR MOMENTS! WE DON'T HAVE A MOMENT!
I WANT TO BE SURE...
BRAKAKAKAK
PEW
PEW
ALL RIGHT. I HAVE IT. I'M READY.
IT'S READY.

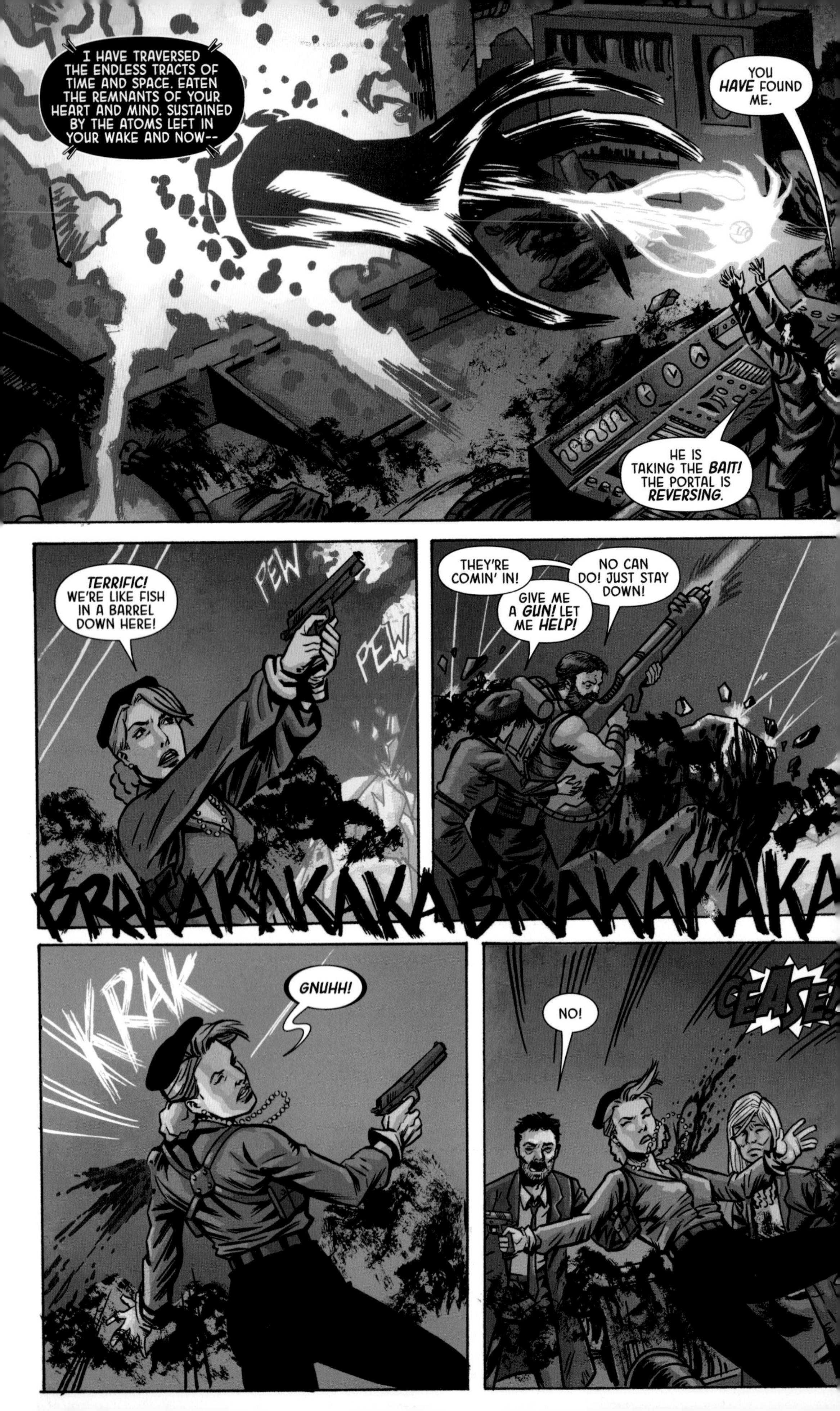
I HAVE TRAVERSED THE ENDLESS TRACTS OF TIME AND SPACE. EATEN THE REMNANTS OF YOUR HEART AND MIND. SUSTAINED BY THE ATOMS LEFT IN YOUR WAKE AND NOW--
YOU *HAVE* FOUND ME.
HE IS TAKING THE *BAIT!* THE PORTAL IS *REVERSING.*
PEW
PEW
TERRIFIC! WE'RE LIKE FISH IN A BARREL DOWN HERE!
THEY'RE COMIN' IN!
NO CAN DO! JUST STAY DOWN!
GIVE ME A *GUN!* LET ME *HELP!*
BRAKAKAKAKABRAKAKAKAKA
KRAK
GNUHH!
NO!
CEASE!

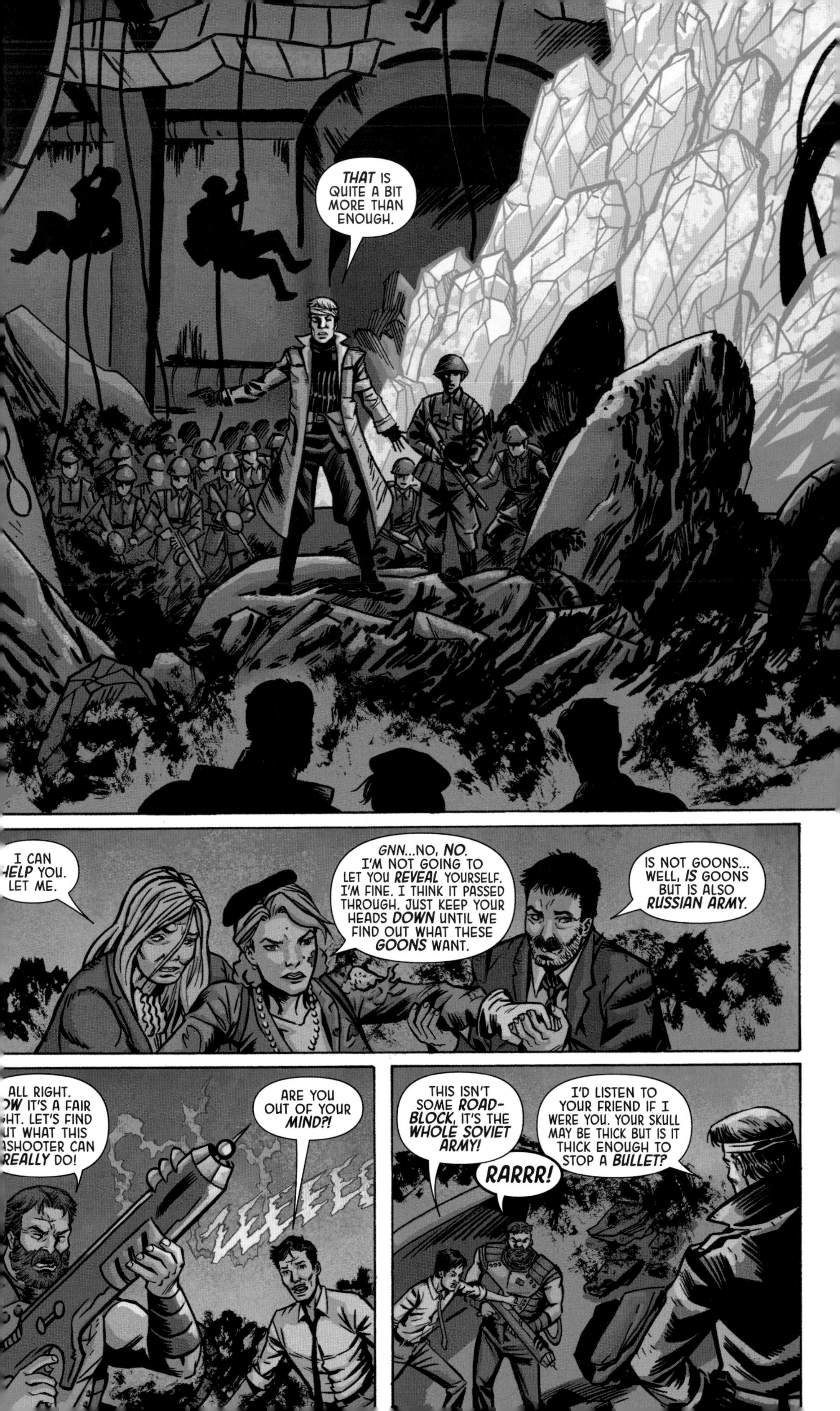
THAT IS QUITE A BIT MORE THAN ENOUGH.
I CAN HELP YOU. LET ME.
GNN...NO, NO. I'M NOT GOING TO LET YOU REVEAL YOURSELF. I'M FINE. I THINK IT PASSED THROUGH. JUST KEEP YOUR HEADS DOWN UNTIL WE FIND OUT WHAT THESE GOONS WANT.
IS NOT GOONS... WELL, IS GOONS BUT IS ALSO RUSSIAN ARMY.
ALL RIGHT. OW IT'S A FAIR GHT. LET'S FIND UT WHAT THIS ASHOOTER CAN REALLY DO!
ARE YOU OUT OF YOUR MIND?!
ZEEEEE
THIS ISN'T SOME ROAD-BLOCK, IT'S THE WHOLE SOVIET ARMY!
I'D LISTEN TO YOUR FRIEND IF I WERE YOU. YOUR SKULL MAY BE THICK BUT IS IT THICK ENOUGH TO STOP A BULLET?
RARRR!

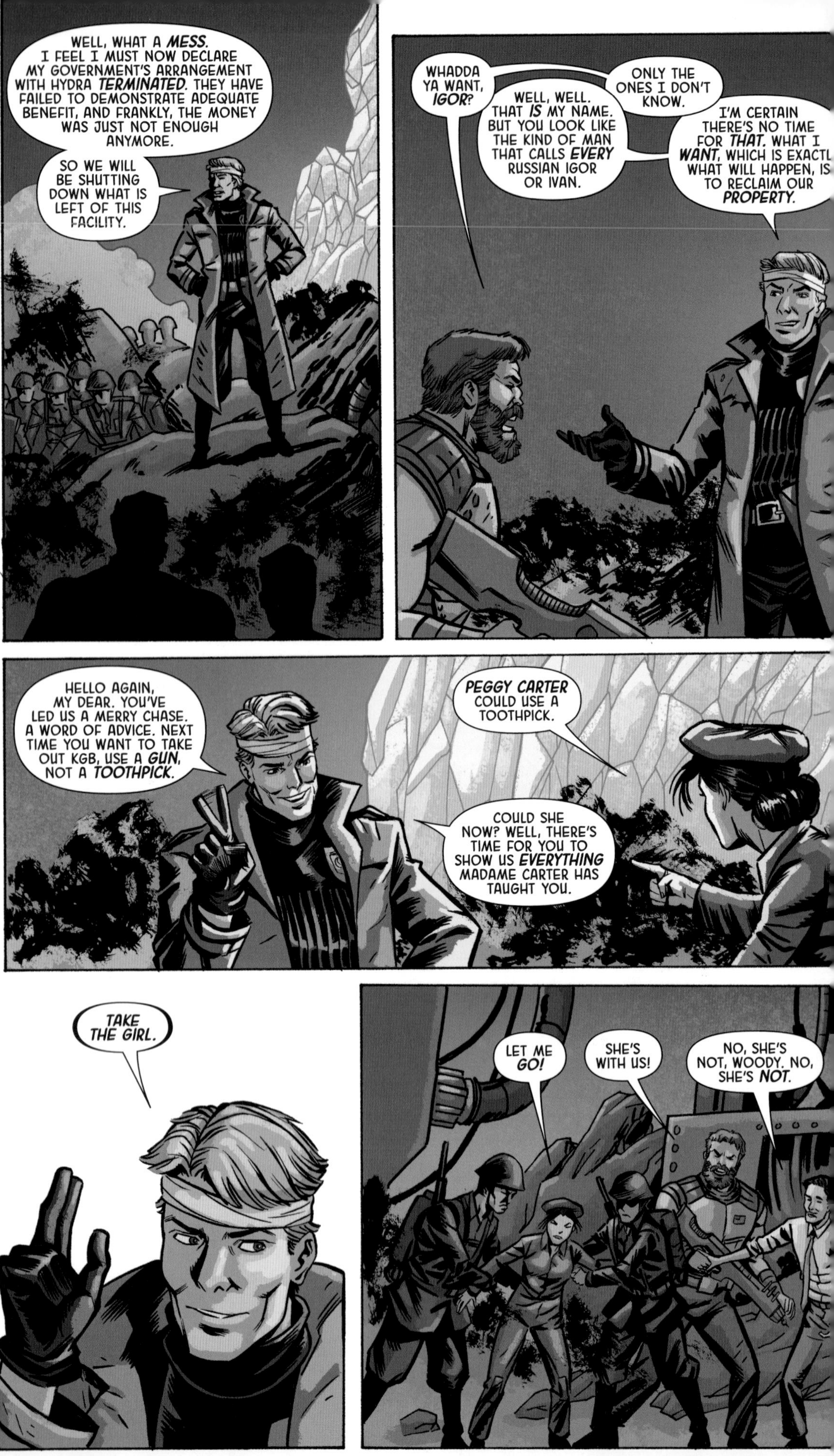
WELL, WHAT A MESS. I FEEL I MUST NOW DECLARE MY GOVERNMENT'S ARRANGEMENT WITH HYDRA TERMINATED. THEY HAVE FAILED TO DEMONSTRATE ADEQUATE BENEFIT, AND FRANKLY, THE MONEY WAS JUST NOT ENOUGH ANYMORE.
SO WE WILL BE SHUTTING DOWN WHAT IS LEFT OF THIS FACILITY.
WHADDA YA WANT, IGOR?
WELL, WELL. THAT IS MY NAME. BUT YOU LOOK LIKE THE KIND OF MAN THAT CALLS EVERY RUSSIAN IGOR OR IVAN.
ONLY THE ONES I DON'T KNOW.
I'M CERTAIN THERE'S NO TIME FOR THAT. WHAT I WANT, WHICH IS EXACTL WHAT WILL HAPPEN, IS TO RECLAIM OUR PROPERTY.
HELLO AGAIN, MY DEAR. YOU'VE LED US A MERRY CHASE. A WORD OF ADVICE. NEXT TIME YOU WANT TO TAKE OUT KGB, USE A GUN, NOT A TOOTHPICK.
PEGGY CARTER COULD USE A TOOTHPICK.
COULD SHE NOW? WELL, THERE'S TIME FOR YOU TO SHOW US EVERYTHING MADAME CARTER HAS TAUGHT YOU.
TAKE THE GIRL.
LET ME GO!
SHE'S WITH US!
NO, SHE'S NOT, WOODY. NO, SHE'S NOT.

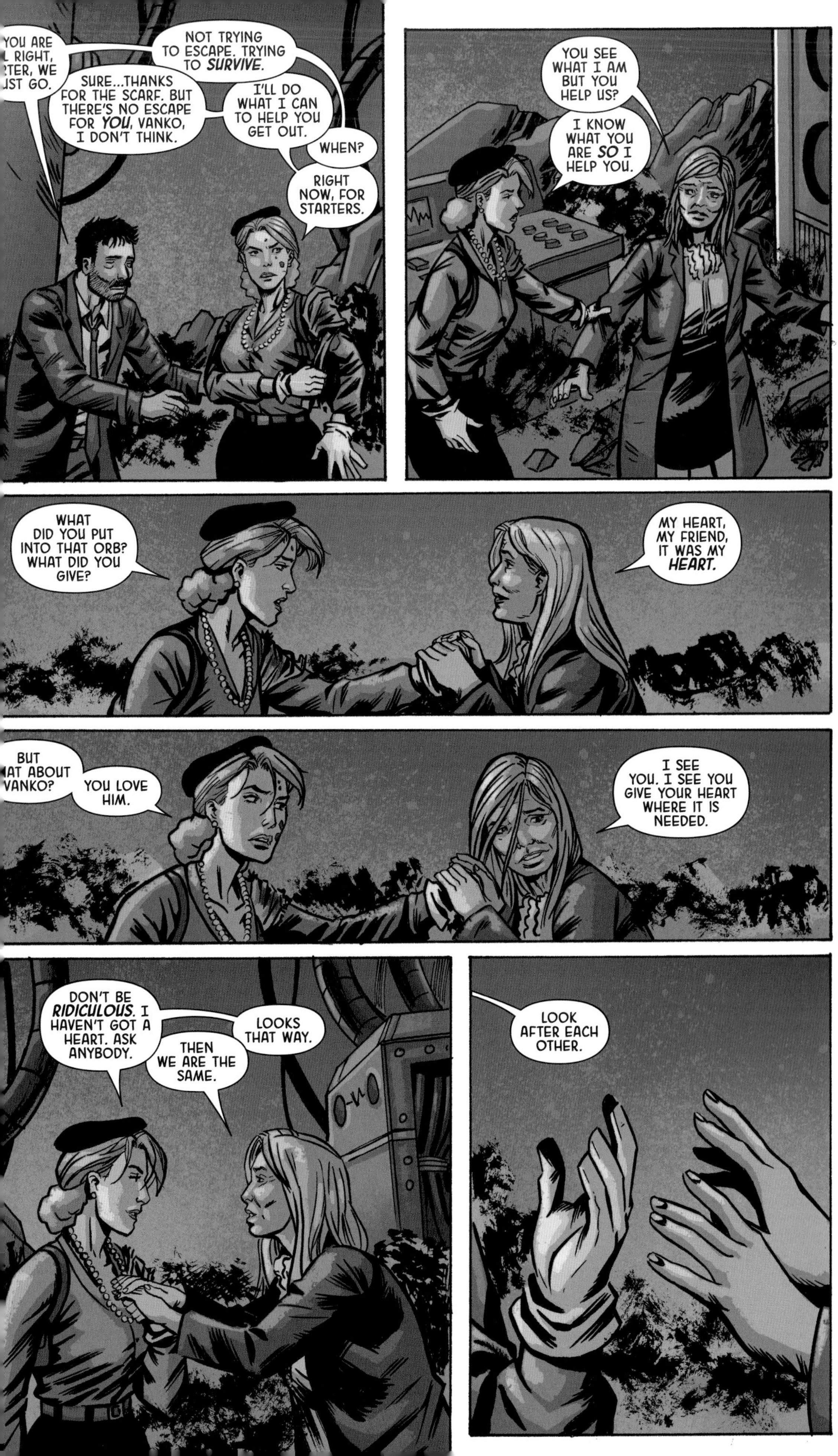

YOU ARE
L RIGHT,
RTER, WE
UST GO.
NOT TRYING TO ESCAPE. TRYING TO *SURVIVE*.
SURE...THANKS FOR THE SCARF. BUT THERE'S NO ESCAPE FOR *YOU*, VANKO, I DON'T THINK.
I'LL DO WHAT I CAN TO HELP YOU GET OUT.
WHEN?
RIGHT NOW, FOR STARTERS.
YOU SEE WHAT I AM BUT YOU HELP US?
I KNOW WHAT YOU ARE *SO* I HELP YOU.
WHAT DID YOU PUT INTO THAT ORB? WHAT DID YOU GIVE?
MY HEART, MY FRIEND, IT WAS MY *HEART.*
BUT
AT ABOUT
VANKO?
YOU LOVE HIM.
I SEE YOU. I SEE YOU GIVE YOUR HEART WHERE IT IS NEEDED.
DON'T BE *RIDICULOUS*. I HAVEN'T GOT A HEART. ASK ANYBODY.
LOOKS THAT WAY.
THEN WE ARE THE SAME.
LOOK AFTER EACH OTHER.

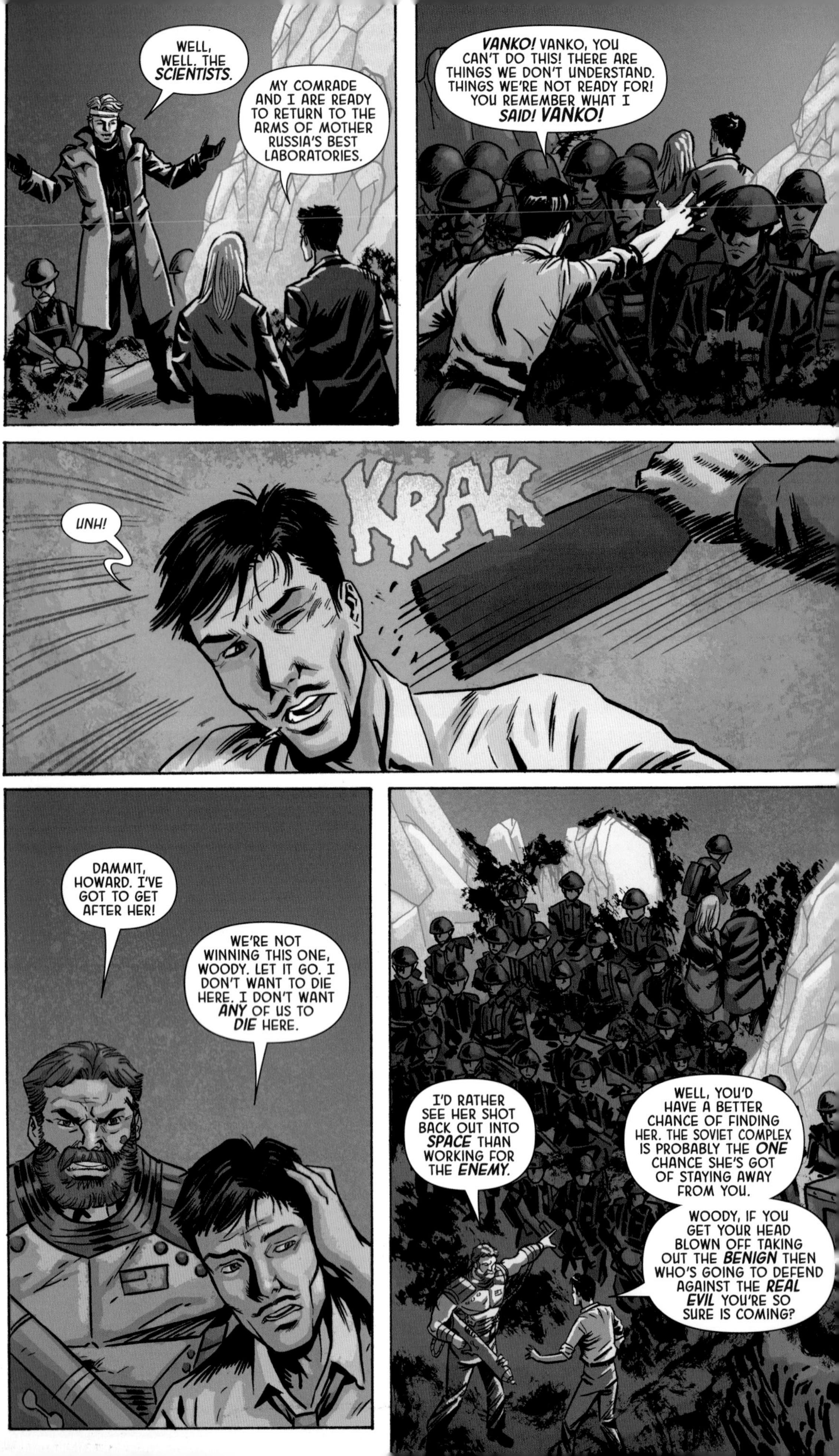
WELL, WELL. THE SCIENTISTS.
MY COMRADE AND I ARE READY TO RETURN TO THE ARMS OF MOTHER RUSSIA'S BEST LABORATORIES.
VANKO! VANKO, YOU CAN'T DO THIS! THERE ARE THINGS WE DON'T UNDERSTAND. THINGS WE'RE NOT READY FOR! YOU REMEMBER WHAT I SAID! VANKO!
UNH!
KRAK
DAMMIT, HOWARD. I'VE GOT TO GET AFTER HER!
WE'RE NOT WINNING THIS ONE, WOODY. LET IT GO. I DON'T WANT TO DIE HERE. I DON'T WANT ANY OF US TO DIE HERE.
I'D RATHER SEE HER SHOT BACK OUT INTO SPACE THAN WORKING FOR THE ENEMY.
WELL, YOU'D HAVE A BETTER CHANCE OF FINDING HER. THE SOVIET COMPLEX IS PROBABLY THE ONE CHANCE SHE'S GOT OF STAYING AWAY FROM YOU.
WOODY, IF YOU GET YOUR HEAD BLOWN OFF TAKING OUT THE BENIGN THEN WHO'S GOING TO DEFEND AGAINST THE REAL EVIL YOU'RE SO SURE IS COMING?

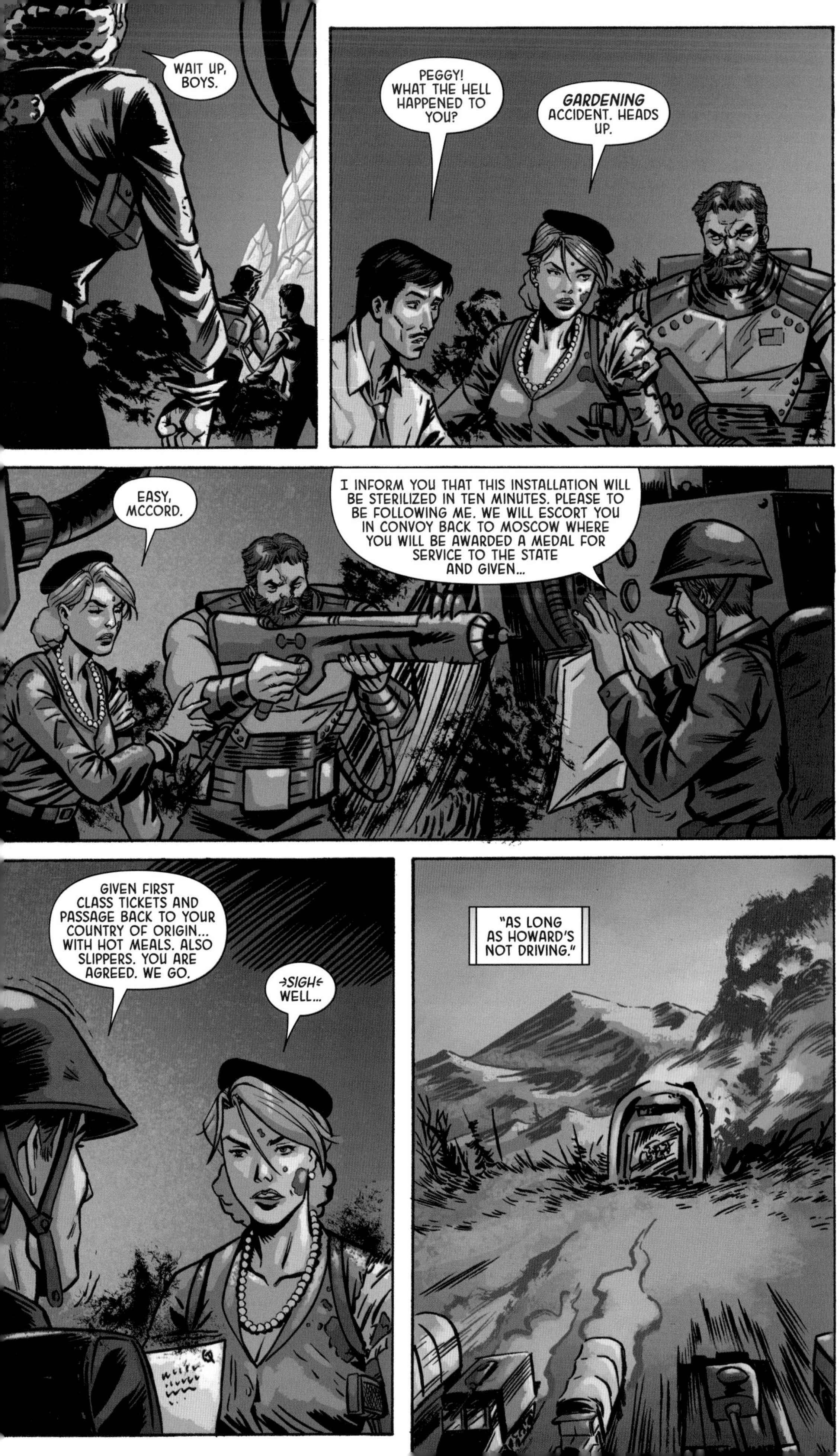
WAIT UP, BOYS.
PEGGY! WHAT THE HELL HAPPENED TO YOU?
GARDENING ACCIDENT. HEADS UP.
EASY, MCCORD.
I INFORM YOU THAT THIS INSTALLATION WILL BE STERILIZED IN TEN MINUTES. PLEASE TO BE FOLLOWING ME. WE WILL ESCORT YOU IN CONVOY BACK TO MOSCOW WHERE YOU WILL BE AWARDED A MEDAL FOR SERVICE TO THE STATE AND GIVEN...
GIVEN FIRST CLASS TICKETS AND PASSAGE BACK TO YOUR COUNTRY OF ORIGIN... WITH HOT MEALS. ALSO SLIPPERS. YOU ARE AGREED. WE GO.
→SIGH← WELL...
"AS LONG AS HOWARD'S NOT DRIVING."

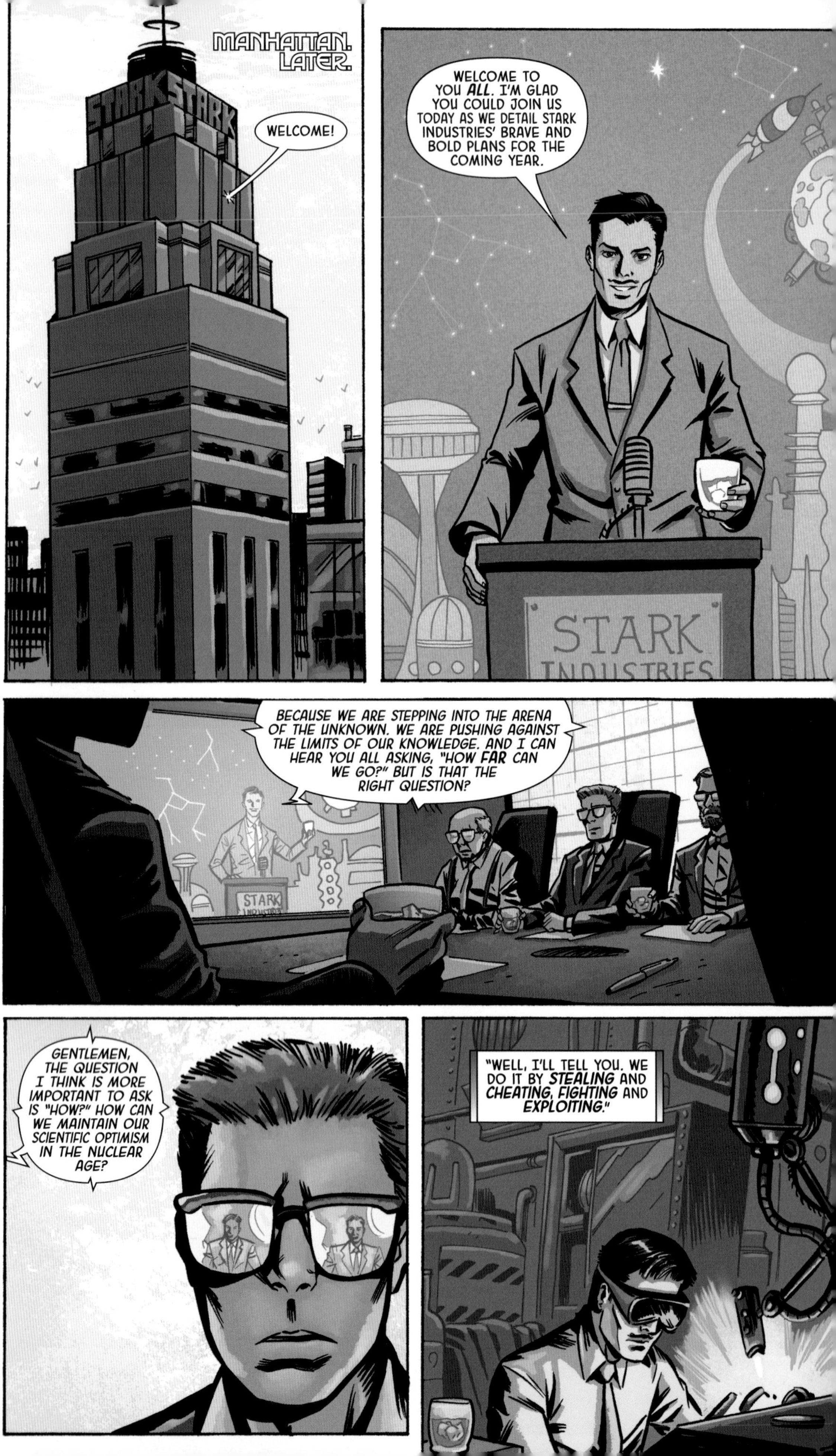
MANHATTAN. LATER.
STARK STARK
WELCOME!
WELCOME TO YOU ALL. I'M GLAD YOU COULD JOIN US TODAY AS WE DETAIL STARK INDUSTRIES' BRAVE AND BOLD PLANS FOR THE COMING YEAR.
STARK INDUSTRIES
BECAUSE WE ARE STEPPING INTO THE ARENA OF THE UNKNOWN. WE ARE PUSHING AGAINST THE LIMITS OF OUR KNOWLEDGE. AND I CAN HEAR YOU ALL ASKING, "HOW FAR CAN WE GO?" BUT IS THAT THE RIGHT QUESTION?
STARK
GENTLEMEN, THE QUESTION I THINK IS MORE IMPORTANT TO ASK IS "HOW?" HOW CAN WE MAINTAIN OUR SCIENTIFIC OPTIMISM IN THE NUCLEAR AGE?
"WELL, I'LL TELL YOU. WE DO IT BY STEALING AND CHEATING, FIGHTING AND EXPLOITING."

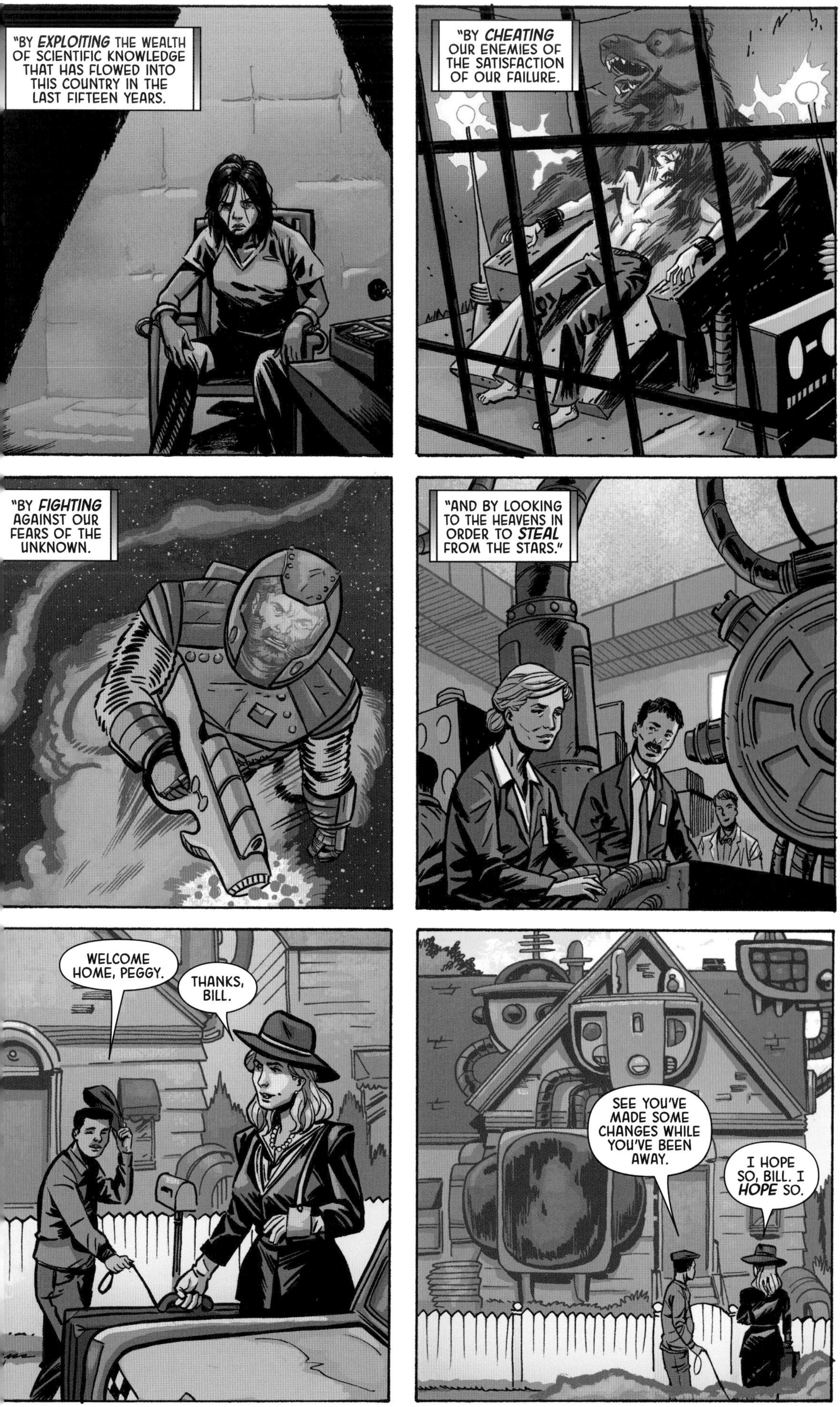
"BY EXPLOITING THE WEALTH OF SCIENTIFIC KNOWLEDGE THAT HAS FLOWED INTO THIS COUNTRY IN THE LAST FIFTEEN YEARS.
"BY CHEATING OUR ENEMIES OF THE SATISFACTION OF OUR FAILURE.
"BY FIGHTING AGAINST OUR FEARS OF THE UNKNOWN.
"AND BY LOOKING TO THE HEAVENS IN ORDER TO STEAL FROM THE STARS."
WELCOME HOME, PEGGY.
THANKS, BILL.
SEE YOU'VE MADE SOME CHANGES WHILE YOU'VE BEEN AWAY.
I HOPE SO, BILL. I HOPE SO.

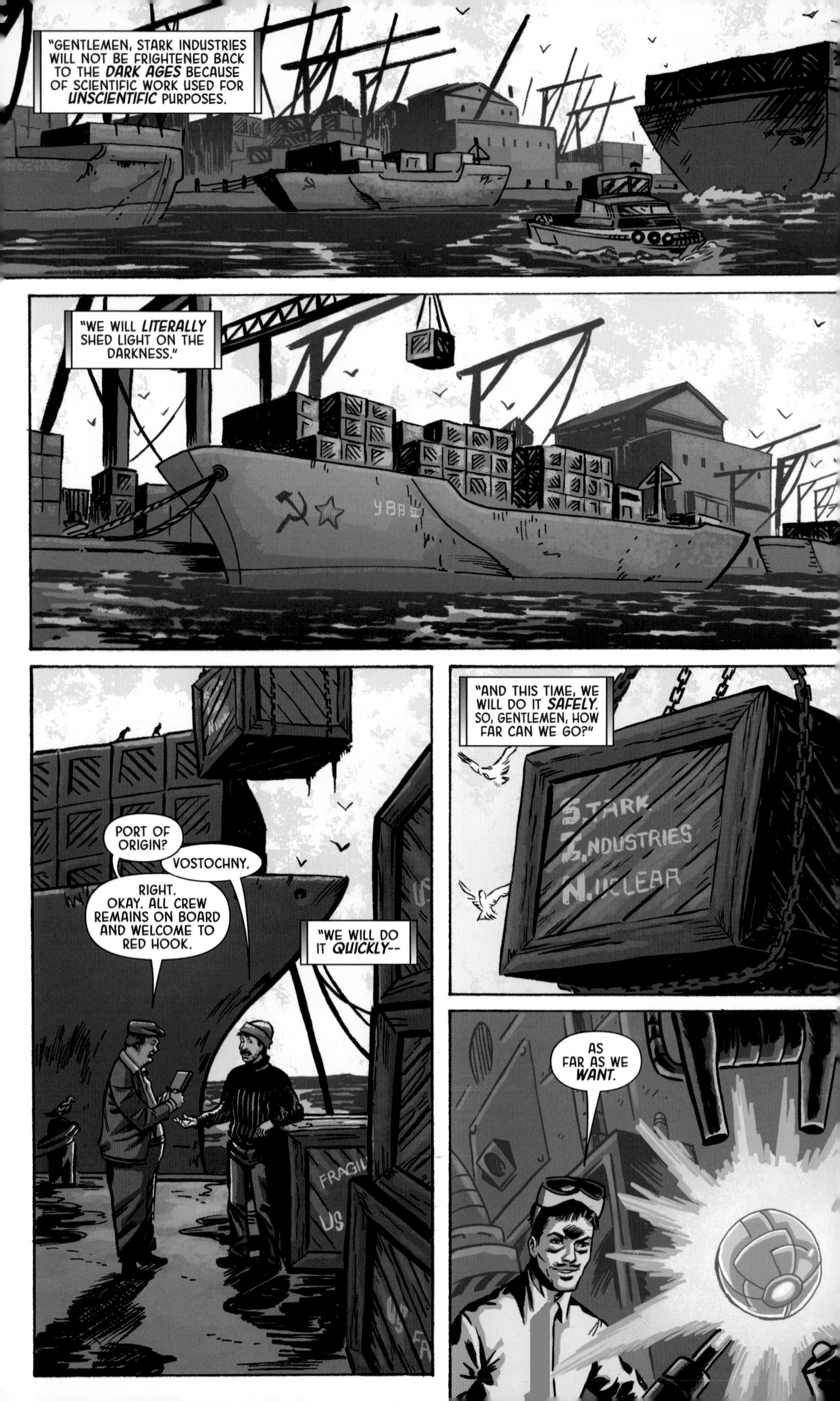
"GENTLEMEN, STARK INDUSTRIES WILL NOT BE FRIGHTENED BACK TO THE DARK AGES BECAUSE OF SCIENTIFIC WORK USED FOR UNSCIENTIFIC PURPOSES.
"WE WILL LITERALLY SHED LIGHT ON THE DARKNESS."
PORT OF ORIGIN?
VOSTOCHNY.
RIGHT. OKAY. ALL CREW REMAINS ON BOARD AND WELCOME TO RED HOOK.
"WE WILL DO IT QUICKLY--
"AND THIS TIME, WE WILL DO IT SAFELY. SO, GENTLEMEN, HOW FAR CAN WE GO?"
S.TARK
I.NDUSTRIES
N.UCLEAR
AS FAR AS WE WANT.

OPERATION S.I.N.
APRIL 1952
SUBJECT: After Action Report
TO: Commanding Officer Moisan

Kathryn: So, Rich. Are you sad it's over? I should get out my thesaurus. Bump up the rhetoric. Hang on a sec...So, Rich, are you feeling atrabilious that we're done here?

Rich: My god yes, finishing the final issue felt like saying goodbye to my friends at the end of summer camp. We spent six months with Peggy and her goofy bunch of weirdos, and had way too much fun.
    I knew I loved Peggy after prepping for the series, but I didn't know that I would get so attached to Woody and the younger cast. Was there anything that really took you by surprise as the series played out?

K: It happens every time, right? You think you know where your affections and loyalties lie and then someone just kind of sneaks up on you. Howard and his general worldview can probably still take a hike but Woody turned out to embody some real tragedy for me...trying to do the right thing in a world where it's increasingly difficult to know what that is. I guess that really goes for all of them. I'd love to somehow revisit Tania/Red Guardian after having done this series.
    I'll tell you what didn't take me by surprise, the fact that you've got "will draw bears for money" at the top of your resume. Ursa Major picking that lock with a claw was an office-wide delight. Everything, really. Moments big and small. I know it's ridiculous, after all the effort that went in, to pick out such a small thing, but you didn't let anything go. Your attention to detail was only outshone by your ability to keep track of the big picture. You're the Michael Mann of comics.
    I know we've both got things that we geek out for relative to this series and time period. I've had a huge fascination with Sergei Korolev, Energomash, and Stalin's idiotic tunnel-to-Japan plan for ages. How did the research go for you?

R: To be honest the research was nothing but fun. You did most of the heavy lifting for a lot of the key set-pieces, so all I had to really worry about was fashion, cars, and props. I always end up researching those no matter what story I'm doing. The most notable fun for me was that everything designed in the '50s is way more fun to draw than modern design.
    One of the things I love about this book was how you weaved some genuinely funny moments into the action. That and the fact that from page one, it was clear that your deep understanding of Peggy meant that she wasn't just a serious badass, but a compassionate and complex person. I could go on at length about my favorite moments, let's just say I really enjoyed getting to draw Howard getting punched. So, in the interest of talking about things we both liked, how much did you love having Jordan coloring the book?

K: Aw, hell. Thanks so much for the words about Peggy. I love her and I love the way you draw her. From the very first sketches, your Peg looked so solid. Her feet just seemed so firmly planted on the ground, literally and figuratively, and I tried to write to what you'd drawn. I think she's a serious person with a lot of internal conflict. I think she's trying to be happy but it doesn't come easily.
    As to Mr. Boyd, what a great match for you on this book. I really believe that the art sells the book but the color gets it to the cash register. We've probably seen more advancement in color in the last decade than in any other aspect of comics and Jordan is able to deploy the practically infinite number of tools with subtlety and control. There was a little bit of throwback quality to everything that all of us did and it wouldn't have been possible without him. Her final outfit made me a little weepy. Thanks a lot (jerks).
One more question. Maybe it's just me, because I'm a child, but do you reward yourself when you're done with a project? And if so, how?

R: You know what, I don't always, but since this was my first big-two miniseries, I absolutely did. I bought myself a fancy knife-sharpening system that I've been ogling for a couple years. Writing it out, that sounds very silly, but I'm a bit of a knife/gear nerd, so I was tickled pink. I also took about a week off and finally let myself play a Dragon Age. I'm curious to know what your version looks like...?

K: Well, if we're confessing, this time it was something small that starts with an "A." ends with "Alexander McQueen." I feel like we've both just gone Christmas shopping for Peg.
    Rich, it's been a distinct pleasure getting to know Peggy Carter with you, thank you to Jon for shepherding the gang (on and off the page) and thank you so much to everyone who rode alongside us. I felt like we were driving a '57 Lincoln...room for all, everybody in the front seat. Let's do it again!

R: Thank you, Kathryn, I couldn't agree more, and I couldn't have said it better myself. So, in closing, I'll steal a line from you, Semper Peg!

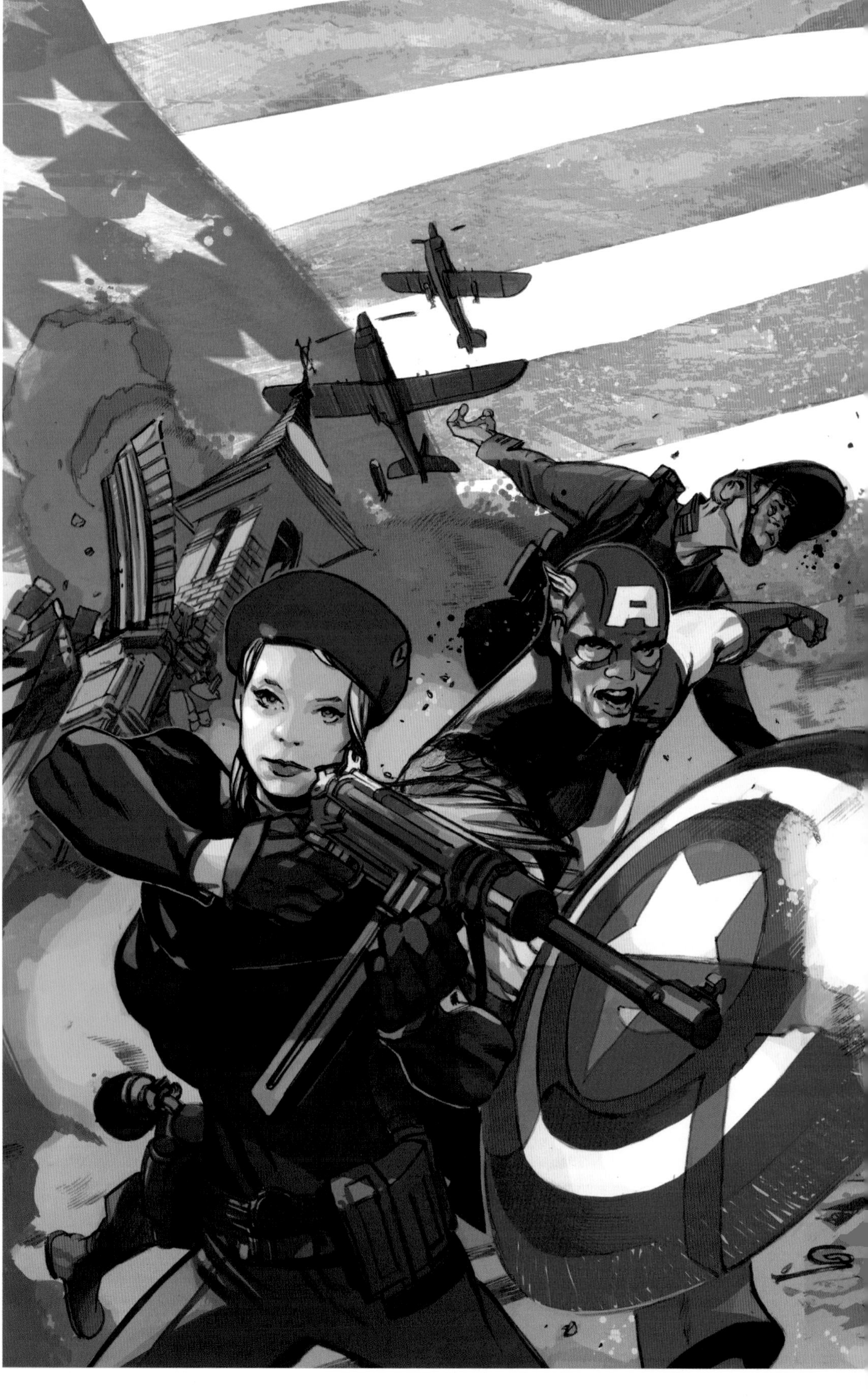

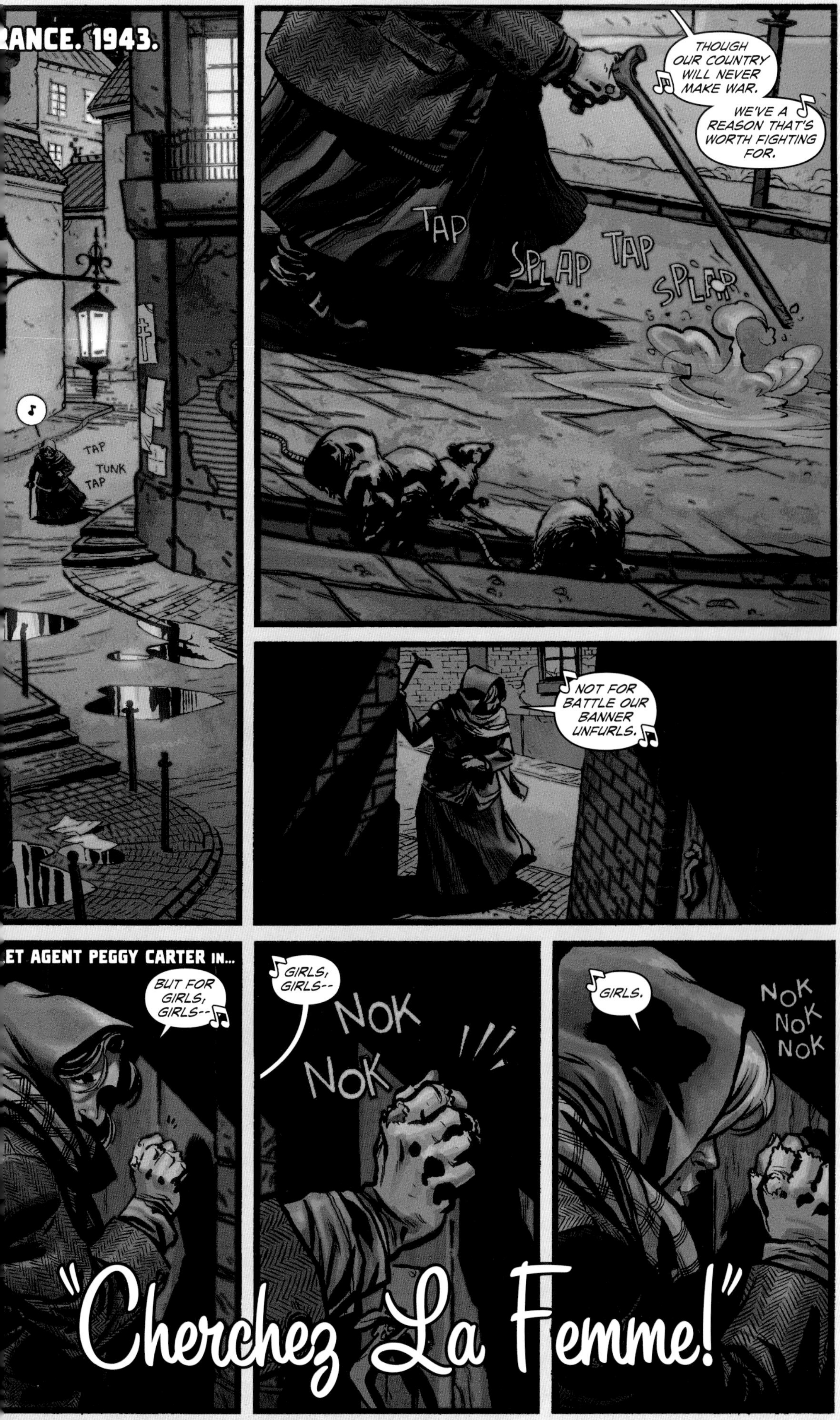

RANCE. 1943.
TAP
TUNK
TAP
THOUGH OUR COUNTRY WILL NEVER MAKE WAR.
WE'VE A REASON THAT'S WORTH FIGHTING FOR.
TAP
SPLAP
TAP
SPLAP
NOT FOR BATTLE OUR BANNER UNFURLS.
LET AGENT PEGGY CARTER IN...
BUT FOR GIRLS, GIRLS--
GIRLS, GIRLS--
NOK
NOK
GIRLS.
NOK
NOK
NOK
"Cherchez La Femme!"

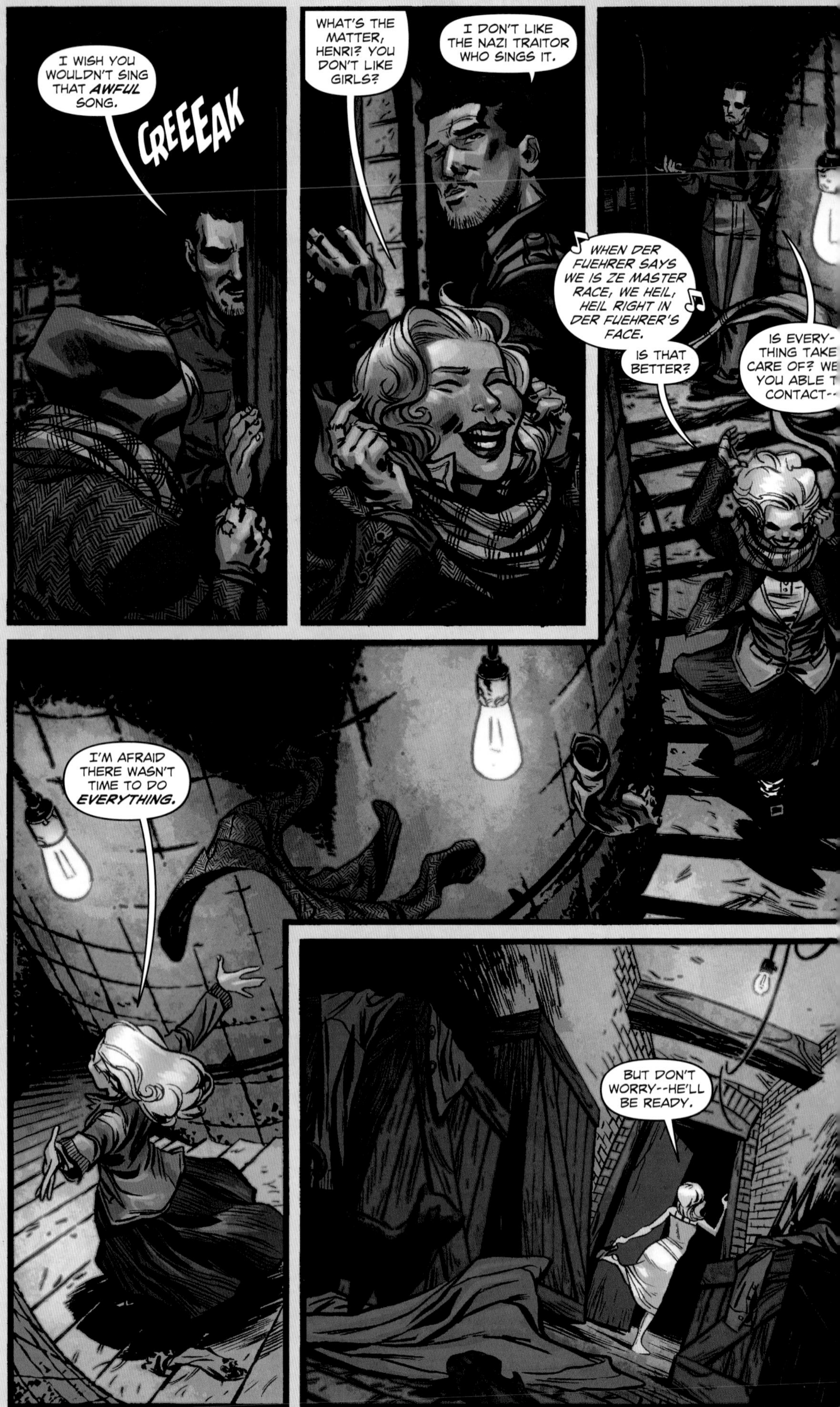
I WISH YOU WOULDN'T SING THAT AWFUL SONG.
CREEEAK
WHAT'S THE MATTER, HENRI? YOU DON'T LIKE GIRLS?
I DON'T LIKE THE NAZI TRAITOR WHO SINGS IT.
WHEN DER FUEHRER SAYS WE IS ZE MASTER RACE, WE HEIL, HEIL RIGHT IN DER FUEHRER'S FACE.
IS THAT BETTER?
IS EVERY-THING TAKE CARE OF? WE YOU ABLE T CONTACT--
I'M AFRAID THERE WASN'T TIME TO DO EVERYTHING.
BUT DON'T WORRY--HE'LL BE READY.

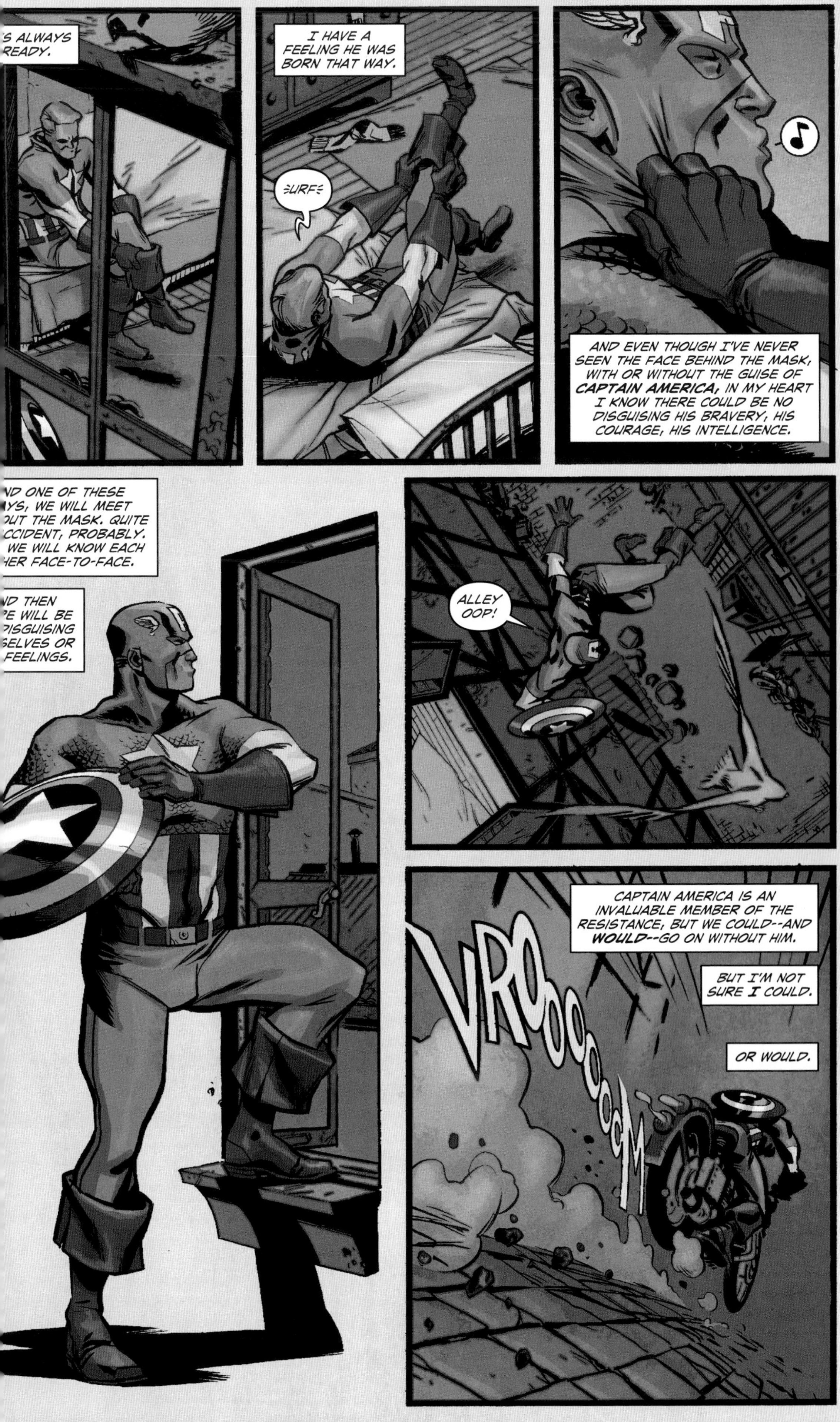
S ALWAYS READY.
I HAVE A FEELING HE WAS BORN THAT WAY.
URF
AND EVEN THOUGH I'VE NEVER SEEN THE FACE BEHIND THE MASK, WITH OR WITHOUT THE GUISE OF CAPTAIN AMERICA, IN MY HEART I KNOW THERE COULD BE NO DISGUISING HIS BRAVERY, HIS COURAGE, HIS INTELLIGENCE.
ND ONE OF THESE YS, WE WILL MEET OUT THE MASK. QUITE CCIDENT, PROBABLY. WE WILL KNOW EACH HER FACE-TO-FACE.
ND THEN E WILL BE ISGUISING SELVES OR FEELINGS.
ALLEY OOP!
CAPTAIN AMERICA IS AN INVALUABLE MEMBER OF THE RESISTANCE, BUT WE COULD--AND WOULD--GO ON WITHOUT HIM.
VROOOOOOOM
BUT I'M NOT SURE I COULD.
OR WOULD.

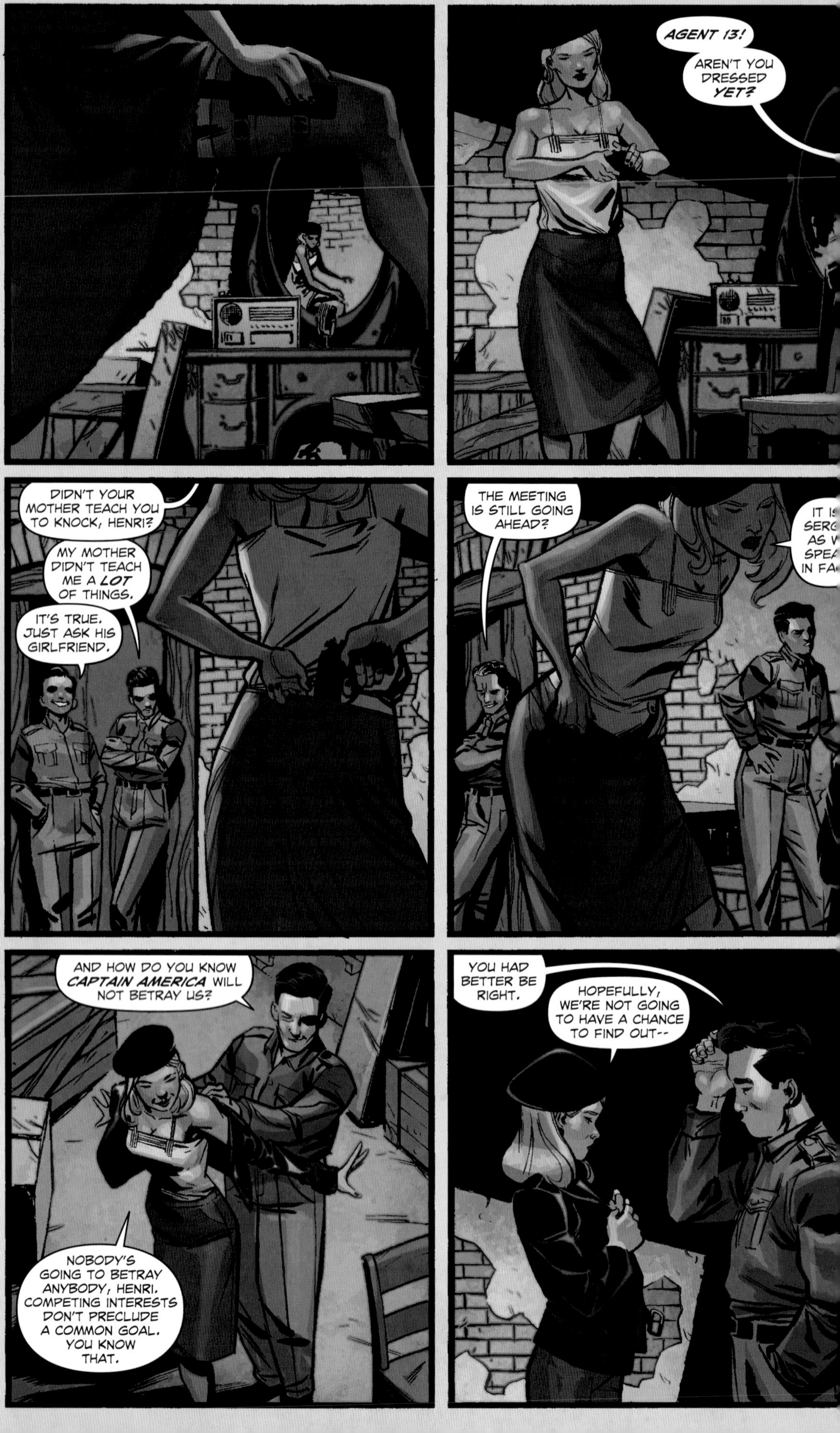

AGENT 13!
AREN'T YOU DRESSED YET?
DIDN'T YOUR MOTHER TEACH YOU TO KNOCK, HENRI?
MY MOTHER DIDN'T TEACH ME A LOT OF THINGS.
IT'S TRUE. JUST ASK HIS GIRLFRIEND.
THE MEETING IS STILL GOING AHEAD?
AND HOW DO YOU KNOW CAPTAIN AMERICA WILL NOT BETRAY US?
NOBODY'S GOING TO BETRAY ANYBODY, HENRI. COMPETING INTERESTS DON'T PRECLUDE A COMMON GOAL. YOU KNOW THAT.
YOU HAD BETTER BE RIGHT.
HOPEFULLY, WE'RE NOT GOING TO HAVE A CHANCE TO FIND OUT--

"I'M SURE THE EXCHANGE WILL GO SMOOTHLY."

IT SURE DOESN'T LOOK LIKE MUCH. ARE YOU SURE IT'S COMPLETE?

IT'S A THERMAL RAY, NOT A PANZERWAGEN. THE JAPANESE TEND TO BE MORE DISCREET IN THEIR DESIGN.

CRAFTY. *TYPICAL.*

NOT CRAFTY ENOUGH, AS IT IS NOW IN OUR POSSESSION. GIVING US THE ABILITY TO TARGET ANY HEAT SOURCE ON THE GROUND, ANY ENGINE IN THE NIGHT SKY.

WELL, I PREFER [W]EAPONS TO LOOK [LIK]E WEAPONS. THAT [W]AY YOU KNOW [W]HO TO SHOOT FIRST.

I ALSO HAVE THE PLANS.

I'LL TAKE YOUR WORD FOR IT, "FRITZ." DO I LOOK LIKE I HAVE X-RAY VISION?

SO, THE DELIVERY IS COMPLETE. I HOPE YOU HAVE A SECURE WAY OUT OF HERE. I NEED TO GET BACK TO MY PEOPLE.

IT'S ALL TAKE--

WHAT IS IT?

WERE YOU EXPECTING COMPANY, MARC?

I TOLD YOU NOT TO CALL ME THAT.

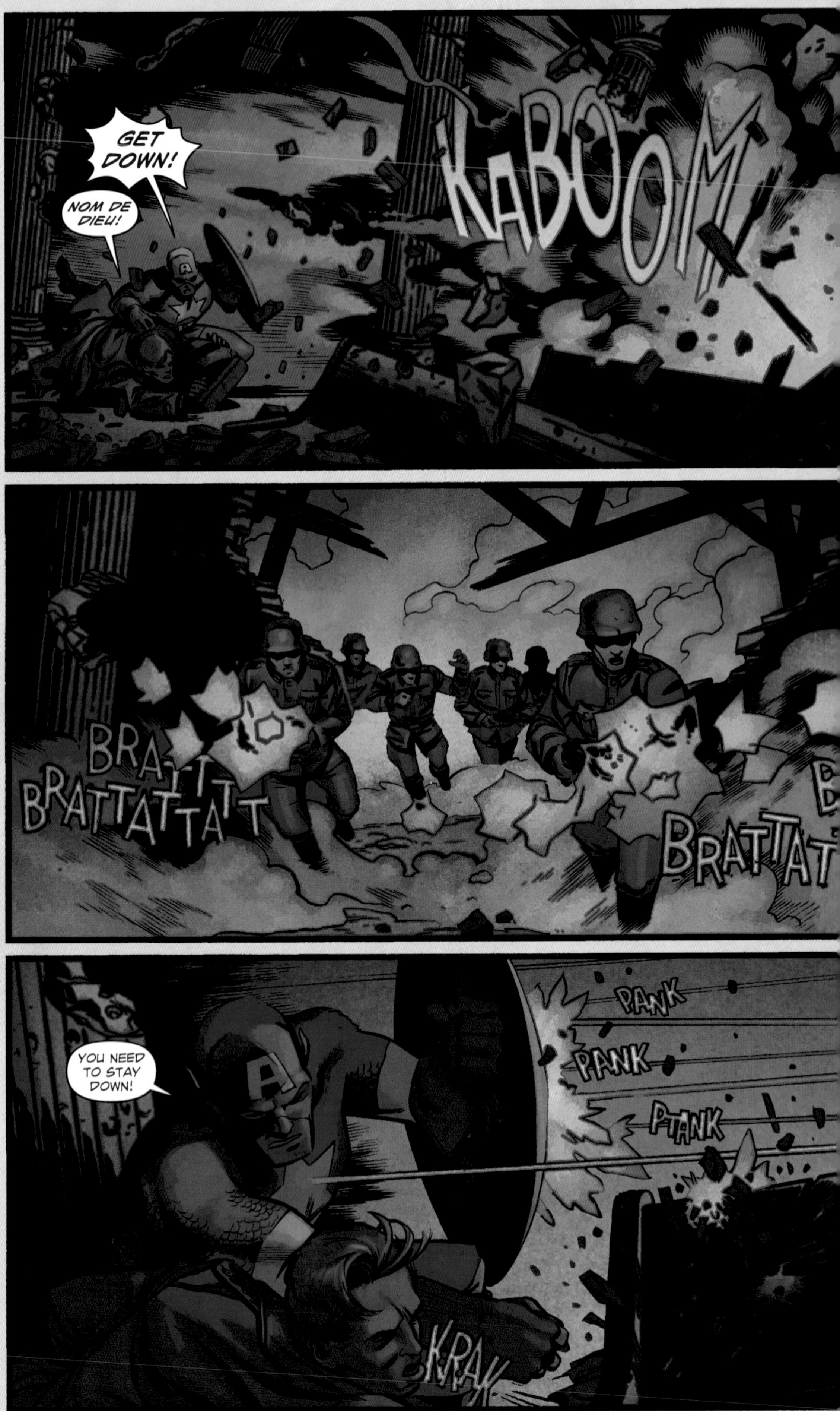
GET DOWN!
NOM DE DIEU!
KABOOM
BRATTATTATT
BRATTAT
YOU NEED TO STAY DOWN!
PANK
PANK
PTANK
KRAK

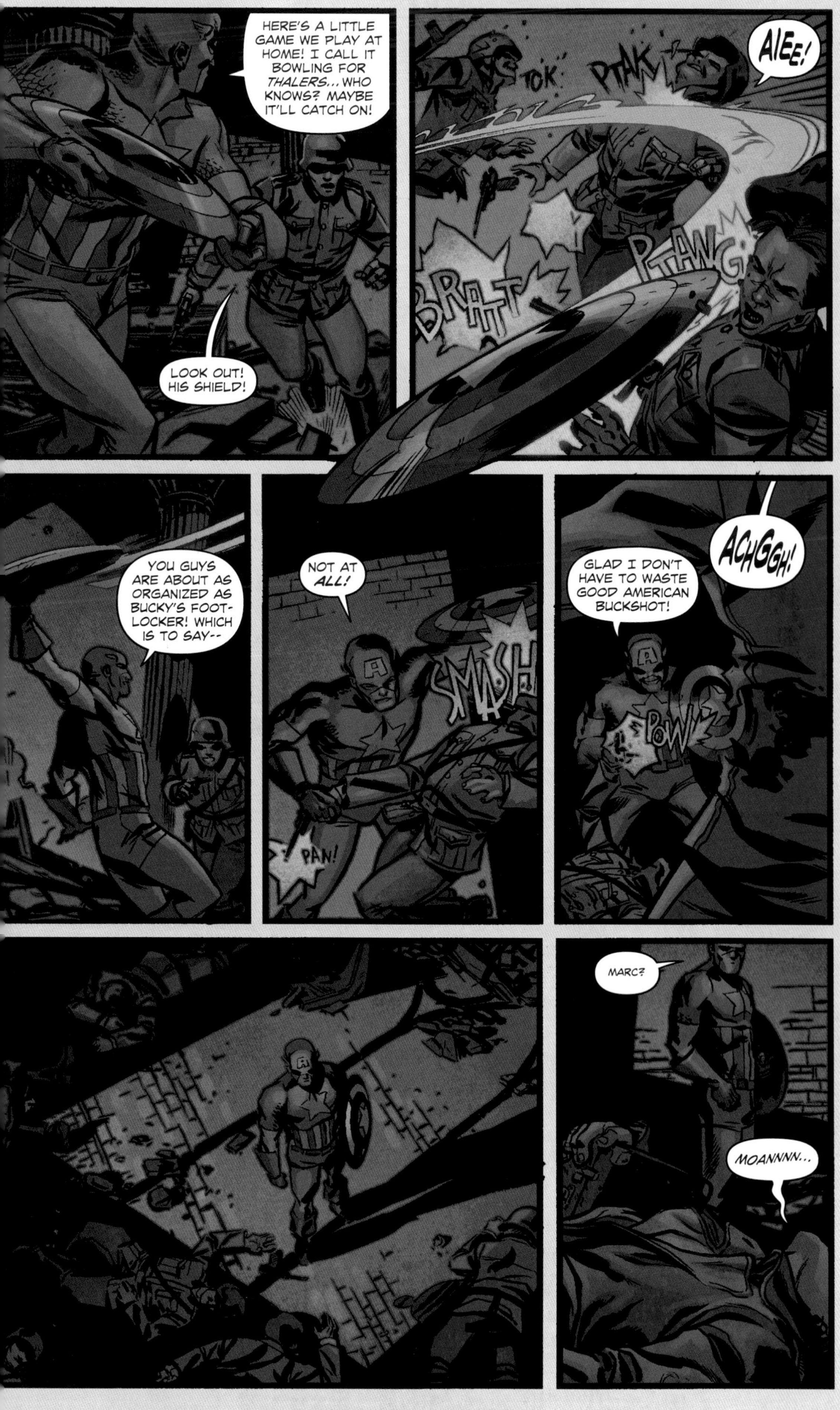
HERE'S A LITTLE GAME WE PLAY AT HOME! I CALL IT BOWLING FOR *THALERS*... WHO KNOWS? MAYBE IT'LL CATCH ON!
LOOK OUT! HIS SHIELD!
TOK
PTAK
AIEE!
BRATT
PTANG
YOU GUYS ARE ABOUT AS ORGANIZED AS BUCKY'S FOOT-LOCKER! WHICH IS TO SAY--
NOT AT *ALL!*
SMASH
PAN!
GLAD I DON'T HAVE TO WASTE GOOD AMERICAN BUCKSHOT!
ACHGGH!
POW
MARC?
MOANNNN...

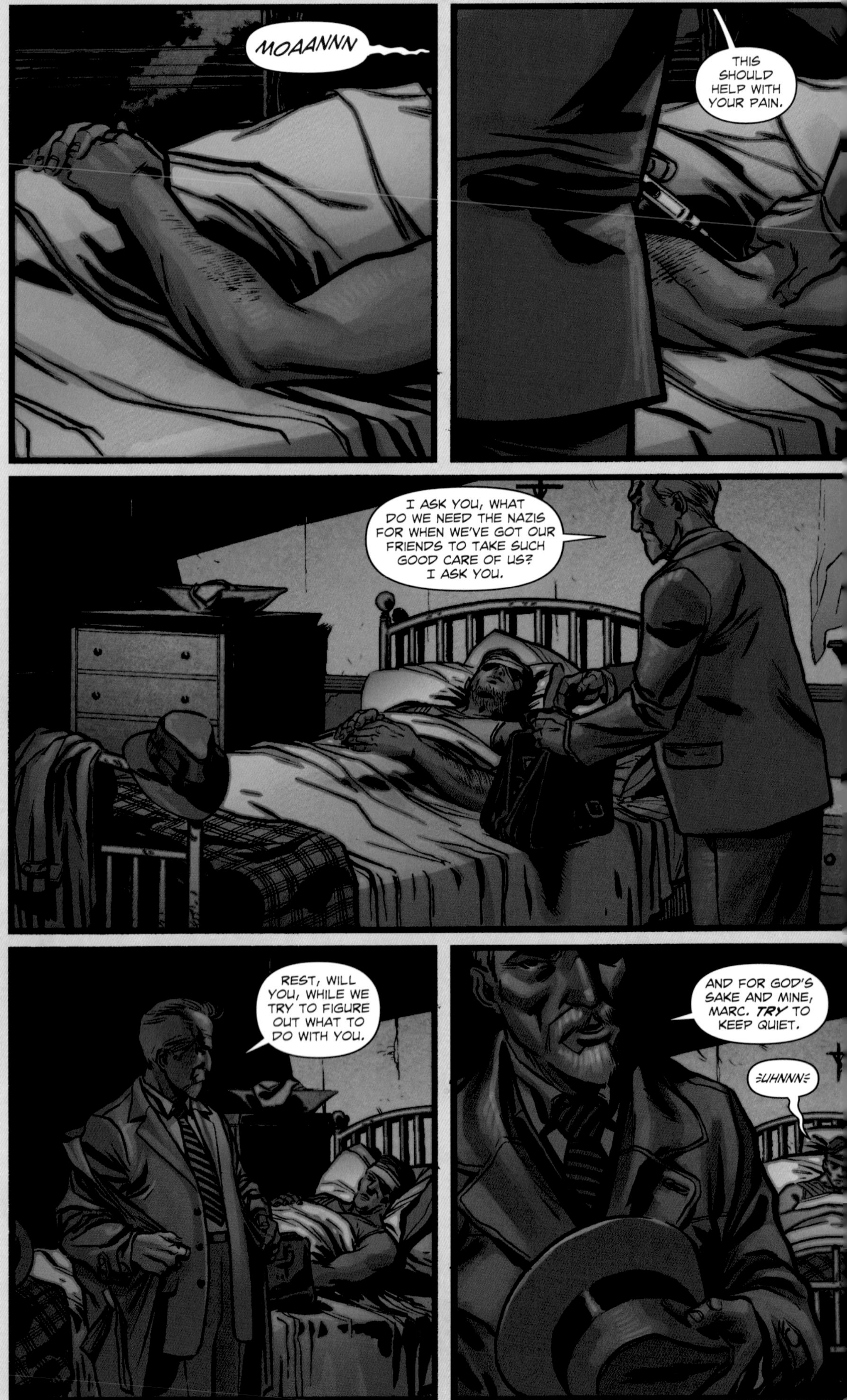
MOAANNN
THIS SHOULD HELP WITH YOUR PAIN.
I ASK YOU, WHAT DO WE NEED THE NAZIS FOR WHEN WE'VE GOT OUR FRIENDS TO TAKE SUCH GOOD CARE OF US? I ASK YOU.
REST, WILL YOU, WHILE WE TRY TO FIGURE OUT WHAT TO DO WITH YOU.
AND FOR GOD'S SAKE AND MINE, MARC. TRY TO KEEP QUIET.
UHHNNN

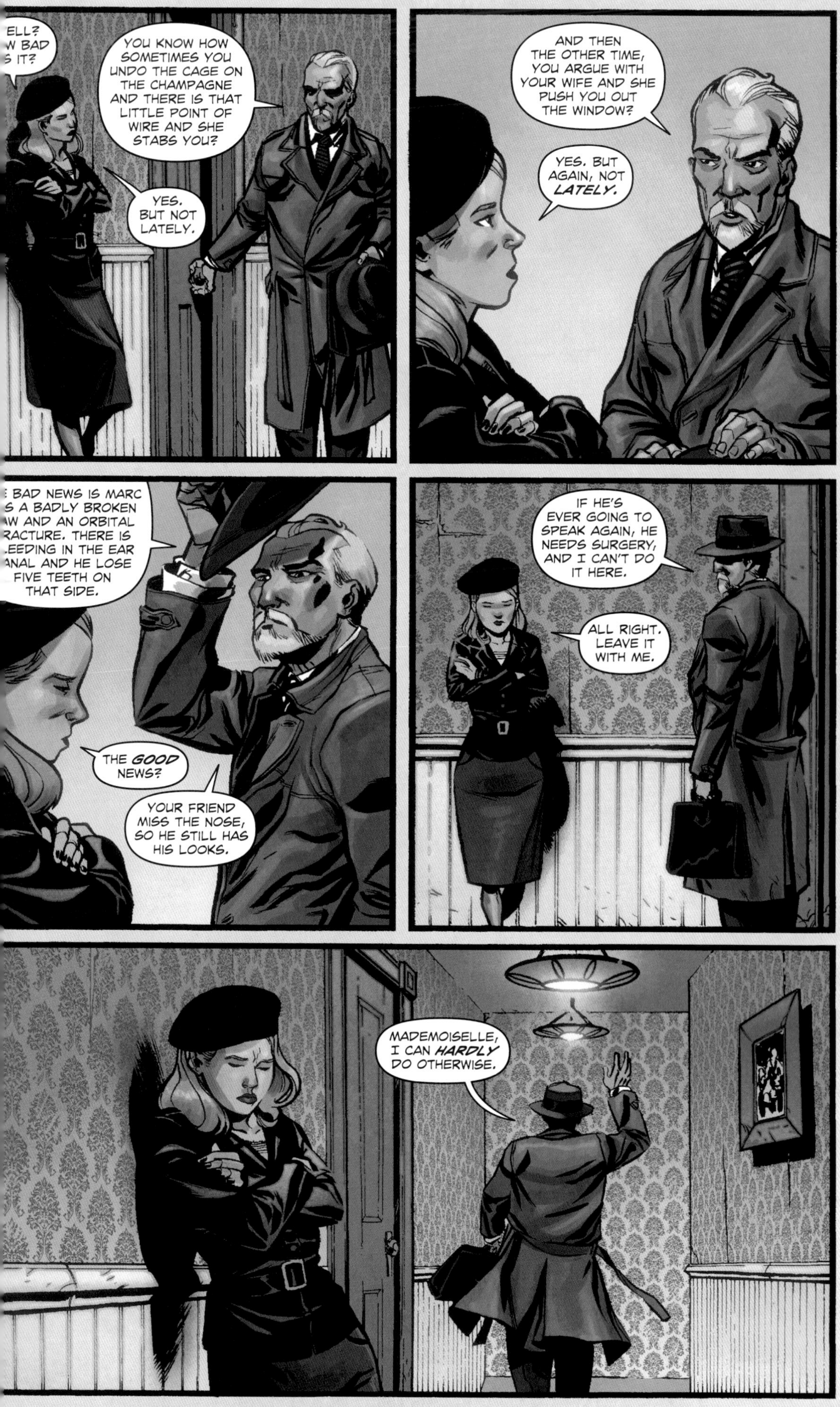
ELL? W BAD S IT?
YOU KNOW HOW SOMETIMES YOU UNDO THE CAGE ON THE CHAMPAGNE AND THERE IS THAT LITTLE POINT OF WIRE AND SHE STABS YOU?
YES. BUT NOT LATELY.
AND THEN THE OTHER TIME, YOU ARGUE WITH YOUR WIFE AND SHE PUSH YOU OUT THE WINDOW?
YES. BUT AGAIN, NOT *LATELY.*
E BAD NEWS IS MARC S A BADLY BROKEN W AND AN ORBITAL RACTURE. THERE IS LEEDING IN THE EAR ANAL AND HE LOSE FIVE TEETH ON THAT SIDE.
THE *GOOD* NEWS?
YOUR FRIEND MISS THE NOSE, SO HE STILL HAS HIS LOOKS.
IF HE'S EVER GOING TO SPEAK AGAIN, HE NEEDS SURGERY, AND I CAN'T DO IT HERE.
ALL RIGHT. LEAVE IT WITH ME.
MADEMOISELLE, I CAN *HARDLY* DO OTHERWISE.

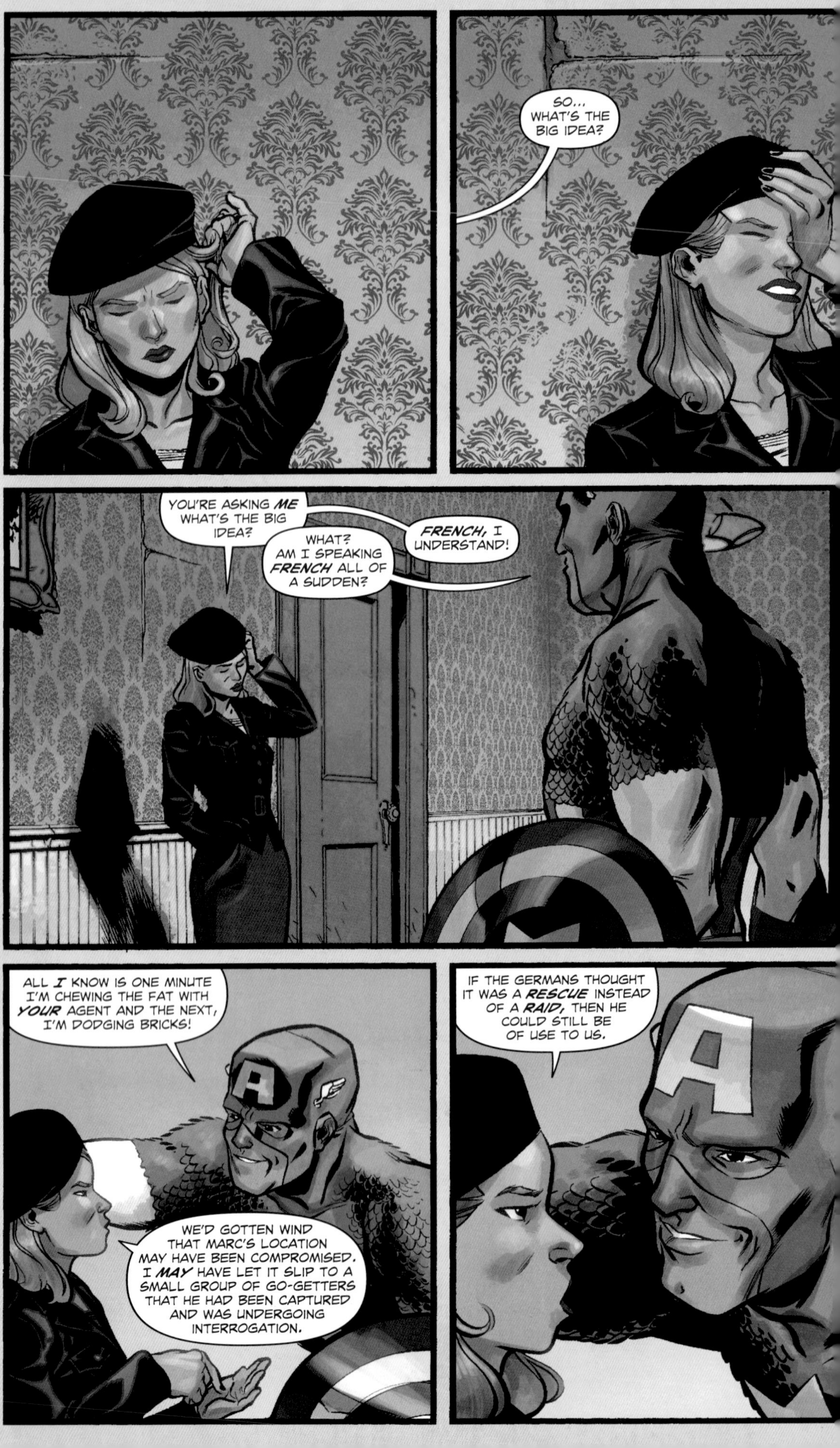
SO... WHAT'S THE BIG IDEA?
YOU'RE ASKING ME WHAT'S THE BIG IDEA?
WHAT? AM I SPEAKING FRENCH ALL OF A SUDDEN?
FRENCH, I UNDERSTAND!
ALL I KNOW IS ONE MINUTE I'M CHEWING THE FAT WITH YOUR AGENT AND THE NEXT, I'M DODGING BRICKS!
WE'D GOTTEN WIND THAT MARC'S LOCATION MAY HAVE BEEN COMPROMISED. I MAY HAVE LET IT SLIP TO A SMALL GROUP OF GO-GETTERS THAT HE HAD BEEN CAPTURED AND WAS UNDERGOING INTERROGATION.
IF THE GERMANS THOUGHT IT WAS A RESCUE INSTEAD OF A RAID, THEN HE COULD STILL BE OF USE TO US.

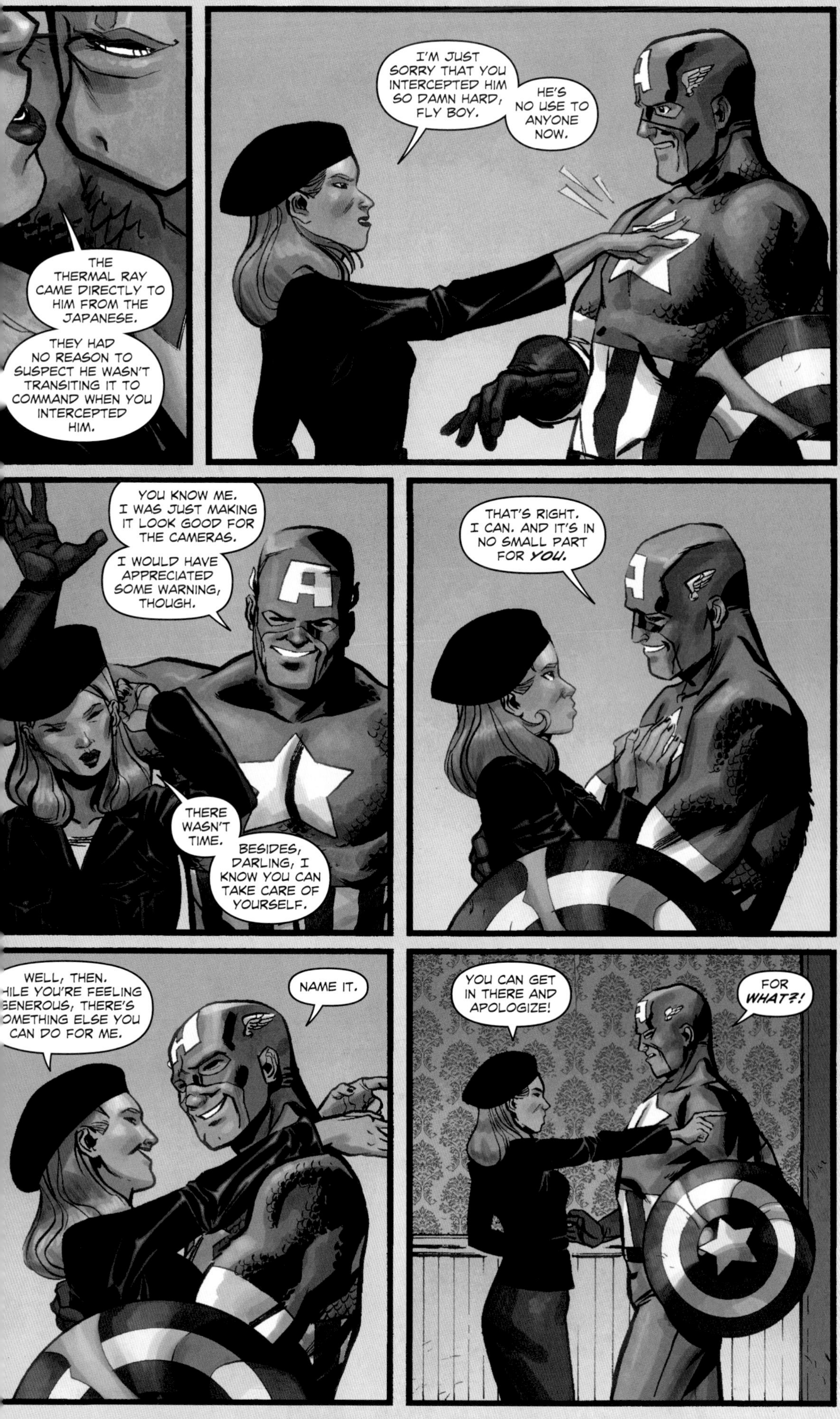
THE THERMAL RAY CAME DIRECTLY TO HIM FROM THE JAPANESE.
THEY HAD NO REASON TO SUSPECT HE WASN'T TRANSITING IT TO COMMAND WHEN YOU INTERCEPTED HIM.
I'M JUST SORRY THAT YOU INTERCEPTED HIM SO DAMN HARD, FLY BOY.
HE'S NO USE TO ANYONE NOW.
YOU KNOW ME. I WAS JUST MAKING IT LOOK GOOD FOR THE CAMERAS.
I WOULD HAVE APPRECIATED SOME WARNING, THOUGH.
THERE WASN'T TIME.
BESIDES, DARLING, I KNOW YOU CAN TAKE CARE OF YOURSELF.
THAT'S RIGHT. I CAN. AND IT'S IN NO SMALL PART FOR YOU.
WELL, THEN. HILE YOU'RE FEELING GENEROUS, THERE'S OMETHING ELSE YOU CAN DO FOR ME.
NAME IT.
YOU CAN GET IN THERE AND APOLOGIZE!
FOR WHAT?!

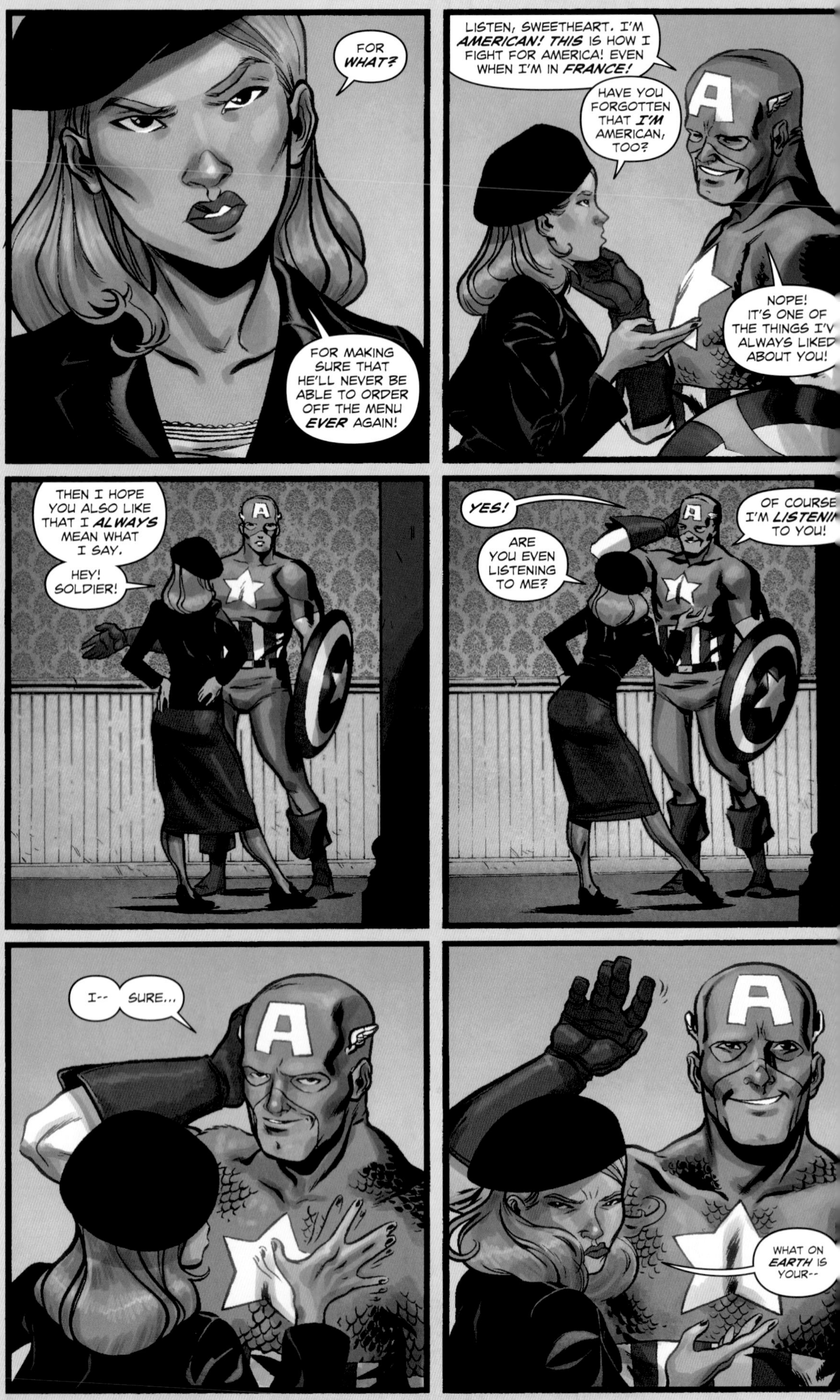
FOR WHAT?
FOR MAKING SURE THAT HE'LL NEVER BE ABLE TO ORDER OFF THE MENU EVER AGAIN!
LISTEN, SWEETHEART. I'M AMERICAN! THIS IS HOW I FIGHT FOR AMERICA! EVEN WHEN I'M IN FRANCE!
HAVE YOU FORGOTTEN THAT I'M AMERICAN, TOO?
NOPE! IT'S ONE OF THE THINGS I'V ALWAYS LIKED ABOUT YOU!
THEN I HOPE YOU ALSO LIKE THAT I ALWAYS MEAN WHAT I SAY.
HEY! SOLDIER!
ARE YOU EVEN LISTENING TO ME?
YES!
OF COURSE I'M LISTENIN TO YOU!
I--
SURE...
WHAT ON EARTH IS YOUR--

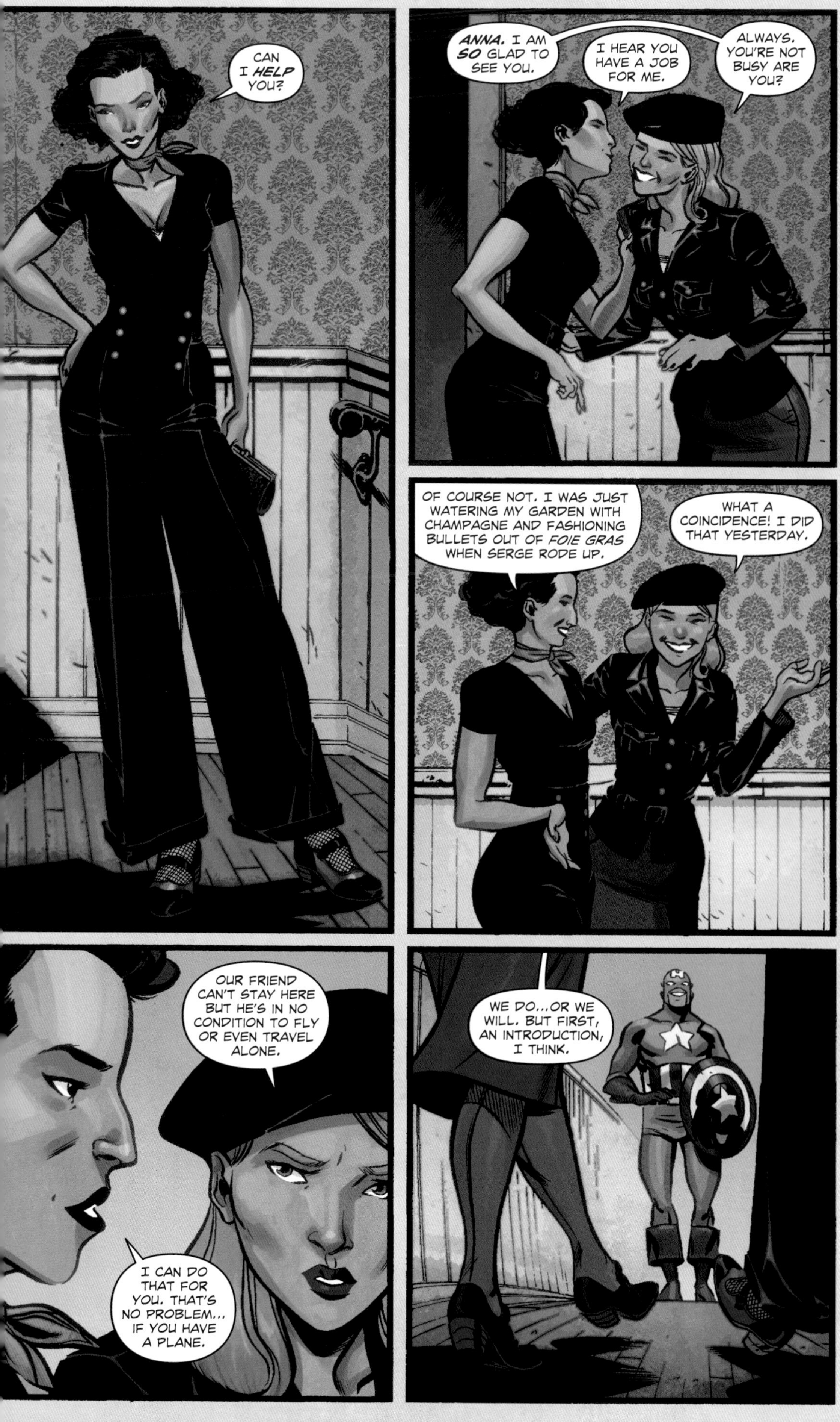
CAN I HELP YOU?
ANNA. I AM SO GLAD TO SEE YOU.
I HEAR YOU HAVE A JOB FOR ME.
ALWAYS. YOU'RE NOT BUSY ARE YOU?
OF COURSE NOT. I WAS JUST WATERING MY GARDEN WITH CHAMPAGNE AND FASHIONING BULLETS OUT OF FOIE GRAS WHEN SERGE RODE UP.
WHAT A COINCIDENCE! I DID THAT YESTERDAY.
OUR FRIEND CAN'T STAY HERE BUT HE'S IN NO CONDITION TO FLY OR EVEN TRAVEL ALONE.
I CAN DO THAT FOR YOU. THAT'S NO PROBLEM... IF YOU HAVE A PLANE.
WE DO...OR WE WILL. BUT FIRST, AN INTRODUCTION, I THINK.

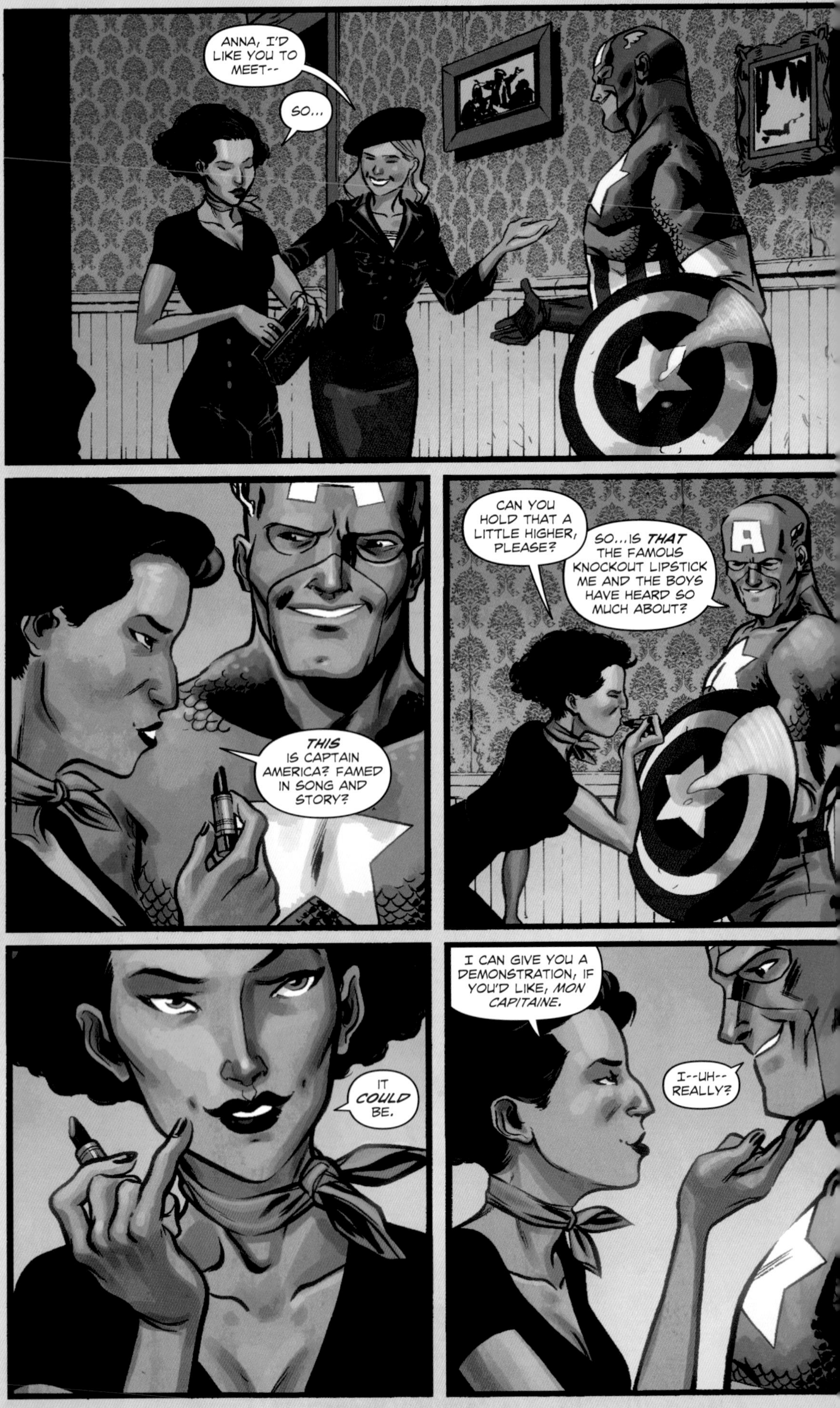

ANNA, I'D LIKE YOU TO MEET--
SO...
THIS IS CAPTAIN AMERICA? FAMED IN SONG AND STORY?
CAN YOU HOLD THAT A LITTLE HIGHER, PLEASE?
SO...IS THAT THE FAMOUS KNOCKOUT LIPSTICK ME AND THE BOYS HAVE HEARD SO MUCH ABOUT?
IT COULD BE.
I CAN GIVE YOU A DEMONSTRATION, IF YOU'D LIKE, MON CAPITAINE.
I--UH-- REALLY?

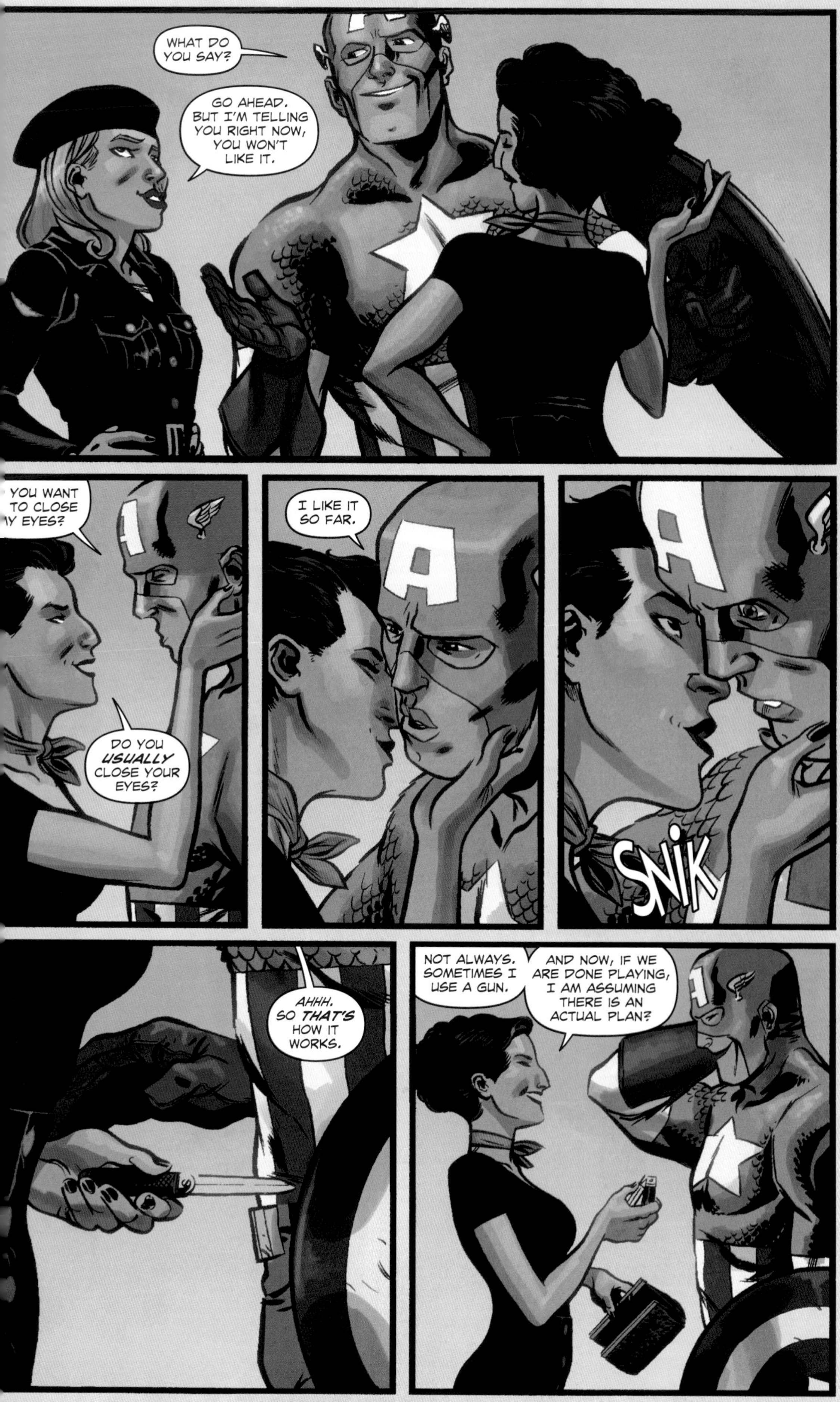

WHAT DO YOU SAY?
GO AHEAD. BUT I'M TELLING YOU RIGHT NOW, YOU WON'T LIKE IT.
YOU WANT TO CLOSE Y EYES?
DO YOU USUALLY CLOSE YOUR EYES?
I LIKE IT SO FAR.
SNIK
AHHH. SO THAT'S HOW IT WORKS.
NOT ALWAYS. SOMETIMES I USE A GUN.
AND NOW, IF WE ARE DONE PLAYING, I AM ASSUMING THERE IS AN ACTUAL PLAN?

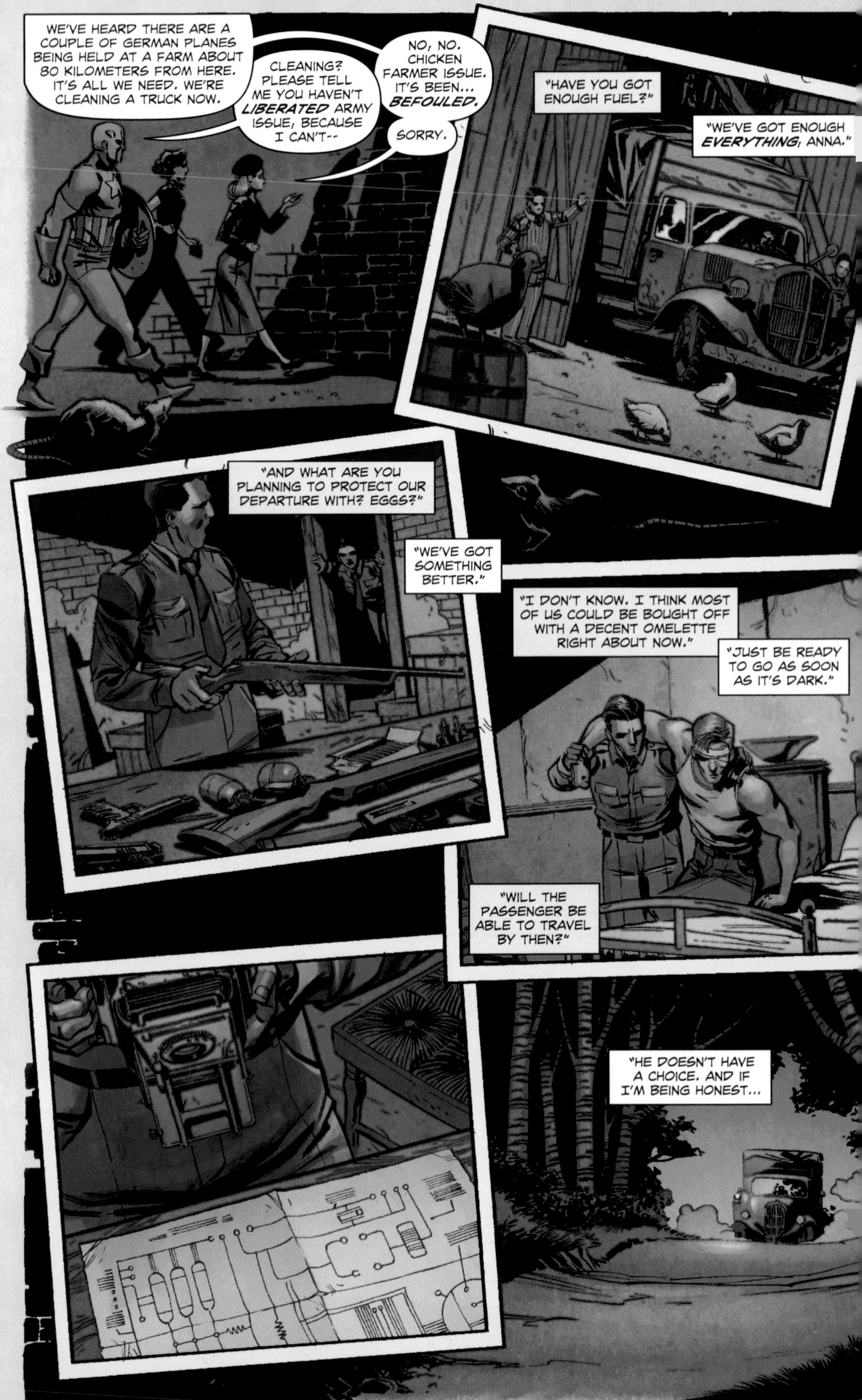
WE'VE HEARD THERE ARE A COUPLE OF GERMAN PLANES BEING HELD AT A FARM ABOUT 80 KILOMETERS FROM HERE. IT'S ALL WE NEED. WE'RE CLEANING A TRUCK NOW.
CLEANING? PLEASE TELL ME YOU HAVEN'T LIBERATED ARMY ISSUE, BECAUSE I CAN'T--
NO, NO. CHICKEN FARMER ISSUE. IT'S BEEN... BEFOULED.
SORRY.
"HAVE YOU GOT ENOUGH FUEL?"
"WE'VE GOT ENOUGH EVERYTHING, ANNA."
"AND WHAT ARE YOU PLANNING TO PROTECT OUR DEPARTURE WITH? EGGS?"
"WE'VE GOT SOMETHING BETTER."
"I DON'T KNOW. I THINK MOST OF US COULD BE BOUGHT OFF WITH A DECENT OMELETTE RIGHT ABOUT NOW."
"JUST BE READY TO GO AS SOON AS IT'S DARK."
"WILL THE PASSENGER BE ABLE TO TRAVEL BY THEN?"
"HE DOESN'T HAVE A CHOICE. AND IF I'M BEING HONEST...

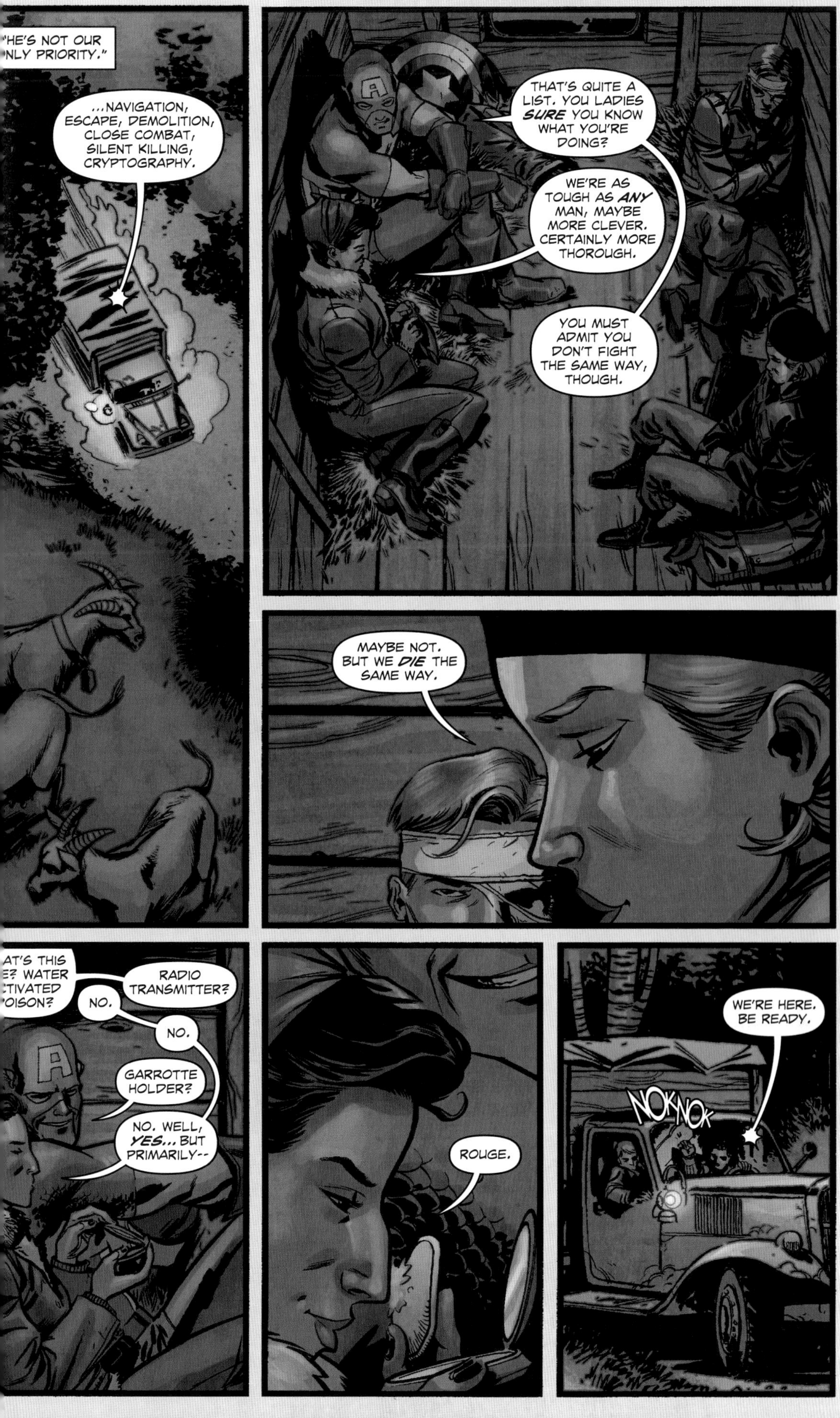
"HE'S NOT OUR
NLY PRIORITY."
...NAVIGATION, ESCAPE, DEMOLITION, CLOSE COMBAT, SILENT KILLING, CRYPTOGRAPHY.
THAT'S QUITE A LIST. YOU LADIES SURE YOU KNOW WHAT YOU'RE DOING?
WE'RE AS TOUGH AS ANY MAN, MAYBE MORE CLEVER. CERTAINLY MORE THOROUGH.
YOU MUST ADMIT YOU DON'T FIGHT THE SAME WAY, THOUGH.
MAYBE NOT. BUT WE DIE THE SAME WAY.
AT'S THIS
E? WATER
CTIVATED
OISON?
RADIO TRANSMITTER?
NO.
NO.
GARROTTE HOLDER?
NO. WELL, YES... BUT PRIMARILY--
ROUGE.
NOKNOK
WE'RE HERE. BE READY.

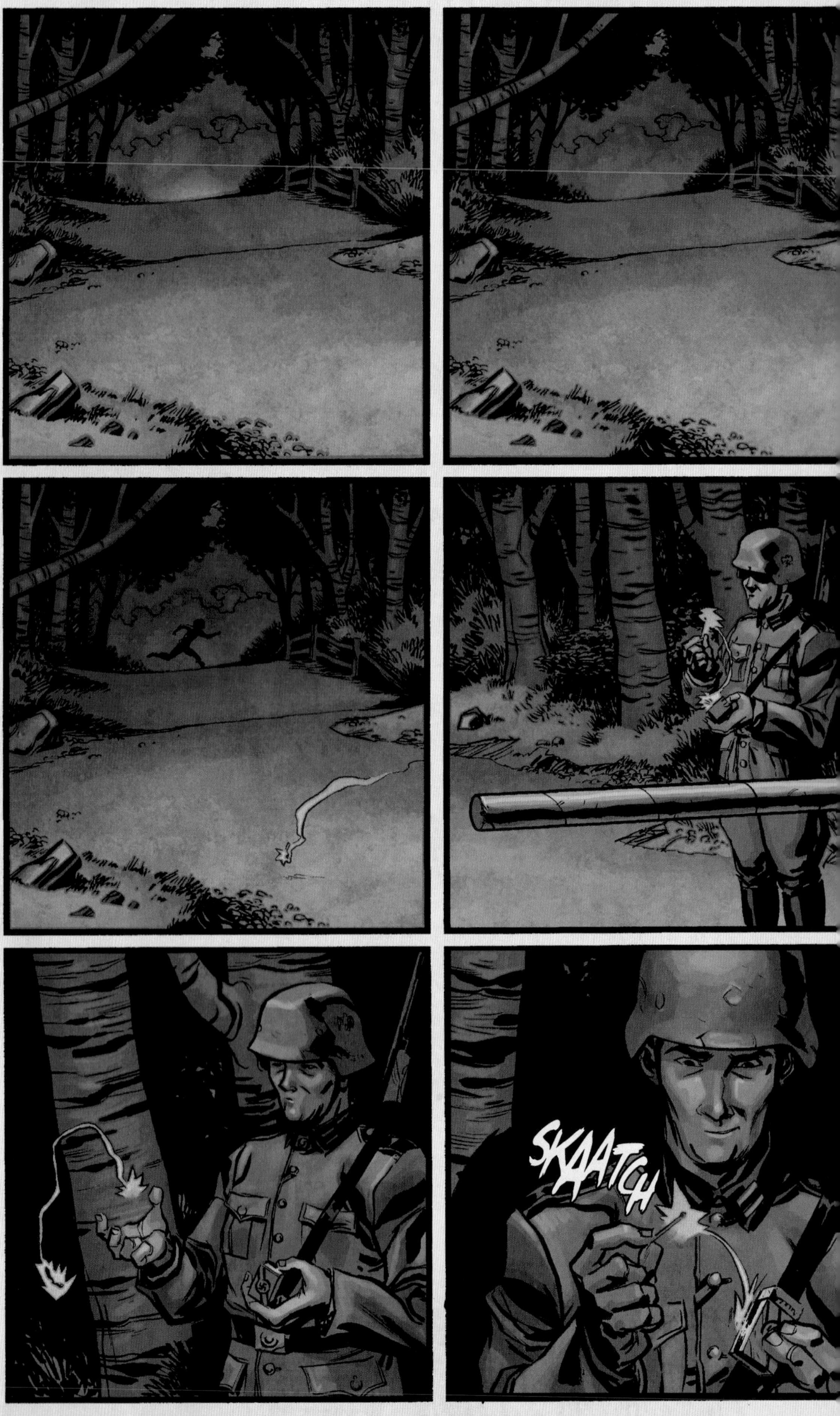
SKAATCH

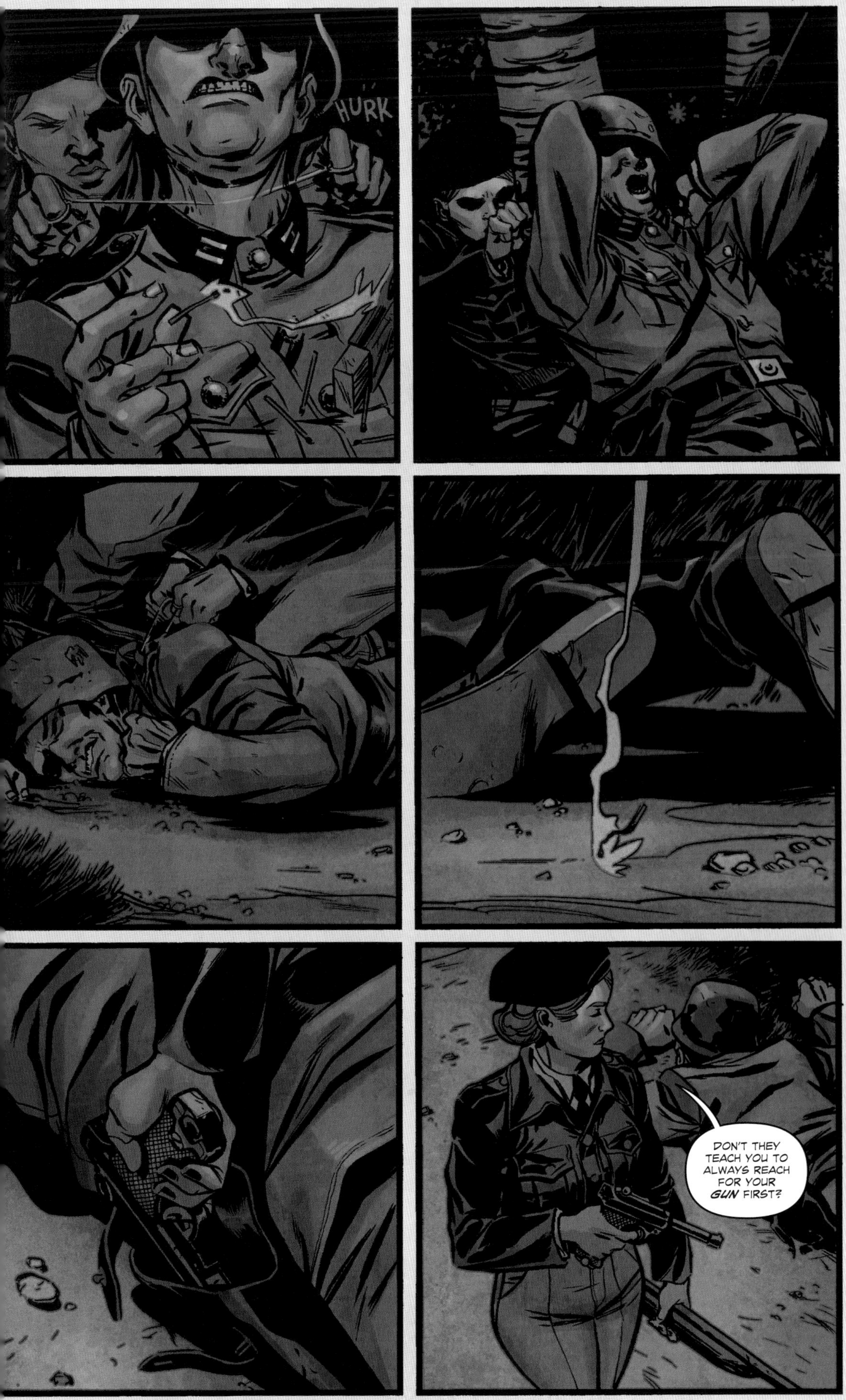
HURK
DON'T THEY TEACH YOU TO ALWAYS REACH FOR YOUR GUN FIRST?

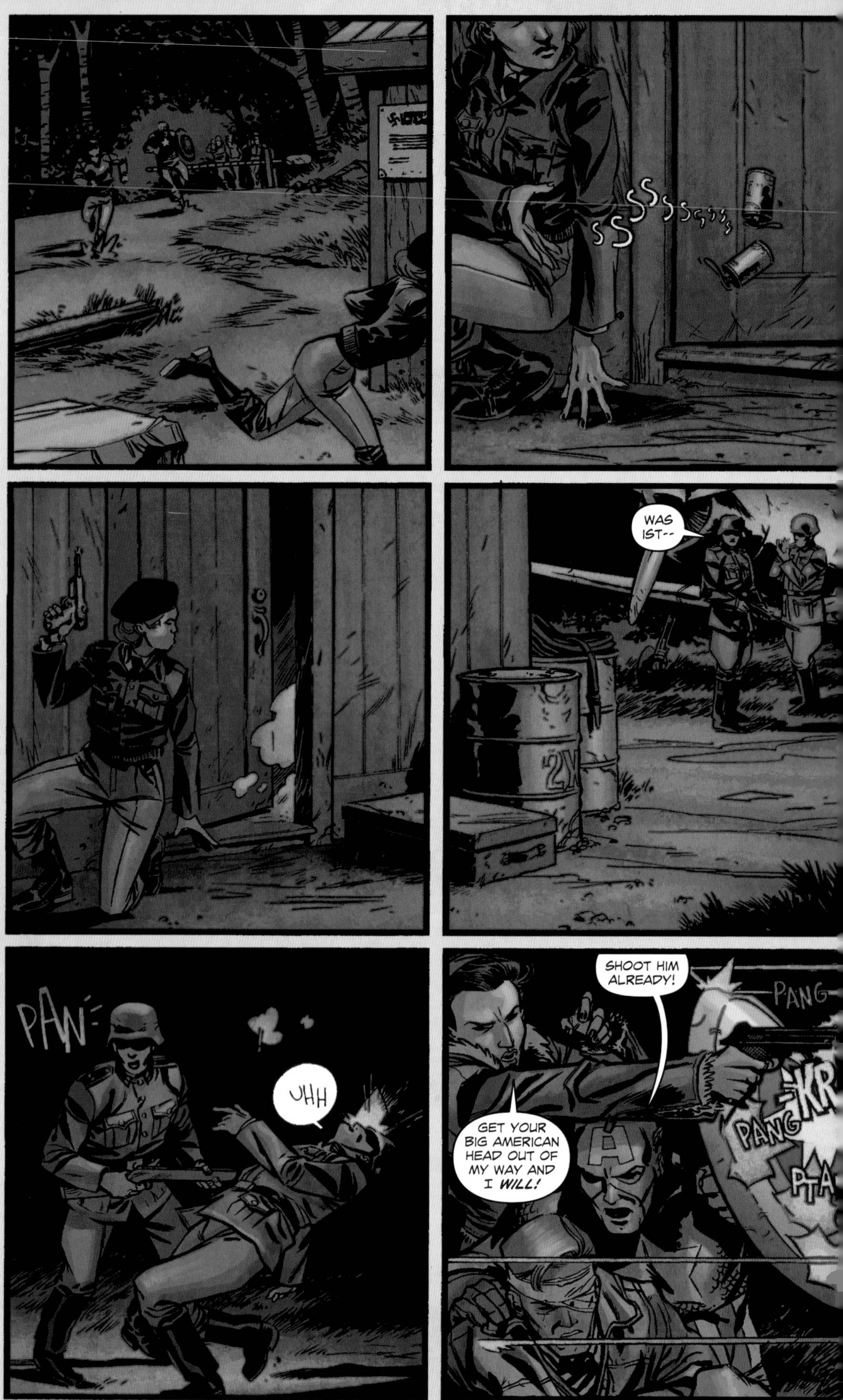
SSSSSSSSSS
WAS IST--
PAW
UHH
SHOOT HIM ALREADY!
PANG
GET YOUR BIG AMERICAN HEAD OUT OF MY WAY AND I *WILL!*
PANG
PTA

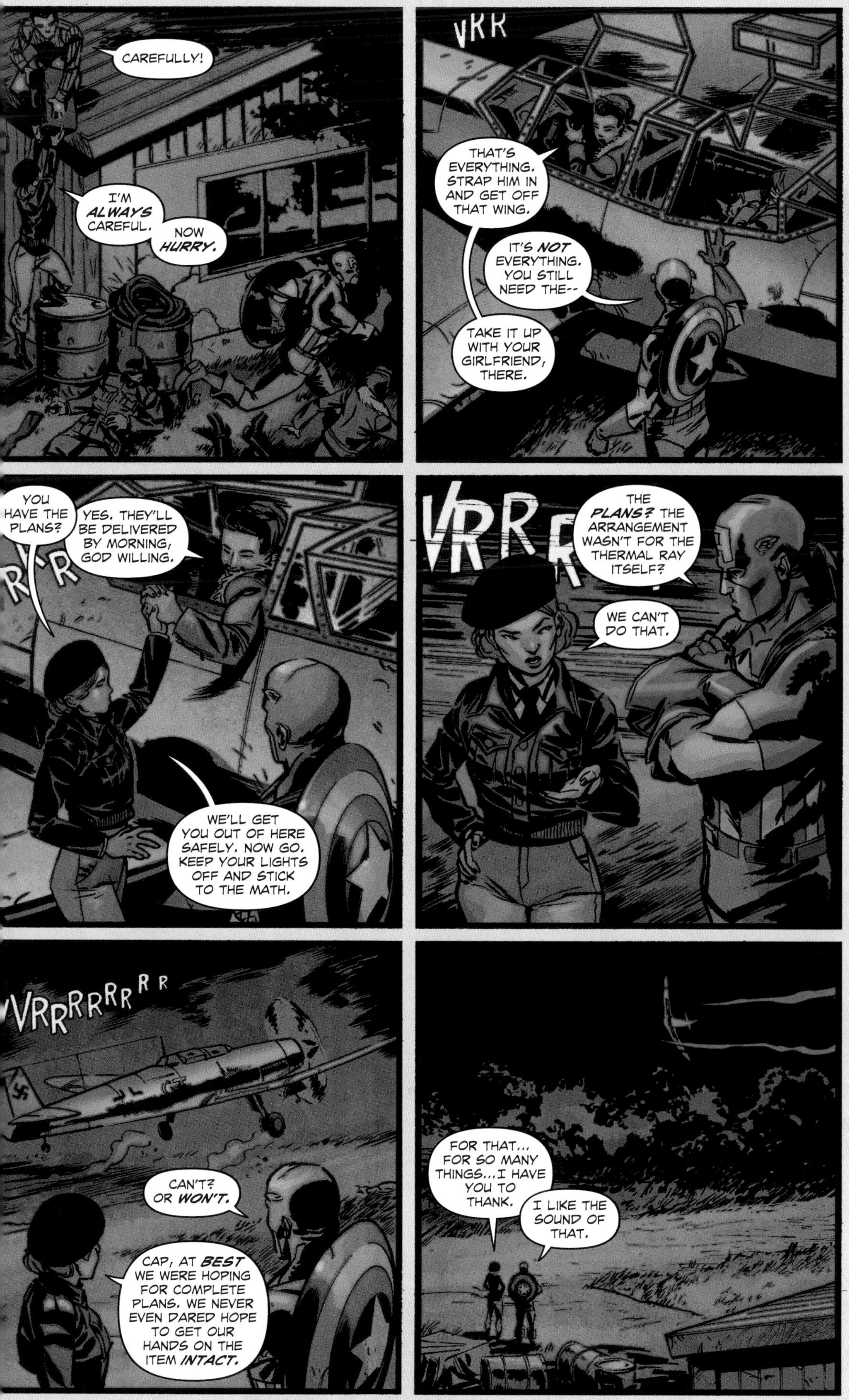

CAREFULLY!
I'M ALWAYS CAREFUL.
NOW HURRY.
VRR
THAT'S EVERYTHING. STRAP HIM IN AND GET OFF THAT WING.
IT'S NOT EVERYTHING. YOU STILL NEED THE--
TAKE IT UP WITH YOUR GIRLFRIEND, THERE.
YOU HAVE THE PLANS?
YES. THEY'LL BE DELIVERED BY MORNING, GOD WILLING.
WE'LL GET YOU OUT OF HERE SAFELY. NOW GO. KEEP YOUR LIGHTS OFF AND STICK TO THE MATH.
VRRR
THE PLANS? THE ARRANGEMENT WASN'T FOR THE THERMAL RAY ITSELF?
WE CAN'T DO THAT.
VRRRRRRR R
CAN'T? OR WON'T.
CAP, AT BEST WE WERE HOPING FOR COMPLETE PLANS. WE NEVER EVEN DARED HOPE TO GET OUR HANDS ON THE ITEM INTACT.
FOR THAT... FOR SO MANY THINGS... I HAVE YOU TO THANK.
I LIKE THE SOUND OF THAT.

HOW LONG UNTIL THEY'RE OUT OF RANGE, HENRI?

ANOTHER MINUTE. THEY'RE THE ONLY THING IN THE SKY, IF THIS CONTRAPTION IS FUNCTIONING PROPERLY.

I NEVER THOUGHT I'D FIND A REASON TO BE GRATEFUL TO THE JAPANESE.

PEOPLE CAN CHANGE, SERGE.

WE ARE ALL CHANGED.

THEY'RE SAFELY AWAY. LET'S GET OUT OF HERE.

DID YOU CLEAN THE BUILDING?

WHATEVER WE CAN USE IS IN THE TRUCK. WE JUST NEED THE OTHERS. WHERE ARE THEY?

LET'S SEE JUST HOW GOOD THIS THING IS AT DETECTING HEAT, SHALL WE?

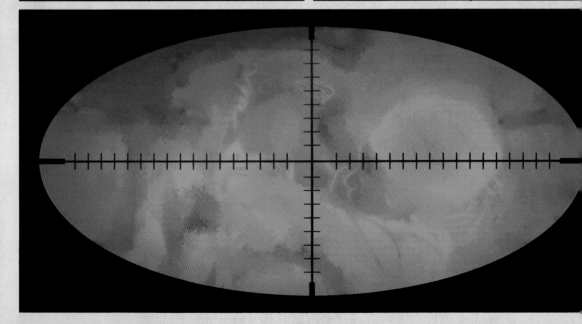

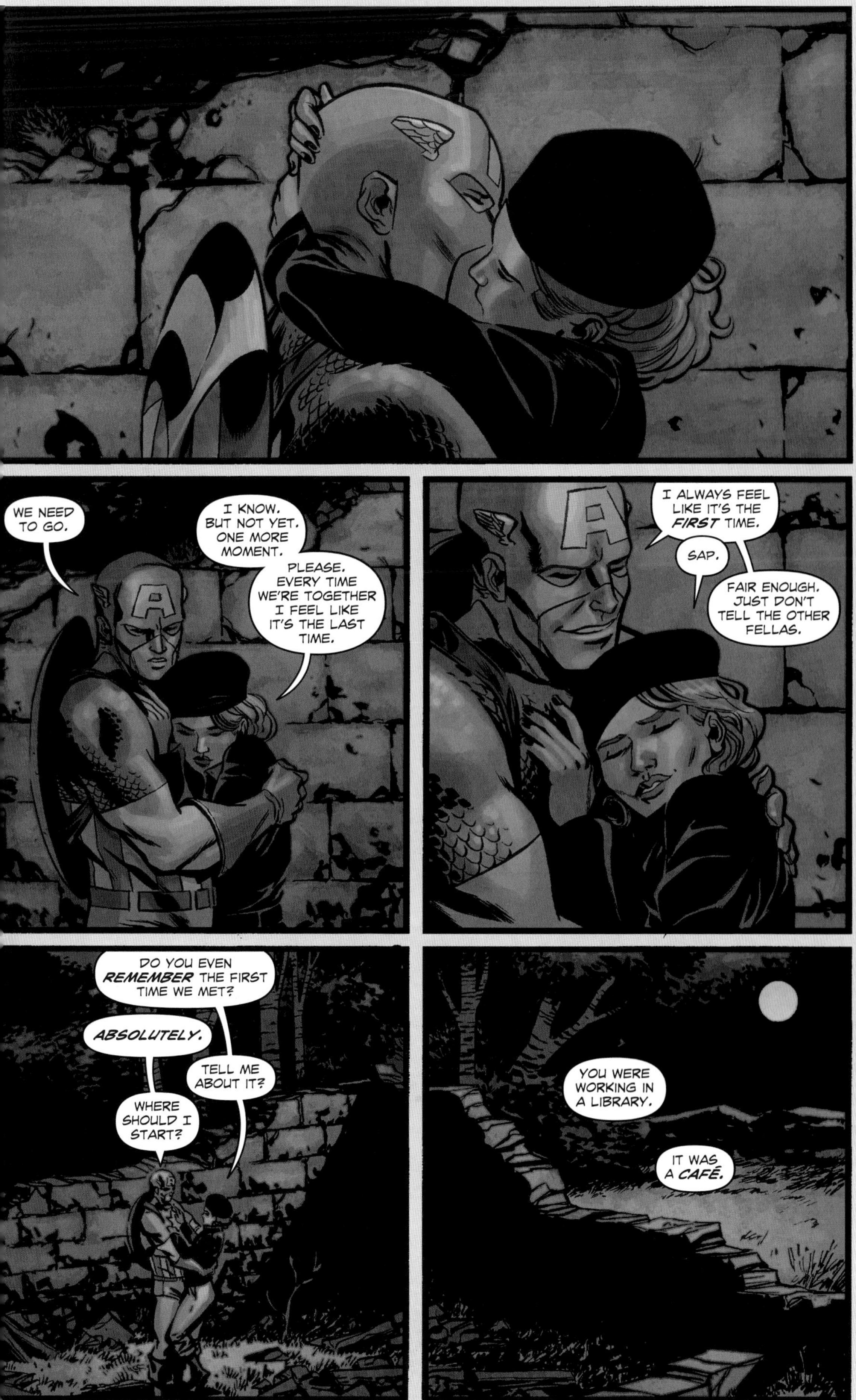
WE NEED TO GO.
I KNOW. BUT NOT YET. ONE MORE MOMENT.
PLEASE. EVERY TIME WE'RE TOGETHER I FEEL LIKE IT'S THE LAST TIME.
I ALWAYS FEEL LIKE IT'S THE *FIRST* TIME.
SAP.
FAIR ENOUGH. JUST DON'T TELL THE OTHER FELLAS.
DO YOU EVEN *REMEMBER* THE FIRST TIME WE MET?
ABSOLUTELY.
TELL ME ABOUT IT?
WHERE SHOULD I START?
YOU WERE WORKING IN A LIBRARY.
IT WAS A *CAFÉ.*

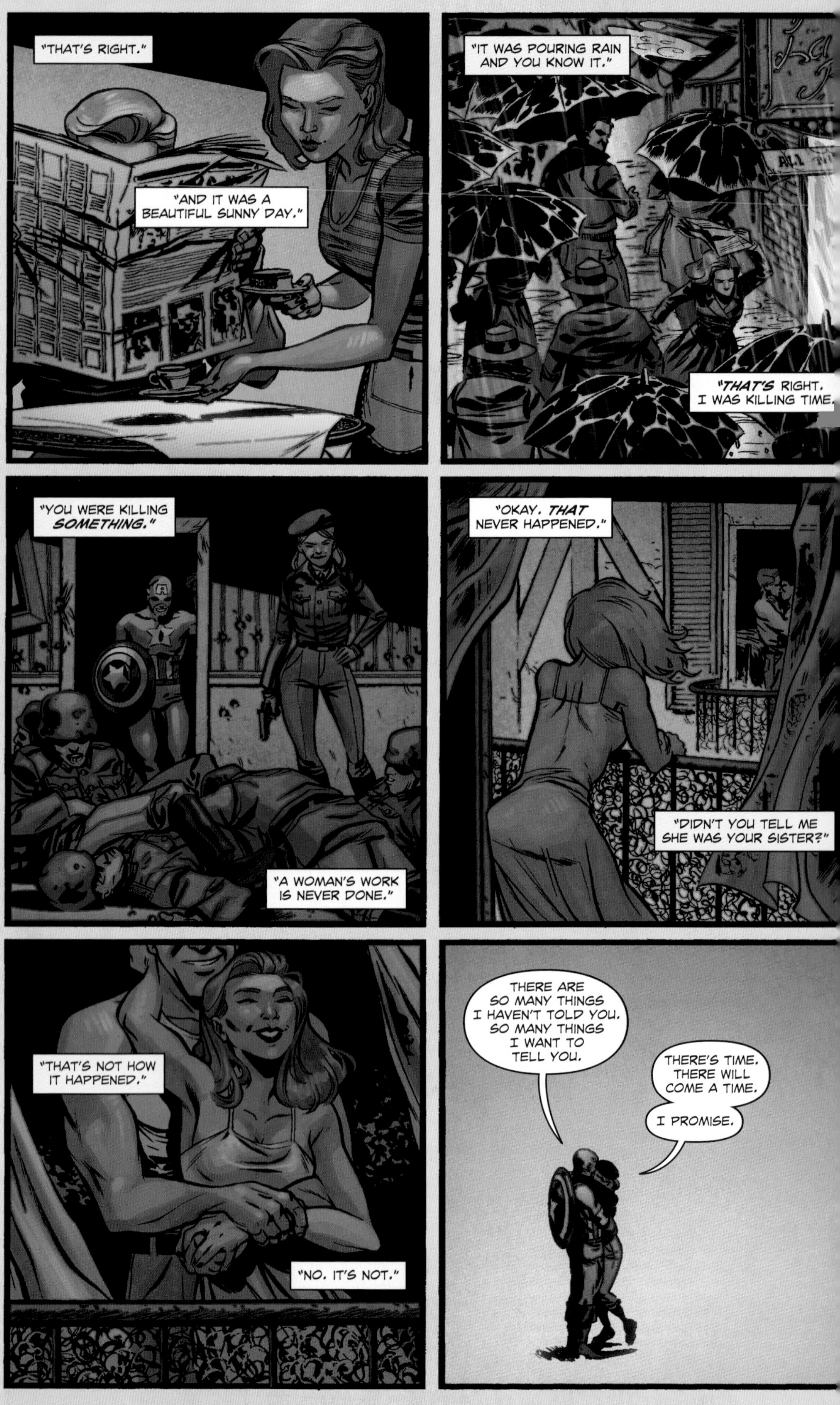
"THAT'S RIGHT."
"AND IT WAS A BEAUTIFUL SUNNY DAY."
"IT WAS POURING RAIN AND YOU KNOW IT."
"THAT'S RIGHT. I WAS KILLING TIME.
"YOU WERE KILLING SOMETHING."
"A WOMAN'S WORK IS NEVER DONE."
"OKAY. THAT NEVER HAPPENED."
"DIDN'T YOU TELL ME SHE WAS YOUR SISTER?"
"THAT'S NOT HOW IT HAPPENED."
"NO. IT'S NOT."
THERE ARE SO MANY THINGS I HAVEN'T TOLD YOU. SO MANY THINGS I WANT TO TELL YOU.
THERE'S TIME. THERE WILL COME A TIME.
I PROMISE.

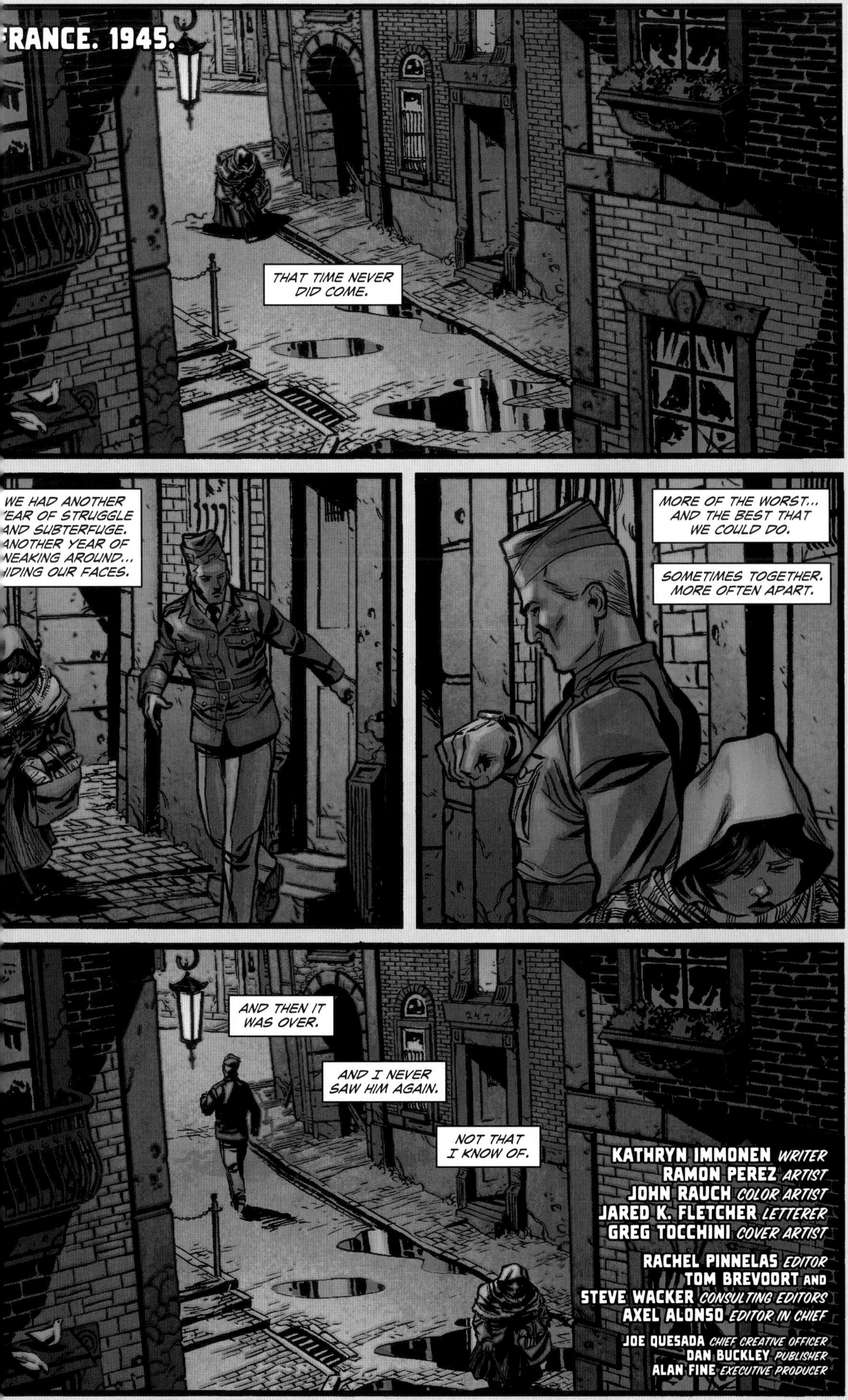

FRANCE. 1945.
THAT TIME NEVER DID COME.
WE HAD ANOTHER YEAR OF STRUGGLE AND SUBTERFUGE. ANOTHER YEAR OF SNEAKING AROUND... HIDING OUR FACES.
MORE OF THE WORST... AND THE BEST THAT WE COULD DO.
SOMETIMES TOGETHER. MORE OFTEN APART.
AND THEN IT WAS OVER.
AND I NEVER SAW HIM AGAIN.
NOT THAT I KNOW OF.
KATHRYN IMMONEN WRITER
RAMON PEREZ ARTIST
JOHN RAUCH COLOR ARTIST
JARED K. FLETCHER LETTERER
GREG TOCCHINI COVER ARTIST
RACHEL PINNELAS EDITOR
TOM BREVOORT AND
STEVE WACKER CONSULTING EDITORS
AXEL ALONSO EDITOR IN CHIEF
JOE QUESADA CHIEF CREATIVE OFFICER
DAN BUCKLEY PUBLISHER
ALAN FINE EXECUTIVE PRODUCER

OPERATION S.I.N.

VARIANT COVER GALLERY

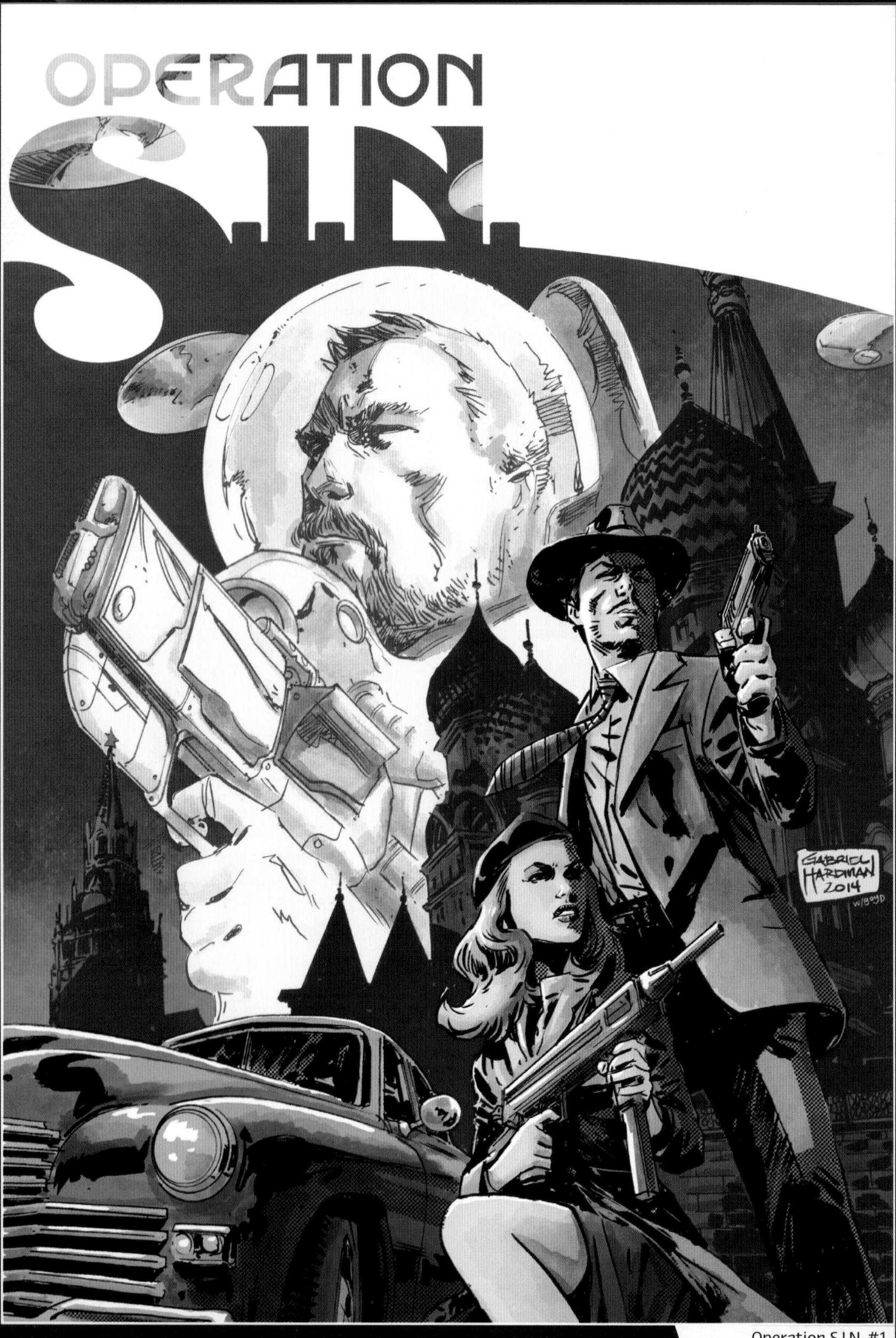

OPERATION
S.I.N.
GABRIEL HARDMAN 2014
W/BOYD

Operation S.I.N. #1
by Gabriel Hardman

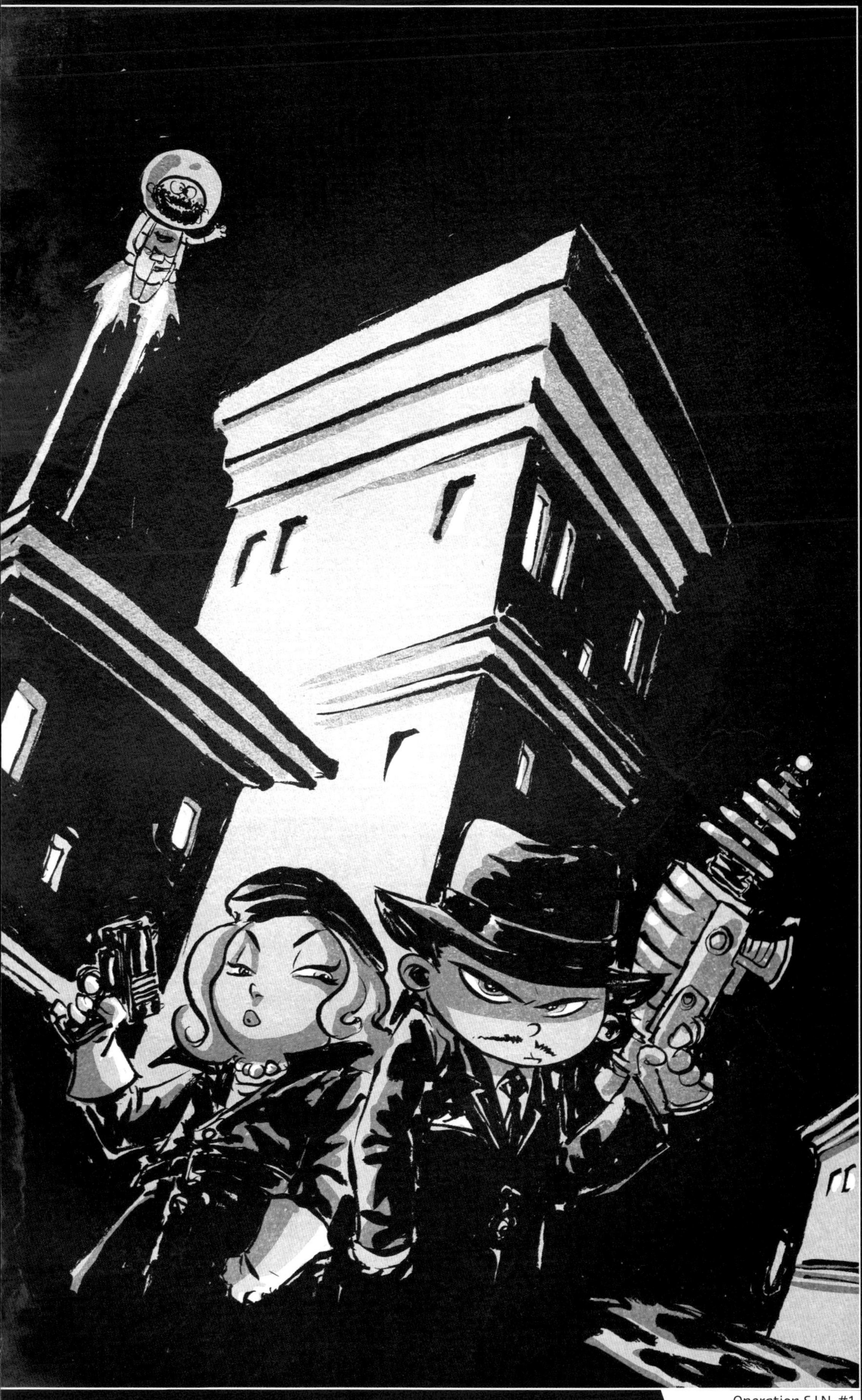

Operation S.I.N. #1
by Skottie Young

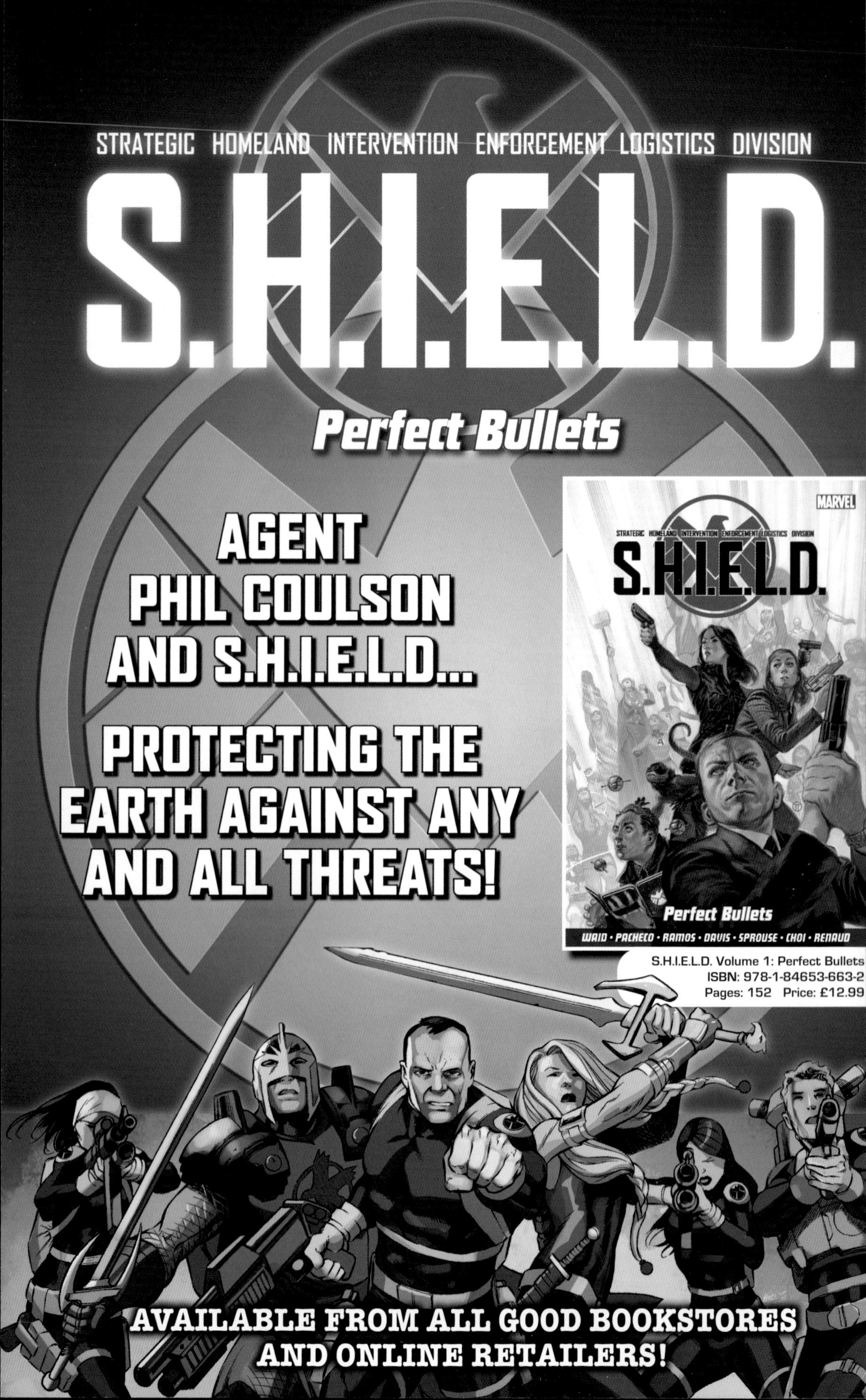
STRATEGIC HOMELAND INTERVENTION ENFORCEMENT LOGISTICS DIVISION
S.H.I.E.L.D.
Perfect Bullets
AGENT PHIL COULSON AND S.H.I.E.L.D...
PROTECTING THE EARTH AGAINST ANY AND ALL THREATS!
MARVEL
STRATEGIC HOMELAND INTERVENTION ENFORCEMENT LOGISTICS DIVISION
S.H.I.E.L.D.
Perfect Bullets
WAID • PACHECO • RAMOS • DAVIS • SPROUSE • CHOI • RENAUD
S.H.I.E.L.D. Volume 1: Perfect Bullets
ISBN: 978-1-84653-663-2
Pages: 152 Price: £12.99
AVAILABLE FROM ALL GOOD BOOKSTORES AND ONLINE RETAILERS!